Date Due

SEP 22 1998

971
.804
0924
Small-R

Rowe, Frederick W., 1912-.   13700
    The Smallwood era / Frederick W. Rowe. --
Toronto : McGraw-Hill Ryerson, c1985.
    245 p. : ill.

Bibliography: p. 221-245.
02299461   ISBN: 007548918X

1. Smallwood, Joseph R., 1900- 2. Prime ministers –
Newfoundland – Biography. 3. Newfoundland –
Politics and government – 1949- I. Title.

THE SMALLWOOD ERA

Frederick W. Rowe

McGRAW-HILL RYERSON LIMITED

Toronto Montreal New York St. Louis San Francisco Auckland
Bogotá Guatemala Hamburg Johannesburg Lisbon London Madrid
Mexico New Delhi Panama Paris San Juan São Paulo
Singapore Sydney Tokyo

THE SMALLWOOD ERA

ISBN   0-07-548918-X

Printed and bound in Canada by John Deyell Company

1   2   3   4   5   6   7   8   9   JD   3   2   1   0   9   8   7   6   5   4

Canadian Cataloguing in Publication Data

Rowe, Frederick W., date
   The Smallwood Era

Bibliography: p.
Includes index.

0-07-548918-X

1. Smallwood, Joseph R., 1900–   2. Prime ministers –
Newfoundland – Biography.   3. Newfoundland – Politics
government – 1949   I. Title.

FC2175.1.S62R6 1984   971.8'04'0924   C85-098068-2
F1123.S62R6 1984

ACKNOWLEDGEMENTS

In writing this book I have received help and encouragement from a
number of people to whom I extend my thanks: Hon. B.J. Abbott, Anne
Alexander, R.L. Andrews, A.C. Badcock, Milicent Bradbury, Marian
Burnette, Derek Bussey, Hon. J.R. Chalker, Roy L. Cheeseman, Mona
Cramm, Hon. H.R.V. Earle, Judy Foote, Thomas Fraize, Rosalind Godfrey,
Stuart Godfrey, Nancy Granville, Denis J. Groom, Dr. Leslie Harris, Anne
Hart, E.P. Henley, Hon. T. Alex Hickman, Gerald I. Hill, Dr. James Hiller,
H.V. Hollett, Edgar House, Barbara Kelland, C.A. Knight, Gloria Kunta,
Monsignor R.J. Lahey, Hon. C. Max Lane, David Leamon, Gordon
MacDonald, Hon. Aiden Maloney, Dr. Keith Matthews (deceased), Eva
Melanson, Elizabeth Miller, Mrs. Carolyn Morgan, Hon. Gerald R.
Ottenheimer, Hon. T. Anthony Paddon, Hon. J.W. Pickersgill, George
Pope, C.W. Powell, Catherine Power, Gordon F. Pushie, Norma J. Richards,
Edward Roberts, Dr. D. Severs, Hon. J.R. Smallwood, Graham Snow,
Eric Spicer, Captain Earle Winsor.

TABLE OF
CONTENTS

To My Parents,
Eli and Phoebe Ann Rowe

Books by Frederick W. Rowe

Extinction: The Beothuks of Newfoundland
Education and Culture in Newfoundland
A History of Newfoundland and Labrador

PREFACE

This book is intended to be neither an apologia nor an exposé. It cannot be seen as a comprehensive biography of Joseph Smallwood and it does not purport to cover all the details of Newfoundland's history during his administration. It is, instead, a more personal work: with Smallwood as the focal point, it is simply a book about certain aspects of the period from 1949 to 1971, chosen and developed by one who was intimately connected with the major political activities of the period. Inevitably, this raises the question of whether such a work can be fair and impartial. The answer is affirmative, albeit with qualifications.

Obviously it is difficult for any writer, no matter how dedicated to maintaining his objectivity, to have played an intimate part in the events about which he writes and yet be totally unbiased. Notwithstanding this, however, it does not change the fact that there is a need for such a study by one who was on the "inside." In fact, since many of the studies done by those on the "outside" are tinged, if not motivated, by their authors' political perspectives, then the need for the inside story becomes all the more necessary.

Sadly, those who constituted the Smallwood cabinet during the first half of the era are disappearing. Of the 1959 cabinet more than one-half are dead. In the normal course, most of those who remain will have died within another dozen years or so. Similarly, many of those making up the senior civil service in 1949 are dead. So far as I have been able to ascertain, none of those ministers and officials now dead left any written records for posterity. Unfortunately, for most of such first-hand accounts, the field has been left to those who have political axes to grind, or to the myth-makers — of which, for whatever reason, Newfoundland has always had an inordinate number. It is not surprising, then, that this book devotes a good deal of attention to the myths and semi-myths that have grown up since 1949 — Smallwood's career, the history of the Trans-Canada Highway, the treatment of Labrador, the resettlement programme, the fishery programme, and so on.

But important as it is to deal firmly with misconceptions and misunderstandings, the premise of this book is not meant to be negative. As Leslie Harris, president of Memorial University, has recently pointed out, "Confederation with Canada brought Newfoundland into the mainstream of North American life and set in train a revolutionary process. In the intervening years that process has wrought changes of enormous significance that have touched every aspect of society." Dr. Harris attributes most of this change to education — a belief which I and many other students of the period share. Indeed, this "revolution" is evident to anyone old enough to compare pre-1949 conditions with the Newfoundland of twenty years later. The revolution was partly physical and material, but most of all it was social. With all the blunders and stupidities that took place between 1949 and 1971, the fact is that by the end of the era much of Newfoundland's historic poverty, isolation and privation had disappeared. In their place, again to use Dr. Harris' words, were "dignity, confidence and competence."

Much of the material in this book is controversial and will undoubtedly be the object of criticism. It is my sincere hope, however, that before passing judgement on either the events or the characters in it, both supporters and critics will read it from beginning to end. This will not, of course, silence my critics; but it may enable those interested to understand and assess what was undoubtedly the most exciting and revolutionary period in Newfoundland's history, and appraise the record of that Newfoundlander — Joseph Roberts Smallwood — who, more than any other in this century, was instrumental in bringing about that revolution.

Frederick W. Rowe
St. John's 1984

1 SMALLWOOD BEFORE 1949

Joseph Roberts Smallwood was born in Gambo, Bonavista Bay, Newfoundland on December 24, 1900. Named for two famous turn-of-the-century figures — Joseph Chamberlain and Field Marshall Lord Roberts — he was the grandson of David Smallwood, who had come to Newfoundland in 1861 from Prince Edward Island, and among other activities had set up a profitable boot and shoe factory. Perhaps sensing the promise of his grandson's future, his relationship with young Joe was particularly close, no doubt playing an important part in shaping that future.

Joe's father, Charles Smallwood, was a lumber surveyor working in Gambo at the time of his son's birth. Unfortunately, due to both a serious alcohol problem and the difficult nature of his work, Charles' large family, thirteen in all, knew almost constant poverty in their early years, as well as the disruption and turmoil of changing residence frequently.

Although Smallwood was born in a small logging and lumbering settlement, he was not, as is often held by the popular imagination, a son of the Newfoundland outports. Joe was only a year old when his family moved from Gambo to St. John's, and it was there that he grew up, went to school, and worked until, as a young man, he left the city to seek his fortune in the United States. It might be said that he did experience a semblance of outport life, but only for a brief period when the family moved a couple of miles outside the city limits and Joe learned to handle horses — especially in the clearing of land. So, too, when the family moved at an earlier time to a house near his grandfather's home, Joe received some training in the planting and growing of ordinary vegetables (potatoes, turnips, cabbage and carrots.) It may have been these experiences which stimulated Smallwood's later interest in farming and agricultural pursuits.

By the time he had reached ten years of age, Smallwood had already attended four schools in St. John's. His Uncle Fred, who had become a prosperous businessman, decided to assume responsibility for his nephew's education and to this end agreed to pay all the costs involved in registering him as a boarding school student rather than as a day student. Under the denominational system of education, each church recognized by law for educational purposes was entitled to own and operate two "colleges" (in the English sense) with places for both day and boarding students, the latter usually being the children of well-to-do outport people. These colleges — in Smallwood's case, Bishop Feild College — had more highly trained teachers and better facilities, especially in sports, than did ordinary schools. The highest grade obtainable was Senior Associate, roughly Grade 12. Although Methodist by denomination, Smallwood had no difficulty in registering at a Church of England college. Indeed, it was the practice of all the colleges to take in students from other churches if there was room. If one may judge from Smallwood's own account of life at Bishop Feild, the experience was a most beneficial one, and certainly a radical change from the poverty and deprivation he had known for the first ten years of his life. It was at school that Smallwood became a voracious reader, and it was perhaps this habit which affected his subsequent years more than anything else. Like Winston Churchill, he was in some respects an indifferent student; however, his taste for reading was destined to offset the deficiencies of his limited formal education and, in time, was to make him (again like Churchill) a master in the use of the English language.

Smallwood left Bishop Feild at the age of fifteen and eventually found work with a number of newspapers between 1915 and 1920, ending with the *Evening Telegram* of which he became acting editor. During his period as a reporter he covered several of the dramatic attempts by aviators to cross the Atlantic.

In 1920 Smallwood left Newfoundland for New York, working for several months en route at newspapers in Halifax and Boston. When he arrived in New York, Smallwood signed on with a well-known socialist periodical, the New York *Call*, and there got his first real taste of political campaigning as a supporter of well-known socialist Norman Thomas in the 1924 presidential elections. Although his New York period was punctuated by several trips back to Newfoundland, Smallwood became well enough established to enable him to make the acquaintance of such notables as English philosopher Bertrand Russell and Will Durant, philosopher and historian. Perhaps even more important to his future were his studies at the Cooper Institute, the Rand School of Social Science and the Labour Temple — all famous left-wing educational institutions — as well as the invaluable experience of extemporaneous sidewalk and other open-air campaigning. The rough and tumble of New York politics served as a priceless apprenticeship for the future Premier, and he learned quickly the art of dealing with hecklers and controlling large crowds at public meetings.

In 1925 Smallwood took what was to prove the most decisive step in the course of his life. That was to accept the challenge posed to him by American labour leader John P. Burke to return to Newfoundland and organize the workers at the paper-mill town of Grand Falls. Typically, Smallwood went far beyond the scope of his original mission, founding not only Local 63 of the International Brotherhood of Pulp, Sulphite and Paper-mill Workers at Grand Falls, but also Local 64 at Corner Brook and, while in Grand Falls, becoming the founding president of the Newfoundland Federation of Labour.

During that same period Smallwood undertook what to many was a more quixotic task. In answer to an appeal from railway section men to help avert a proposed reduction in their 25-cent-an-hour wage, Smallwood organized the group by walking almost the entire length of the nearly 800-mile line. It was probably the threat of having the railway closed that led the government to rescind its original intention.

Smallwood's cross-country walk was the occasion of another decisive step: in Corner Brook he had met a very attractive

3

young lady, Clara Oates, from a well-known Carbonear family. Shortly afterward they became engaged, although the wedding had to wait until Smallwood had completed his marathon trek across the island.

Close on the heels of his railway success Smallwood founded a weekly newspaper, but gave it up to accept the editorship of what was really the official organ of the Liberal party of Newfoundland — the *Daily Globe*. There was no socialist party in Newfoundland, but Smallwood had no difficulty in reconciling his own beliefs with the philosophy of the Liberal party, which he considered to be the nearest thing to socialism that was likely to be found in Newfoundland.

Smallwood encountered a more serious personal ambivalence in his attempts to outline a Liberal philosophy and line of action in the newspaper, anticipating that a general election was likely to be held in 1928. Two of his heroes, Sir Richard Squires, who had been prime minister from 1919 to 1923, and Sir William Coaker, founder of the great Fishermen's Protective Union (FPU), had become increasingly antagonistic towards each other over the years. Smallwood felt that only with Squires as leader could the Liberal party dislodge the Conservative administration which had been elected to power in the 1924 contest. But he felt that the active co-operation of Coaker and his union would be essential for a victory under Squires' leadership. The two were not on speaking terms, however, when Smallwood made his first visit to London in 1927.

While in London, Smallwood wrote his first book, a biography of Sir William Coaker which detailed how he had founded his union in 1908 and had been a power in both the economic and political life of Newfoundland for nearly two decades. Coaker had withdrawn his support of the Liberals in the 1924 election and for a period had demonstrated a particular unwillingness to have anything further to do with Squires. According to Smallwood, it was his unremitting efforts in London and later in St. John's that brought the two together and led to a 28-to-8 electoral victory for the Liberals.

Upon his return from England, after having spent several productive and enjoyable months there, Smallwood went to Corner Brook and obtained work from the owner of the great paper mill — then the International Power and Paper Company. But journalism was still in his blood and before long he had founded a tabloid newspaper, the *Humber Herald*. It soon became clear that Smallwood's decision to take this step was motivated as much by political as journalistic ambitions. His mind was on winning the Liberal nomination for the Humber district which, as a result of the great mill established there five years earlier, was now one of the largest, most prosperous and most Liberal in the country.

To ensure his nomination, Smallwood did not rely on his newspaper alone. For months prior to the election he visited every community, gave speeches and visited homes, using every available mode of conveyance — often at considerable personal risk — in his attempts to get to remote parts of the district. It was when his nomination was virtually a foregone conclusion that he received a telegram from his leader, Squires, the man who had "put the hum in the Humber" (a reference to Squires' leading role in getting the paper mill on the Humber River), informing him that Squires himself had decided to run. According to Smallwood, in conversation with me, this was the worst blow he had ever received in his political life. But he swallowed his bitter disappointment, became Squires' campaign manager, and had the vicarious satisfaction of seeing Squires elected by an overwhelming majority in November, 1928.

Following the election, Smallwood continued as editor of the *Humber Herald* until early 1930 when Squires invited him to become editor of a Liberal paper, the *Watchdog*, to be published in St. John's. But with the effect of the Depression worsening every week, compounded by disastrous fisheries, time was running out for Squires and the Liberals. In April, 1932, a riot took place in St. John's at the Colonial Building, then the seat of the legislature. Taking advantage of the public parade to present a petition to the legislature, unruly elements attacked the building and endangered the lives and safety of those inside. In June a general election was held, resulting in the near extinction of the Liberal party, which elected only two members: Roland Starkes of Green Bay, and Gordon Bradley in Humber. Smallwood, running in Bonavista South, was roundly defeated.

Undaunted, Smallwood set out to try to fill the vacuum created by the decline of Coaker's FPU. He and his family moved to Bonavista where they lived for the next five years. There he formed the Fisherman's Cooperative Union, with a peak membership of 8000. But even the small membership fee of fifty cents was too much for a good many members and the total collected after expenses was inadequate to allow Smallwood to support his family. The time came when he had no choice but to return to St. John's and try to get work of one kind or another.

Smallwood's next venture was once again journalistic in nature. His second book, *The New Newfoundland*, had been published in 1931. Now the time had come when he felt he should undertake a far more ambitious task — the compilation and publication of a two-volume encyclopaedia of Newfoundland which he would call *The Book of Newfoundland*. Given the capital outlay required by such a project, and having no money at all, he applied to his friend Ches Crosbie, who agreed to help. The result was probably the most remarkable feat of journalism that Newfoundland has ever known — two large, well written books (Smallwood had edited or rewritten most of the articles), covering almost every aspect of Newfoundland's history and culture. Unfortunately for Smallwood, Newfoundland was too poor in 1937 to absorb the relatively large printing (10,000 sets), and he and Crosbie had to wait until World War II, with the advent of American bases there, before getting a return on their investment of time and money.

With nothing else in sight, Smallwood turned once more to a newspaper — this time as a columnist for the St. John's *Daily News*. As an experiment he got permission to put his column on radio for a week or so. It attracted the attention of Frank M. O'Leary, a progressive St. John's businessman, who agreed to sponsor it under its original title, "The Barrelman."[1] The programme's sub-title was "making Newfoundland better known to Newfoundlanders" — which was quite literally what Smallwood did. No aspect of Newfoundland was ignored. In particular, Smallwood told of Newfoundlanders who had performed brave or mighty deeds, and he was especially successful in digging up information about Newfoundlanders who had achieved prominence in other countries — educators, politicians, mayors, businessmen, artists, actors, and so on.

---

[1] The name derives from the barrel near the top of a ship's mast where a member of the crew would stand while scanning for ice, seals, whales or other ships.

Also, in addition to collecting those stories and accounts sent in to him by his listeners, Smallwood spent part of every summer travelling around Newfoundland gathering information — and in the process making not only Newfoundland, but Joe Smallwood, better known to Newfoundlanders. Long before he retired from the project, he was probably the best-known living Newfoundlander. What no one foresaw at the time was that Smallwood had a built-in audience on which he could call if the appropriate occasion arrived.

Although better known for his interest in journalism with its various off-shoots, Smallwood was also interested in anything to do with agriculture. It is difficult to judge which of two widely diverse occupations appealed to Smallwood more. What is interesting is that during most of his life in Newfoundland, no matter what his principal occupation happened to be, he maintained his contacts with the good earth — root crops, ranching, pig raising and mink farming. During his "barrelman" period, for example, he farmed on the outskirts of St. John's. It should not have occasioned too much surprise, therefore, when Smallwood decided to accept an offer from the commanding officer at Gander to operate a pig farm, using edible swill for food for the animals. This undertaking was soon expanded from simply raising pigs for pork to the processing of ham, bacon, sausages and other by-products. An unexpected stroke of fate was the decision of the British government that when a national convention was convened, candidates would have to be *bona fide* residents of the districts for which they ran. To operate a piggery, Smallwood had to live in Gander. This meant that he was eligible to run for Bonavista Centre which contained that part of the town of Gander in which Smallwood lived. Had he been living in St. John's it is almost certain that, as an advocate of confederation, he could not have been elected.

Smallwood was visiting Montreal when he read a newspaper announcement by British Prime Minister Atlee that the people of Newfoundland were to be given the chance to elect a national convention which would recommend what form or forms of government should be voted on by means of a referendum. He resolved to obtain all the information he could about confederation with Canada — something which Newfoundland had considered on several occasions only to reject it for one reason or another. After reviewing all the literature he could obtain, he arrived at the conclusion that Newfoundland's future lay in joining Canada, and it was then that he decided he would try to get a majority of Newfoundlanders to agree with him. He launched his campaign for confederation in March, 1946, when he wrote a series of fourteen letters to the *Daily News* outlining the benefits which would accrue to Newfoundland in the event of joining Canada. This was followed by a campaign in Bonavista Bay where he received enthusiastic support for his candidacy and for the cause of confederation.

Election to the convention was held on June 2, 1946. Smallwood received 2129 votes against 277 for his opponent. Of the forty-five members, it was clear to Smallwood almost from the beginning that only a minority would favour confederation with Canada. This being so, Smallwood was left with two tasks: first, to get the convention to agree to obtain from Canada the terms Canada would be prepared to offer Newfoundland to induce the latter to join; and, second, to educate the people of Newfoundland as to the benefits of union to the point where they would demand a chance to vote on the proposal, notwithstanding the feeling of the national convention. This latter was speeded on its way by a decision made apparently by the Commission of Government and without any prodding or scheming on the part of Smallwood. This was to broadcast on the government radio station all the proceedings of the convention verbatim.

Smallwood was now in his element. All his years of experience in speaking extemporaneously, all his months of studying confederation, would now yield dividends. With his superb oratorical skills and his matchless memory, he dominated the convention. But it was not the convention that concerned him most; it was the people of Newfoundland to whom he was preaching. And it was the people who stayed up night after night, clustered around the battery radios, listening to their David attack and defeat the goliaths arrayed against him. The convention had a number of well-known citizens, held in high regard by the public or by some sections of it. Most of these opposed confederation and favoured a return to responsible government. Among these were Edgar Hickman, son of a former prime minister, and a leading St. John's businessman; Major

8

Peter Cashin, former finance minister, orator and specialist in political invective; Malcolm Hollett, Rhodes Scholar, senior magistrate, veteran of World War I and first-class debater; Kenneth M. Brown, union leader, former minister of the crown and also skilled in debate; Chesley Crosbie, probably the most popular merchant in Newfoundland; R.B. Job, highly respected head of one of Newfoundland's oldest mercantile families; Gordon F. Higgins, whose father had been a prominent politician and later justice of the Supreme Court, himself a skillful lawyer in his own right.

On the side of confederation was the former solicitor general, of imposing presence and matchless oratory, Gordon F. Bradley. Another former politician was the respected Twillingate merchant Thomas Ashbourne. Two firsts were registered in the person of the Reverend Lester Burry, a United Church minister in Labrador. He was the first clergyman to be elected to a national assembly, and his election marked the first time that Labrador was given the franchise. Two other members supporting Smallwood and destined to become well-known were union leader Charles Ballam, and William J. Keough, a co-operative field worker who, before the convention was dissolved, emerged as a first-class phrasemaker and public speaker. Another former public figure who supported Smallwood was Roland G. Starkes.

In October 1946, Smallwood introduced his first resolution. Essentially it was a request for the convention to investigate what Canada's attitude towards union with Newfoundland would be and what terms and conditions Canada would stipulate to effect such a union. The speech that Smallwood gave when introducing his motion was considered by many to be one of the most moving pieces of oratory ever delivered in the historic Colonial Building. But it was not enough. The resolution was defeated 25 to 18. To many observers this appeared to signal the death of the confederation movement. But not to Smallwood.

R.B. Job's abiding interest was the future of the frozen fresh fish industry. Like Bond before him, Job felt that its fortunes would be inextricably linked to those of Newfoundland, and that the continuing existence of the American bases in Newfoundland gave her a splendid position of strength from which to negotiate an agreement favourable to Newfoundland's in-

9

terests. Smallwood knew that a number of responsible government supporters in the convention favoured approaching the British government to ascertain what help Britain would be able to guarantee in the event of a return to responsible government. Consequently, Job agreed with Smallwood's suggestion that the Commission of Government be approached to (*a*) determine how an approach could be made to the United States regarding a tariff concession on fish; (*b*) how to find out what Canada would offer regarding federal union; and (*c*) what Britain would do if responsible government were restored. The resolution containing the above was moved by Job and seconded by Higgins, and was carried 13 to 8. Thus Smallwood was enabled to initiate discussions with Canada.

In the subsequent discussions between the convention and the Commission of Government, the latter pointed out that under no condition could a Newfoundland convention approach a foreign power such as the United States; only a government could do that. But there was nothing to prevent the convention, with the blessing of the Commission of Government, from approaching London and Ottawa to obtain the necessary information. Thus it was that in March, 1947, the convention passed resolutions authorizing delegations to proceed first to London and then to Ottawa.

The delegation to Britain was soon greeted with some bad news: as far as the British government was concerned, Newfoundland could only return to responsible government if it was self-supporting; in other words, if it did not need help from Britain or anyone else. Responsible government and assistance from Britain could not be lumped together. The report submitted to the convention was, not surprisingly, rather gloomy and pessimistic, but it lent considerable strength to the hand of the confederation supporters.

In the months that followed, supporters of responsible government argued that since Newfoundland was now self-supporting, the British government had both a moral and, possibly, a legal obligation to observe that section of the *Newfoundland Act* which promised a return of responsible government to the people. Newfoundland had had surpluses for several years and, with a good nest egg built up, was now self-supporting. Responsible government should be returned.

The confederates argued that in making such a demand the

Responsible Government League was conveniently leaving out an important element of the restoration clause which gave the people the right to choose. Properly read, the clause said that responsible government would be restored upon request from the people of Newfoundland. The fact that Newfoundland might now be self-supporting (an arguable point, since the surpluses had resulted from artificial wartime prosperity) did not mean that responsible government should automatically be restored.

The delegation to Ottawa arrived in late June, just as a debilitating heat wave settled over the city. Nevertheless, the group, of which Bradley was chairman and Smallwood secretary, persevered during the long summer, in spite of several urgent and peremptory demands from those members left in Newfoundland, most of whom were anti-confederate, that the delegation return forthwith. This they refused to do on the grounds that they had not completed their assignment. When they did return after three months, the responsible government group attempted to censure Bradley, who had been appointed convention chairman following the death of the original chairman, Cyril Fox. But in anticipation of such a move, Bradley simply resigned — an action which was greeted with approval by the ever-increasing number of confederates throughout the country. Another chairman, John B. McEvoy, was appointed and the convention got down to work shortly after.

Here again was Smallwood's chance. Day after day, week after week, Smallwood led the debate during which the federal terms were discussed and analysed. In all, counting the earlier debates, a total of thirty-four convention days were devoted to the subject of confederation, as compared with four days devoted to responsible government. Finally, on January 23, Smallwood introduced his motion that confederation be placed on the ballot paper in the forthcoming referendum. The motion was defeated 29 to 16, and for thousands of Newfoundlanders the fight was over. But Smallwood had not yet used his ultimate weapon—the majority support of the outport people. It was not long before radio listeners heard the stentorian voice of Gordon Bradley, in a speech written by Smallwood, denounce the "dictators" in the convention who had prevented the ordinary people from showing their preference. But their plans could be frustrated, he continued, if enough

Newfoundlanders telegraphed their demands that confederation be placed on the ballot paper. These telegrams would be forwarded immediately to the British government.

Within hours of Bradley's speech, responses began pouring in, and within a week telegrams bearing some 50,000 names were submitted to the governor for conveyance to his superiors in England. The next several weeks were of interminable length to Smallwood. Then came relief: the British government announced its decision that the Newfoundland people should not be deprived of their right to choose in this matter. Therefore, the option of confederation would go on the ballot paper along with responsible government and Commission of Government.

Smallwood's victory paved the way for the much bigger fight for votes that would follow. But here Smallwood held the advantage: the Confederation supporters were united under one leader, unlike their opponents, who were divided in their aims and lacked political leadership. Nevertheless, a threat to Smallwood's forces did exist in Ches Crosbie's formation of movement called "Economic Union with the United States." Crosbie, who was a most inarticulate speaker, enlisted the talents of a young radio announcer, Donald Jamieson,[2] to convey his message. Economic Union could not, of course, go on the ballot paper, but Crosbie sought to overcome this disadvantage by linking it with responsible government. In other words, once Responsible Government had been restored, the economic union would be negotiated. Although apparently far-fetched, Crosbie's idea was given a degree of respectability by the tacit endorsement of a number of United States senators who had been contacted and expressed interest in the

In the months preceding the first referendum, Smallwood probably worked harder than at any time in his life—travelling, speaking, organizing, publishing for the cause of confederation. The newspaper *The Confederate* was a particularly effective weapon, thanks in part to the caustic wit of Smallwood's close friend, Gregory Power, who was devastating in his ridicule of both the Responsible Government League and the Economic Union movement. Also assisting the cause of confederation was the creation of the Newfoundland Confederate Associa-

---

[2] Jamieson eventually entered public life, becoming Canada's minister of external affairs and later Canadian high commissioner in London.

tion, with "vice-presidents" in every part of Newfoundland. Smallwood was, of course, president. Other positive factors included the close ties between the non-conformist churches, notably the United Church which represented over 20 percent of the total population, and their religious colleagues in Canada. Another was the large number of Newfoundlanders who in the decades before 1948 had emigrated to Canada but who kept in close touch with their relatives and friends at home.

Smallwood's opponents gave unwitting aid as well by allowing the words "as it existed in 1934" to go on the ballot paper as qualifiers to "Responsible Government." Finally, although perhaps only apparent in retrospect, the opposition's attempts to prevent confederation from going on the ballot paper were bound to provoke the angry indignation of many voters who would otherwise have been lukewarm in their support of it.

In spite of all the factors favouring it, confederation received a defeat in the first referendum on June 3, 1948. Responsible Government received 69,400 votes, confederation 64,066 and Commission of Government 22,311. Clearly, with Commission of Government dropped, the confederation supporter would have to get a good majority of former Commission votes, or convert a significant number of those for responsible government. Smallwood's group tried, and were successful, in doing both. First, by persuading a group of St. John's merchants, of whom Sir Leonard Outerbridge was the most prominent, to come out and support confederation, they broke what had been regarded as a solid phalanx of support for responsible government by the mercantile sector. Second, and probably even more significant, was the recruitment of the three Newfoundland commissioners. Two of them — Herman Quinton, an Anglican, and Dr. H.L. Pottle, probably the best-known United churchman in Newfoundland — also went on radio to pledge their support for confederation. The result of these two developments was that many small businessmen, civil servants, and professional people who had supported Commission of Government were influenced to throw their allegiance to confederation.

An unfortunate by-product of the confederation debate was the resurgence of sectarianism in politics. What started it is difficult to pin-point, although it was well known that the beloved and revered Roman Catholic Archbishop Roche was against confederation as was Bishop O'Neil of the Harbour Grace Diocese. (The reasons for the archbishop's opposition are still a mystery to many, both Catholics and Protestants.) In any case, when the results of the first referendum were made known, it was clear that most of the Catholic settlements on the Avalon Peninsula had voted almost unanimously against confederation and for responsible government. Rightly or wrongly, most Protestants attributed this one-sided return to the enormous influence wielded by the archbishop and to the unremitting anti-confederation campaign waged by the Roman Catholic church periodical, *The Monitor*. These beliefs of clerical influence were encouraged by developments on the west-coast diocese of St. George's where Bishop O'Reilly, while not taking a strong stand, had indicated a personal preference for confederation — with the result that many Catholic communities voted strongly for confederation, while others were fairly evenly divided. Taking this as proof that the Archbishop and the *Monitor* had invoked church loyalties to induce the Catholic people to vote against confederation, the Grand Master of the Orange Order sent out a letter to all lodges calling attention to the *Monitor*'s campaign and urging Orangemen "to bring such attempts to naught." This letter was widely applauded by many Protestants and bitterly resented by most Roman Catholics.

The second referendum was held on July 22, 1948. When the results were tallied confederation had collected 78,323 votes (52 percent) and responsible government 71,334 votes (48 percent). The Responsible Government League tried to contest the result by appeal to the Supreme Court and to the British government but these attempts were to no avail. For better or worse, Newfoundland had decided to join Canada. The decision became an official act on March 31, 1949, and on April 1 of that year, Joseph Smallwood became premier of Newfoundland.

2 INDUSTRIALIZATION AND ECONOMIC DEVELOPMENT

When the Smallwood administration took office in April, 1949, World War II had been over for nearly four years. All the servicemen who intended to remain permanently in Newfoundland had done so and had been absorbed into the everyday life of the erstwhile dominion. The American bases were still in operation, although not so actively as they had been a few years earlier, nor as they would be two or three years later. The full-scale employment of the later war years was now a thing of the past. Once more, thousands of able-bodied Newfoundlanders were either without work at all or could find only seasonal jobs fishing, in construction or logging — after which they had to apply for more government support. But there was a difference between the unemployed man on relief in 1939 and his counterpart in 1949. Thousands of Newfoundlanders had been abroad and had seen the difference between the standards at home and those in Canada or Scotland. Thousands more, while working full-time on the bases or at the mines in St. Lawrence, Buchans and Bell Island, had known the security of having cash-in-pocket month in and month out. In short, having only experienced poverty and deprivation prior to 1939 or 1940, they had experienced a new way of life and liked it. In many cases, having had the freedom to *choose* one of several available purchases, families were determined not to go back to the old way of life. They would sooner go where opportunities were better. For many, that meant moving to Canada or the United States.

Such attitudes were nothing new. Although there had been a falling off in emigration during the Depression, it was not for a lack of Newfoundlanders who wanted to relocate. The fact was that many did not have even the modest amount required to get to Toronto and, in any case, neither Canada nor the United States encouraged newcomers who might simply add to the economic burdens of those countries. But in the first three decades of the century, with some interruption during World War I, there had been massive and continuous movement of Newfoundlanders, most often to New York, New England, Nova Scotia and Ontario. This explains why Newfoundland's population, despite having the highest birth rate of any western country, had increased at only a snail's pace, and why so many communities — such as Greenspond, Wesleyville, Fogo, Trinity and many others — had actually suffered a decline in population during those decades.

The history of my own home town of Lewisporte, in Notre Dame Bay, typifies that of many towns in Newfoundland. It had been founded in the 1870s by fishermen who left Fogo, Twillingate and New World Islands to move up to the bottom of the bay, where they were nearer to supplies of wood and lumber, and where there was land to cultivate. With the building of the trans-insular railway and the branch to Lewisporte in the late 1890s, more settlers began to arrive and, being both a railway and steamship terminal, it soon became a relatively prosperous community. Nevertheless the number of jobs available was strictly limited. The population in 1911 was 514, growing to 588 in 1921 and 699 in 1935. The relatively modest increase did not reflect the birth rate, however, as many young people, having reached adulthood, were unable to support themselves. Some became loggers in the camps operated by the two paper companies, a number of young women became teachers, and a few found work in the commercial stores. But the simple fact remained that there were not enough jobs in or near Lewisporte to provide for the normal increase in population. And so they left Newfoundland for Toronto and New York, to such an extent that by 1930 there were probably as many former Lewisporte citizens in those two centres as there were remaining in Lewisporte.

It is paradoxical that one reason for this large exodus to the mainland was the comparatively high standard of education available in small towns like Lewisporte, Trinity and Greenspond. Since those places had schools with two or three or even four classrooms, any industrious students could obtain high school standing. Having done this, however, young women were reluctant to take work "in service," and the young men looked askance at a life in the fishing boats. And so, in their hundreds — and, some years, in their thousands — they left Newfoundland to pursue such careers as store and bank clerks, typists, carpenters, steel workers and tradesmen in those exciting mainland centres. Regularly they would return to Newfoundland for vacations and to visit their relatives back home, and just as regularly they would persuade other members of the family to take the plunge. It was clear to many Newfoundlanders that their relatives and friends who had gone to Boston or Toronto enjoyed a more affluent life than those who were left behind. How else could one explain the expensive return trips, the fine clothes, as well as their ability to send cash and other forms of support back to their families? These facts were not forgotten when the choice for confederation was being considered years later.

Going to Canada or the United States in the period before 1939 was not a simple matter. Admittedly, Newfoundland and Canada were sister dominions, enjoying equal status in the Commonwealth, and there were occasions when Canada treated Newfoundland almost as if it were another province. To a lesser extent this was also true of the attitude of the United States. But friendliness — even generosity — notwithstanding, Canada was still a separate country and, especially during the 1940s, subjected incoming Newfoundlanders to such bureaucratic deterrences as customs and immigration requirements, medical screening and so on. Nevertheless this did not significantly discourage those who wanted to emigrate.

Many of the families that had left Newfoundland in the years prior to 1949 were the more ambitious and energetic residents of the twelve or thirteen hundred outports around Newfoundland. Their leaving only increased the problem of those small and usually isolated communities, making it harder to supply educational and social services to them. From the first days of his administration, Smallwood made no bones

17

about his fears that, with easier access to Canada and with increasing unemployment in Newfoundland, a serious — or possibly fatal — hemorrhage might set in which would drain Newfoundland of its best blood. History had shown that the one way to prevent such a disaster was to provide jobs.

Although the new province had a nest egg of just over $45 million — a lot of money to those whose memories went back to the 1930s when Newfoundland's total revenue for a year was only a quarter of that amount — there were two obstacles to Newfoundland's programme of economic development and industrialization: a lack of qualified personnel to organize it, as well as a lack of basic scientific knowledge regarding Newfoundland's resources and whether they could be developed economically. There was the potential of the Hamilton River, of course, and many hoped that some day its great falls could be developed, but nobody knew for sure. Also, several mines were working on the island and it was widely assumed, if only by the law of probability, that other deposits could be profitably developed. But again, this was mere speculation.

It was in the person of a Latvian named Alfred Valdmanis that Smallwood thought he had solved his first problem. Although the details of his background were somewhat murky,[1] Valdmanis profoundly impressed Smallwood as an able man whose talents could be used for Newfoundland's benefit, and he was subsequently made director of economic development — at a higher salary than anyone else who worked for the government. In this capacity he recommended that the Newfoundland government build two plants at Corner Brook: one for cement, the other for gypsum. The government also built a birch plywood plant at Donnovan's just west of St. John's, followed by a particle-board plant nearby. Generally, it can be said that these ventures, by making use of natural resources such as cement, gypsum, birch and conifers, received strong public support.

Given that there was a limit to the amount of money the province could invest in new industries, Smallwood, through Dr. Valdmanis, encouraged the participation of German industrialists in the economic development of Newfoundland. The basic plan was that in return for financial assistance, German

---

[1] There is evidence that Valdmanis served as minister of economics and finance in the pre-war government of Latvia for nine months.

industrialists would locate the necessary machinery and qualified personnel to those key areas in the province designated by the Newfoundland government. As a result of this policy, Newfoundland would establish a manufacturing sector which generated a wide variety of items such as rubber products, leather goods, chocolates, woolen knitwear, and car batteries. It soon became apparent, however, that while government funding made it fairly easy to construct these plants, it was quite another matter to operate them at a profit or even on a break-even basis. Almost without exception, the owners came back to the government for a transfusion of operating capital and, at first, rather than see them close down, the government came across. Eventually, however, there was no choice but to let some of the plants fold.

Critics of the government argued that its policy of economic development, particularly in the face of what happened with the German industries, was irresponsible and foolhardy; that the government allowed itself to be used for hare-brained schemes which had no relation to Newfoundland's natural resources and its economy and were, therefore, pre-ordained to failure; and that the government was being swindled right and left by Valdmanis and his German friends. On this latter charge, at least, a degree of confirmation was not long in coming.

Although he had often praised Valdmanis generously and, in the minds of his strongest critics, extravagantly, there was evidence by 1952 that Smallwood's admiration had begun to diminish somewhat. But in 1953, when he was given evidence that substantial sums of government money meant for the new industries had ended up in Valdmanis's pockets, this disenchantment turned to cold fury. Smallwood immediately contacted the RCMP who, after careful investigation, laid charges. Valdmanis pleaded guilty and was given a four-year prison sentence.

That the government's economic policy was a misguided one became even more apparent to its critics following an investigation made at the request of the government by the firm of Arthur D. Little, which revealed that several industries were uneconomic, and which led to their subsequent closing. The government was not without arguments to help defend its economic policy, however. While admitting the obvious, it pointed

19

to the millions that had been spent in construction, in wages and in local material. The alternative for many of the several thousand employed directly and indirectly in the projects would have been public relief at the government's expense. A second argument was that at the time the policy was implemented in the 1950s, no one could predict which industries would fail and which would succeed. That some did succeed (although several in modified form) was as Smallwood stated in his book *I Chose Canada*, to the benefit of the province overall. Smallwood could also point to other provinces such as Nova Scotia and Manitoba which, following Newfoundland's example, had lost huge sums of public money investing in unsuccessful industries. But the indiscretions of other provinces could not be invoked to justify what, in retrospect, often proved to be ill-considered judgements and costly failures.

In an effort to speed up resource development and to avoid federal corporation taxes, the government created the Newfoundland and Labrador Corporation (NALCO), a Crown corporation in which the province invested $900,000 and other shareholders invested $100,000. But a million dollars was woefully inadequate to undertake the exploration, surveying and development needed both on the island and in Labrador. It was equally clear that the Newfoundland government itself could not find the vast amounts needed for exploration and development.

In order for the corporation to discharge its mandate the government introduced a bill to give it exploration and development rights to large tracts of Crown land, including water, forests and mineral rights in Newfoundland and Labrador. There was strong opposition to the legislation both in and outside the legislature. But Smallwood and his supporters in the House, desperate for development, were adamant, and the bill was passed. Sir William Stephenson, a Canadian, of *Intrepid* fame and with wide industrial contacts, became the first chairman. It was hoped that his many contacts in the United States and elsewhere would bring in the needed investment capital for exploration and related activities. But this did not happen and NALCO became something of an orphan in the storm. Eventually it was sold to Canadian Javelin, a company which, under the control of John C. Doyle, was to play an important role in two major developments in Labrador and Newfoundland. The first of these was the iron ore mine in the Wabush area of Labrador.

Under its agreement with the province the Iron Ore Company of Canada — made up of major American and Canadian steel interests — had to shed periodically a proportion of its concession area. The richest ore in its concession was that in the Knob Lake-Ruth Lake area straddling Labrador's boundary with Quebec, in the northwest corner. It was this area that the company decided to develop and, accordingly, it built the 365 miles of first-class railway from the port of Sept Isles to Shefferville,[2] the name given to the town which serviced their mining operation.

In 1952 the Iron Ore Company handed back some 2400 square miles in the Wabush Lake area of west Labrador. This ore was known to be around 35 percent compared with the 55 percent which obtained in their northern concession. Hence their decision to develop to the north.

In the meantime Canadian Javelin, through Doyle, applied for the rights to the area relinquished by the Iron Ore Company — a request which was ultimately granted. Very soon it became apparent that a new benefication process together with developments in pelletization, and coupled with the shorter distance to tide water, made the Wabush development an economically viable proposition. But in order to make it still more attractive, Doyle requested that the Newfoundland government guarantee a $16.5 million bond issue to enable Doyle to build the branch railway from the main line to Lake Wabush. Against the strenuous objections of opposition members in the House of Assembly and a large segment of the public, the government and the House approved the guarantee. Happily, as it turned out, the guarantee was not one that Newfoundland was called on to redeem. The branch was built, a great consortium of American and other steel interests entered into an agreement with Canadian Javelin, and so Wabush mining came into being. Around the same time, the Iron Ore Company decided that it would develop its still unshed concessions in the Wabush area, taking advantage of the new benefication processes as the Javelin group had done. The result was another great mine — this one, like Wabush, wholly

---

[2] To Newfoundland's disappointment, the IOCC decided to build its town across the border in Quebec.

in Newfoundland — as well as the ultra-modern communities of Labrador City and the City of Wabush.

Whether the Iron Ore Company would ever have developed the Labrador City area if Doyle had not been interested in the Wabush development is uncertain. Whoever or whatever was responsible for the decision to proceed with the development, it was one which, unlike that which involved Knob Lake-Schefferville, brought both satisfaction and profit to the Newfoundland government and to the province as a whole.

If there was one project which preoccupied Smallwood more than any other, it was the possibility of getting a third paper mill either on the island or in Labrador. This obsession was understandable, given that the Grand Falls paper mill had created an oasis of prosperity amidst difficult conditions for forty years, giving both permanent and seasonal work to thousands of Newfoundlanders. On an even larger scale, the great mill at Corner Brook had virtually transformed and revitalized the whole west coast. Moreover, those great enterprises had been, respectively, the brain-children of two of Smallwood's political heroes, Sir Robert Bond and Sir Richard Squires, the Liberal prime ministers. Thus sentiment served to strengthen his determination to do what would otherwise be dictated by common sense and political acumen. But there were problems.

It was clear that in Labrador there was enough wood to support two or more paper mills like those on the island. Indeed, the casual visitor to Sandwich Bay, and especially to Lake Melville, could view from a boat the rolling hills and lush valleys, covered by millions of cords of black spruce and other species, some of which were larger and far superior to anything on the island of Newfoundland. What was not known, however, was whether the wood could be economically harvested and the pulp or paper shipped to markets at acceptable cost — particularly given the rough terrain, climate and, above all, the prevalence of local and drift ice for as much as seven months of the year. The availability of power was of considerably less concern, however, since all the Labrador rivers flow from a high plateau, and any one of a dozen could be harnessed to meet the need.

The island of Newfoundland presented another set of problems. Sufficient power could probably be obtained from the Gander or Terra Nova rivers, and if these were inadequate, then from the South Coast rivers centring on Bay d'Espoir. But there were few large areas of suitable pulpwood, and many of the small patches were in difficult country. Moreover, many areas of prime pulpwood had been destroyed by fire in the preceding decades, largely caused by sparks from steam locomotives. In other words, it was uncertain that there was sufficient economic pulpwood on the island to justify a third paper mill. If not, there was the unappealing alternative question of whether Labrador pulpwood could be economically brought to an east or west coast site on the island. Regrettably, the Commission of Government, which had been charged with responsibility for the economic rehabilitation of the dominion, had done almost nothing to develop such natural resources as forestry, minerals, and hydro power, despite having had fifteen years in which to do the measuring, surveying, exploration and prospecting required.

After becoming minister of mines and resources in the spring of 1952, I was not long in discovering that we knew very little about the potential of the resources that we all took for granted. It was this fact that motivated me in going to the premier in late 1953 and suggesting that we set up a royal commission on forestry to ascertain, among other things, whether a third mill was feasible. Smallwood accepted the suggestion immediately and asked me to include a recommendation to set up, as well, a royal commission on agriculture. In fact, it was chiefly due to his enthusiasm that we were able to secure the services of a notable Canadian, General Howard Kennedy, a professional forester as well as an outstanding soldier, to head up the forestry commission, and another nationally recognized specialist and administrator, Dean A.M. Shaw of the University of Saskatchewan, to head up the agriculture commission.

The forestry commission brought in its report in 1955. One of its chief findings was that the island of Newfoundland could, for the time being, support a third mill, but that this would require some rationalizing of the wood reserves of the two existing paper companies. A third mill, they suggested, could best be set up by the two mills acting together. If, in the course of time, the island's stock showed signs of becoming depleted, then the deficit could be made up by wood from southern Labrador — just as Bowater's had been shipping wood from White Bay around the top of Newfoundland and down the west coast to Bay of Islands. To our deep regret, neither of the two Newfoundland mills showed any interest in the commission's recommendation.

This disappointment in no way diminished Smallwood's determination to establish a third mill. Contacts were made with a number of the world's leading paper and related companies and, on several occasions, success appeared near. Among the interested parties were Crown Zellerbach of California, Cuneo of Chicago, and Snia Viscosa of Italy. But nothing materialized.

Among the assets held by NALCO (i.e. Canadian Javelin) were timber rights to large areas in Labrador, and Doyle had the idea of putting a mill in Labrador. Various sites for the mill were considered, as were the options of setting up for either pulp, paper or linerboard[3] production. The Labrador site had to be abandoned, however, because of the shipping problems caused by ice. Eventually, with strong opposition from the people of Labrador, it was decided to put the mill at Stephenville, where the facilities and infra-structure of the large American air base had recently reverted to Newfoundland. The final plan was to build a linerboard mill there and to supply it — in part, at least — with wood from the Lake Melville area of Labrador. In addition to Canadian Javelin, the enterprise included financial interests in Britain and Germany, as well as the Newfoundland government. At the time of its inception, the cost of the huge linerboard mill was estimated at $72 million. When the Smallwood administration met defeat in early 1972, however, the estimated cost on completion had risen to $135 million, of which the Newfoundland government was responsible for over $90 million. Subsequently the mill was nationalized by the Moores administration, later achieving some measure of stability when it was acquired by Price-Abitibi, which converted it into a newsprint mill.

Another enterprise which started out with great promise but left a sour taste in the mouths of some Newfoundlanders was a chemical (phosphorus) plant established by the British firm of Electric Reduction, at Long Harbour in Placentia Bay. The initial investment required by the decision to locate at Long Harbour was the building of a road at provincial expense. But far more burdensome to the government, in the minds of

---

[3] A term referring to paper used in packaging, such as cardboard.

many critics, was its promise to supply cheap electricity, without which the company would not have built in Newfoundland. The worst result, however, was that after several years of operation, both the water and atmosphere in the vicinity of Long Harbour were polluted as a result, so many believed, of chemical emissions from the plant.

It was clear to many observers that the government had paid too high a price for the economic benefits of the plant, and that it had acted too precipitously in agreeing to supply power at a price that was soon below cost of production and on conditions which made no provision for escalation. This matter is explored in more depth in the following chapter concerning the Brinco and the Churchill Falls agreements. Against these charges the government argued that it could not have anticipated the pollution, nor could it have foreseen the astronomical increases in the cost of oil and the proportionate increase in the value of hydro and thermal power. This was borne out by the experience of other governments at the time. In addition, the company had not been obligated to come to Newfoundland, but could have gone elsewhere in Canada or the United States. The building and operation of the plant provided permanent work at good wages for several hundred Newfoundlanders who would otherwise have had to rely on government relief, or would have had to go outside Newfoundland for work.

At the time of union with Canada, there were four active mines in operation: the big iron mine at Bell Island, supporting a population of over 10,000; the zinc-lead-gold mine at Buchans, employing 600 to 700 men in a closed community of around 3000; and the two fluorspar mines at St. Lawrence on the Burin Peninsula, also supporting a population of around 3000. Other mineral deposits were known to exist, however, and these remained unexploited. There was coal at several sites on the west coast, and oil could be seen bubbling at Parson's Pond north of Bonne Bay. On the Baie Verte Peninsula and the off-shore islands, copper mines had been developed at a number of sites during the second half of the nineteenth century. In fact, the first and largest of these had been opened in 1864 at Tilt Cove, and had operated successfully for nearly fifty years before being forced to close because of competition from Ontario and other richer and more accessible deposits.

One of the early actions of the government following confederation was to invite large mining companies such as Falconbridge to accept a lease of a promising area in return for their undertaking to expend a minimum amount on prospecting and exploration. Periodically, the company would be required to "shed" a proportion of its holdings, in the same way as had the Iron Ore Company in Labrador. Several well-known companies accepted the offer, but after meeting their obligations each withdrew without taking out development licences. In the meantime, the government's Geological Division continued drilling and exploration. These efforts were supplemented in 1953 by a massive, government-sponsored magnatometer survey.

It was during the early 1950s that one of Canada's most successful prospectors and developers, M.J. Boylen, came to the attention of Premier Smallwood. At the latter's invitation, Boylen came to Newfoundland and took out exploration and development leases on a large segment of the Baie Verte Peninsula. Using government data, and by drilling at selected sites, Boylen was able to reactivate the old Tilt Cove copper mine, open two new copper mines at Rambler, and develop at Baie Verte one of the largest and richest asbestos mines in the world. In addition, he was able to reactivate a copper mine at Little Bay and open another at Great Gull Lake. Other developments were Brinco's copper mine at Whalesback, located near that in Little Bay, and a small pyrophyllite mine near Manuels in Conception Bay.

Some of the mines did not last very long, partly because the stock-piling which had resulted from Cold War tensions began to decline and, in turn, led to smaller markets and lower prices. Others, such as Tilt Cove, found that the quality of their ore dwindled to the point that mining it became uneconomic. While they lasted, however, they poured many millions of dollars into the Newfoundland economy, giving several thousand Newfoundlanders employment. Unfortunately for the province, factors beyond the control of the government eventually resulted in the closing of most of these mines, and effectively brought to an end what was undoubtedly Newfoundland's most rewarding mining era.

3 BRINCO AND CHURCHILL FALLS

O f the many projects and enterprises initiated by the Newfoundland government during the Smallwood era, the largest, most promising — and, to some, the most disappointing — was the development of the hydro power potential of the Churchill (formerly Grand, later Hamilton) River in the heart of Labrador. The existence of the great falls on the river had been known to Europeans since around 1840, and the possibility of eventual development had been discussed for more than half a century. One reason for the enormous effort that Newfoundland made in trying to prevent Labrador from becoming part of Quebec was the vision that some day the Hamilton Falls would be a source of extraordinary wealth.

The British Newfoundland Corporation (Brinco) was created in 1952 following visits to England by Premier Smallwood. With the help of Lord Beaverbrook, Smallwood met with Prime Minister Churchill and succeeded in arousing the prime minister's interest in the idea of forming a company along the lines of the Hudson's Bay Company and the East India Company of earlier centuries, with a mandate to explore and develop the resources of Newfoundland and Labrador. In addition to Beaverbrook and Churchill, other well-known British leaders, including Lord Leathers, Sir Eric Bowater, and, perhaps most important of all, Edmund de Rothschild of the famous banking house, were fascinated by the possibilities that

Smallwood held out. At a time when Britain's position in the world appeared to be on the decline, here seemed a chance to achieve a twofold goal — develop the resources of the oldest part of the Commonwealth (that had also made great sacrifices in Britain's behalf in two world wars), and secure opportunities for British capital and expertise to be invested in one of the most stable parts of the world.

The Rothschilds brought together a group of some of the world's largest companies, eventually numbering twenty in all. Among them were Hambros Bank, Morgan Grenfell, Prudential Insurance, Rio Tinto, Imperial Chemical Industries and English Electric company. From the first the company name was shortened in popular use to Brinco. The winter of 1953 was occupied in negotiations between the Newfoundland government and the Rothschilds. L.R. Curtis, the attorney general, and I, as minister of Mines and Resources negotiated on behalf of the government, and the Rothschilds were represented by Peter Hobbs, one of their senior directors, and Hillary Scott, an eminent London lawyer. In March of that year the necessary legislation was passed in the House of Assembly by which Brinco was given exploration and development rights to most of the Crown lands and water power in the province. These included all mineral and forest rights on the leased land, which amounted to 50,000 square miles in Labrador and 10,000 square miles on the island of Newfoundland. The concession areas were large, although not as rich as might have been thought, since Nalco and other companies had selected what they considered to be the most promising tracts, the paper companies had most of the economic forests on the island, and the iron ore deposits of western Labrador held by the two great companies were about to come into production. Accordingly, in order to compensate for this deficiency of resources, the Hamilton River Falls was transferred from Nalco to Brinco. Other Nalco assets were similarly transferred when occasion demanded.

In return for its concessions, Brinco agreed to give Newfoundland 8 percent of its profits before taxes and fifty cents per horsepower of hydro energy developed. Royalties paid to the government for any mineral or forestry developments would be calculated as follows: 5 percent on the profits from mineral development; 12.5 percent on profits from oil or natural gas; and one dollar per cord (128 cubic feet) on any timber cut for export. Two other conditions applied to the new company: a minimum of $1.25 million had to be spent on the concessions every five years, and periodically a portion of the concession area had to be "shed" (returned to the Newfoundland government). The general feeling at the time of the signing was that the agreement which gave so many great corporations an interest in the development of the province was a good thing.

Under its general manager, A.W. Southam, the company started mapping, surveying and prospecting. But the results of the company's geological activities, strenuous and dedicated as they were both on the island and in Labrador, were somewhat disappointing. Only two ore bodies were discovered and only one was economically viable — the copper deposit at Whales Back in Notre Dame Bay. The other, a uranium deposit in the Makkovic area of northern Labrador, could not be developed given the decline in world markets for the ore. In the forest areas located chiefly in the Lake Melville area of Labrador, all efforts to find entrepreneurs willing to invest in development failed, despite the abundance and excellent quality of the wood. Then, as during subsequent investigations, the fact that ice blocked access to the coast for half the year ruled out the possibility of establishing a pulp or paper mill in Labrador; also, given the distance involved, transporting the wood or wood products to a site on the island of Newfoundland was equally uneconomic. In time it became clear that if Brinco was to live up to expectations, it would have to develop the Hamilton Falls.

Apart from the St. Lawrence, the Hamilton was probably the largest river in eastern Canada flowing into the Atlantic. But it was more than the size of the watershed that attracted would-be developers. Much of Labrador is a plateau, ranging from one to two thousand feet in height. At the falls, and within a few miles of it, the river water has to fall from a height of over 1000 feet. It was this combination of watershed plus "head" that gave the falls the potential of driving the largest single hydro development in North America, perhaps the world.

Three basic questions confronted Brinco: first, from an engineering standpoint, was it feasible to harness (Churchill's

29

phrase was "put a bridle on") this vast amount of water; second, could the power be channelled into electrical energy at a price that would make it competitive with other hydro, nuclear, or thermal generators in eastern Canada and New England; and third, assuming the first two conditions could be met, where would the market be found to consume from five to ten million horsepower of energy — several times as much as the total power production of Niagara and enough to meet the total energy needs of three cities the size of Montreal.

The logistical problems were formidable. To the west, the nearest neighbours were Labrador City and Wabush on the railway line running from Sept Isles to Knot Lake — as the crow flies, a distance from the line of 150 miles, although much longer by an actual ground route. To the east, Goose Airport was the nearest settlement — a distance of 180 miles in a straight line, but again somewhat longer by ground. One thing was clear: any development of the falls would necessitate a rail line or an all-weather road to the existing railway or to Goose, and a bridge across the great river, either of which would be a major undertaking. But geography and topography were not the only physical factors involved. Long winters, with temperatures frequently ranging from $-20°$ F to $-40°$ F, made outdoor construction a nightmare. The Iron Ore Company got a real education in this when they undertook to build the railway from Sept Isles to Knob Lake, 360 miles over and through some of the most difficult terrain in the world. But it had been done and served as an example to Brinco of what could be done when money, engineering and determination were directed towards a common end.

The physical layout of the site itself posed a very big question mark. Would the topography allow for the creation of a reservoir and cachement basin (almost as big as the island of Newfoundland) to hold and regulate the supply of water to the turbines? Previous speculation had never addressed this problem and it was clear that scientific surveys would be needed to tell Brinco just what the possibilities were. To this end, Southam was authorized to commit the company to an expenditure of $3 million to carry out these surveys, and two of Canada's leading engineering companies were engaged — Montreal Engineering and Shawinigan Engineering. Work actually started in the winter of 1954, as surveyors were flown in, using the thick ice of the lakes for runways.

The question of Brinco's eventual markets, although as yet academic, still had to be addressed. It was becoming clear that, given the increasing rate of electrical energy consumption in Quebec, New England and New York, these areas would soon be facing a critical power shortage. How could these needs be met? Already the northeast United States was depending on nuclear energy for some of its power. But two factors had to be considered: generally, while nuclear power was cheaper in 1950 than it had been a few years before, it was still more expensive than that generated by traditional hydro and thermal sources. Then, too, the residents of New England and New York were becoming increasingly anxious and suspicious about environmental problems, especially the danger of radioactive leaks, and the finding of safe nuclear waste disposal procedures.

In Quebec itself three options were being considered: continued reliance on thermal power, despite its growing cost; beginning plans for the development of the James Bay watersheds; or co-operation with Brinco in attempting to develop the Hamilton watershed. As it turned out, Hamilton power would be cheaper than James Bay, but no one was sure of that in 1954. One thing was certain: Newfoundland itself could not serve as the total market for the Hamilton power. Even if another paper mill was established, such a facility would require no more than a hundred or two hundred thousand horsepower. And the minimum that could be developed economically on the Hamilton was probably four million. Moreover, even if Newfoundland's power needs warranted it, any thought of massive transmissions to the island could be virtually dismissed by the difficulty of putting power lines across the ten-mile Strait of Belle Isle which, with its tides, winds, fog and above all, its pack ice and icebergs, is one of the most dangerous bodies of water in the world.

In the early years of Brinco, the Province of Ontario was frequently mentioned as a possible customer for Hamilton Falls power. This, of course, would mean transmitting the power across the Province of Quebec — a notion quickly squashed when that province's government made it abundantly clear that Quebec would never permit "outsiders" to put a power

31

line across its land. In other words, to reach any potential customer to the west, Hamilton River power would have to be
sold to Quebec at the Quebec-Labrador border. I was present
with Premier Smallwood when we met with the premier of
Quebec to discuss the issue. When Smallwood hinted that Newfoundland might go to the federal government to have the
transmission line declared "in the national interest," the
Quebec premier pointedly asked how we would deal with the
problem of sabotage.

As noted earlier, the answer to the question of markets
presupposed the viability of engineering and economic considerations, and these were not long in forthcoming. In April
1955, reports were received showing that a "channel" scheme
of development was entirely feasible from an engineering
standpoint. This "channel" scheme was simply a diversion of
the river's waters above the falls and rapids to a man-made
channel which would send the water plummetting over 1000
feet to the waiting turbines below. The reports also showed
that the topography was "favourable" to the development of
a large reservoir and an underground power house, all of which
were economically feasible. The words used were: "The cost
per horsepower of the ultimate development will be very low."

The years following 1955 brought forth a mixture of hope
and frustration. With Quebec adamant over the transmission
issue, the Newfoundland government, at heavy cost, had a
survey made by the respected British firm of Preece, Cardew
and Rider to determine whether it was feasible to circumvent
Quebec by bringing the lines down through southern Labrador to the Strait of Belle Isle, across the Strait (by tunnel if
need be) and down the entire west coast of Newfoundland,
across the 62-mile Cabot Strait to Nova Scotia and thence
through Nova Scotia and New Brunswick to New England.
Although the report suggested that such a plan was possible,
Brinco and other interested parties refused to accept it, citing
that it would involve engineering and technical problems for
which there were no precedents. Admittedly, power was being
transmitted under water in Europe and elsewhere, but nowhere
had there been climatic and geographical obstacles such as
those with which the Brinco developers would have to contend. In any case, the ultimate cost of the power would be

well beyond what customers in the United States would be willing to spend for it.

On several occasions talks between the governments of Newfoundland and Quebec, as well as between Brinco and Quebec Hydro, broke down. Frequently the two premiers, LeSage and Smallwood, attacked each other publicly. Some of LeSage's demands were so extreme that they appeared almost frivolous. In fact, a number of times he had to retreat from what were patently absurd positions. Repeatedly he demanded the nationalization of Brinco which, he claimed, would save at least $20 million annually, a saving which would enable Newfoundland to offer Quebec the power at a lower rate than would otherwise be possible. Smallwood rejected this suggestion outright on the grounds that it would be a complete breach of faith on Newfoundland's part if, after having invited this great consortium to come to the province to develop its resources, the government then arbitrarily and unilaterally, nationalized the entire project.

Quebec made a number of additional demands which Newfoundland considered preposterous. Priority had to be given to Quebec workmen on the construction of the project. Material used in construction had to be purchased from Quebec sources. But the one demand which most aroused the ire of Newfoundland people was that, as part of the overall agreement, there should be an adjustment of the Quebec-Labrador border. Since all Newfoundland interpreted this as being an attempt to undo, in part at least, the Privy Council decision giving Labrador to Newfoundland, the government lost no time in informing Premier LeSage that rather than accede to such blackmail the falls would remain undeveloped indefinitely.

The accusations, innuendos and antagonisms ceased for a while and, although there was no official agreement, Brinco, now the Churchill Falls Labrador Corporation, gambled huge amounts of money on preliminary projects. This was based on the assumption that Quebec, faced with a deepening crisis in electrical supply, would have to sign. LeSage was defeated in the June 1966 election, and his successor, Premier Daniel Johnson, recognized that his situation was untenable: if he persisted as LeSage had done in attaching extravagant conditions to an agreement, there would be further delays, thus making a power shortage in Quebec inevitable. Accordingly, in October of that year, Hydro-Quebec was authorized to sign a letter of intent with Brinco to purchase Churchill Falls power.

The negotiations had taken fourteen years and had involved the best efforts of some of the world's top business leaders. Among them were B.C. Gardiner, Robert Winters and Donald McParland (killed in a tragic crash of the Brinco company jet in 1969). During his years as head of Brinco, Winters laboured unendingly in the face of severe tension and frustration. In the minds of some, he was martyr to the cause of Churchill Falls development, for, had he continued his political career instead of immersing himself in the Churchill project, it is possible that he might have had the extra margin of support to have won the Liberal leadership in 1968. Others involved were Donald Gordon, former head of the CNR, Henry Borden, Robert D. Mulholland, William Mulholland, Sir Val Duncan and Edmund de Rothschild, whose never-flagging interest and enthusiasm caused him to make, reputedly, over 200 round-trip crossings from London to Canada on behalf of Brinco.

The sod-turning ceremony for the Churchill Falls development was held in June 1967, and the official opening took place five years later. During that time, the largest and probably most difficult project in Canada's history had been completed at a cost of over a billion dollars. Some 12,000 Newfoundlanders had been employed at wages higher than any of them had known previously. The company estimated that over the forty-year contract period the province would receive around $700 million in royalties and taxes. And to these benefits Newfoundland could add the many purchases made in Newfoundland, the contracts awarded to Newfoundlanders amounting to nearly another hundred million dollars, as well as a small but modern town, 300 miles of road and a fine airport, all at no expense to the province.

There were nevertheless opponents of the Churchill Falls deal, and they found a ready spokesman in John C. Crosbie who became minister of finance in the Moores administration in 1972. Speaking in the House of Assembly in June of that year, Crosbie astounded many Newfoundlanders by declaring that the Upper Churchill development was " far from a great benefit to the province" and that the various concessions made by Newfoundland to expedite the enterprise meant that the province would not receive the $15 million annual profit until the year 2002. Partly because of the reduction in tax equalization payments Newfoundland would, instead of benefitting from the development, actually realize a loss in the net return, a situation which Crosbie described as "absolutely incredible." Brinco could refute some of Crosbie's charges, but not others. But worse was yet to come.

What no one could foresee when the agreement was signed was that in the 1970s the price of oil would skyrocket to the point where some of the poorest nations in the world became, almost overnight, among the richest. Quebec, on the strength of its long-term agreement with Brinco, could resell the power to the United States at many times the purchase cost. While Quebec reaped windfall profits amounting in time to hundreds of millions, Newfoundland would receive nothing more than its fixed 50 cents per horsepower and its 8 percent tax on profits — paltry, indeed, by comparison.

Many Newfoundlanders became infuriated as they saw the growth of the Quebec bonanza and, not surprisingly, they looked around for scapegoats. The obvious target was the Liberal administration, and in particular, the premier, who had made the agreement with Brinco in the early 1950s. Over and over, the charge was made that Smallwood had given away Newfoundland's resources for a mess of pottage, and that Brinco had been interested only in its own profits and had shown no concern for Newfoundland.

For his part, Smallwood stressed that Newfoundland's actions in respect of Brinco were identical to those taken by Bond, Squires, Monroe and other premiers in their efforts to bring about development in Newfoundland. Basically, an agreement was put through the legislature giving the developer access to resources in return for certain conditions. The Anglo-Newfoundland Development Company, for example, was given timber and power rights to enable it to build and operate a paper mill. The Commission of Government followed similar practices with respect to Labrador west. But at no time did the legislature or the government try to tell the company to whom it should sell the paper and at what price. Similar agreements were made by Squires with regard to the Humber, by Monroe regarding Buchans, and so on. Never did any government interfere regarding prices once the agreement had been signed. That Quebec happened to strike a bonanza was a piece of luck that no one could have foreseen. The same factors which drove the value of the Churchill power to astronomical heights caught every country in the world by surprise. Theoretically, the same could have happened with respect to any one of the agreements made by Newfoundland governments during the past hundred years.

Some critics have argued that the Newfoundland or Brinco negotiators should have seen the possibility and insisted on an escalator clause which would have protected Newfoundland's interests. But in view of the protracted negotiations spread over nearly two decades, the times when negotiations faltered and even broke off, the ever-threatening possibility of competition from other sources, Brinco has argued that it struck the only bargain acceptable to both parties, considering the one indisputable fact that the only customer on the horizon was Quebec. For Brinco (and Newfoundland) to have waited until Newfoundland itself became a market for Churchill Falls production might well have meant waiting indefinitely.

Harry W. Macdonnel, Q.C., became president of Churchill Falls (Labrador) Corporation in 1972, several years after the Churchill Falls agreement with Quebec was signed. In a letter written to me in mid-1983, he put forward a number of cogent explanations regarding the arrangement which, quoted here, will aid in providing a more balanced view of the Churchill Falls agreement for the sale of electric power to Quebec. Macdonnel stated: "I nevertheless feel strongly that the agreement was a good agreement from a 1966-68 perspective. I am also of the view that the Churchill project was a highly successful project, having been completed ahead of time and within budget. It is profitable and this cannot be said of a number of mega-projects executed in the last decade." Macdonnel stressed that the Churchill project could only be constructed when it was on the basis of a contract with Hydro-Quebec. At that time, he said, there was no other customer prepared to purchase power at the price offered, or even at lower prices.

Macdonnel stated further that it is misleading not to recognize that had the project been delayed to take advantage of world-market increases in oil prices, it "would also have had to contend with inflation, decreasing markets, a utility credit crisis in the United States and adoption of alternative generation by Quebec." Moreover, while it is true that the price for electrical power would have been significantly higher had the project been started in the late 1970s rather than in the late 1960s, there is no certainty that it would have been built at all or that, if built, it would have been profitable. "The basic lack of fairness in the criticism levelled against the Churchill-Hydro Quebec contract," said Macdonnel, "lies in the fact that the critics point to the very high current price for energy and relate it to a project which was built in a relatively non-inflationary environment."

Macdonnel reiterated that had the Churchill project not been financed on the basis of a take-or-pay contract with Hydro-Quebec in the non-inflationary environment of the late 1960s and early 1970s, it is doubtful that, on the basis of export contracts to the United States, it could have been built at all. Moreover, had it been built on this basis, it is quite possible that it would have been even less profitable than it is. Macdonnel concluded, however, with his belief that " there is a case for Newfoundland to ask for an adjustment of the terms of the Quebec contract since there is a certain windfall to the Province of Quebec."

For thirteen years C. Terrill Manning, Q.C., was with Brinco, for a period as vice-president and general counsel. From a lengthy letter which he sent me recently I extract the three final paragraphs:

> The power was priced against cost of construction and materials and a return on equity, somewhat better than then accorded by regulatory authorities in the environment of the sixties and against the background that the significant installations and equipment should have a relatively trouble free life of 40 or 50 years. Newfoundland was a 10% owner and also benefitted from an 8% net profits royalty before tax. The Newfoundland labour and materials priority was carefully adhered to and many hundred Newfoundlanders were given the opportunity of work, training and widening prospects for the future.
>
> It was the belief that development would continue and that downstream sites at Muskrat Falls and Full Island would only be delayed a short time. Certainly, the last thing that occurred in the minds of those concerned was any concept that Newfoundland was being prejudiced by the development.

No-one thought of what inflation might do to the price of resale of surplus power but rather could we make a deal on the Lower Churchill quickly enough to contract with Hydro Quebec for the lion's share before they started developing some of their Quebec potentials.

Earlier in this chapter I cited some of the arguments used by John C. Crosbie following his split with Smallwood in 1971, because of his strongly held belief, among other reasons, that Newfoundland had made a bad deal with Quebec over sale of the Churchill Falls hydro power. Recently, when I asked Mr. Crosbie for his views regarding some of the statements appearing in this chapter as well as on the correspondence from which I have included extracts, he essentially summarized his opinions of a decade ago: the agreement concluded with Quebec had been a bad one from the point of view of Newfoundland. Crosbie found no fault with Brinco for its planning and physical implementation of the Churchill project. But, he said, it became clear in time that, "the value of that project to the Province of Newfoundland was not very significant." Provisions had not been included in the agreements that would have allowed either Newfoundland or Brinco to benefit from later circumstances arising out of the worldwide energy crisis.

"By the summer of 1968," as C. Terrill Manning stated in his letter to me, "Brinco had exhausted its funds and its credit with the Bank of Montreal." As a consequence of this, Crosbie contends, "Brinco had to reach an agreement with Quebec-Hydro no matter how onerous the terms Quebec-Hydro insisted upon. The alternative for Brinco was bankruptcy."

It was this situation, in Crosbie's opinion, that left Brinco (and Newfoundland) no alternative to concluding these agreements and the present power contract, although these contracts would take no account of the effects of inflation or events during the succeeding sixty-five years.

Crosbie's criticism of the Smallwood government's policy in these negotiations included the view that the government should have accepted the suggestion made by Premier René Levesque of Quebec early in the 1960s — that Newfoundland and Quebec should undertake jointly the Churchill project rather than have Newfoundland place the project in the hands of a private developer. Such an arrangement, in Crosbie's opinion, would have opened the way for a sharing of risks and profits. Under such an arrangement, Crosbie pointed out, Newfoundland would have shared equally in the "windfall profits" which, since 1973, have fallen to Quebec alone. As I have already related, however, Premier Smallwood rejected this suggestion on the ground that, because of their long association with him in the scheme and their commitment to it, he was obligated to the Brinco principals.

Perhaps one of the most severe criticisms levelled by Crosbie was that Smallwood "played this matter close to his vest and only the minimum of information even went to his cabinet colleagues." Among the implications of this, in Crosbie's view, was that Smallwood did not properly consider all factors, and that he did not permit proper examination of all factors by officials and his cabinet ministers. Crosbie believes that had Smallwood consulted fully with his professional staff and his cabinet throughout the negotiations, Newfoundland would not have concluded the deal with Hydro-Quebec. This did not happen and, to use Crosbie's words, "Newfoundland gave away one of its greatest resources for very minimal revenues that declined in real value every year."

The charges and counter-charges regarding the Churchill Falls Labrador Agreement are likely to continue indefinitely, but amidst the acrimony and bitterness we risk losing sight of two facts — one provincial, the other national. Brinco did far more than develop Churchill Falls. As Manning pointed out in his letter to me, the company carried out massive exploration, mapping and aeromagnetic surveys of large areas of Labrador and the island; it brought the Whalesback copper mine into production, and it carried out hydro-electric surveys which were of great value to the Newfoundland government in planning its own hydro development. All this meant that Brinco poured millions of dollars into the economy of the province.

In our anxiety to see the province grow and benefit, we Newfoundlanders sometimes overlook that we are part of a nation, and that what benefits Canada sooner or later will benefit Newfoundland. As Winston Churchill put it, the underlying philosophy of Brinco was "a great imperial concept." It has not yet benefitted Newfoundland as much as we had all hoped. But it is a great British-Newfoundland-Canadian achievement that will be part of Canada's economic life for centuries to come.

4 FISHERIES AND AGRICULTURE

FISHERIES

For much of the nineteenth and the first half of the twentieth centuries, Newfoundland fishermen engaged in three salt cod fisheries: the inshore, the Labrador and the bank — all of them based on salt- and sun-cure. By the 1930s, however, two of these fisheries — the Labrador and the bank — had started to decline, a process accelerated by World War II with its attendant disruptions and opportunities for alternative employment. By the time Newfoundland joined Canada, the bank fishery had disappeared, and the Labrador fishery was only a shadow of its former self. But European participation in the off-shore Newfoundland fisheries was steadily increasing as Russia, Portugal, Germany and France sent their trawlers, draggers and factory ships to Newfoundland waters. In 1949 Newfoundland's share of the North Atlantic fisheries was 20 percent. By 1964, it was down to 10½ percent, despite a production increase by Newfoundland fishermen.

Of the numerous myths associated with the Smallwood period, one of the most persistent is that both the man and his government grossly neglected the fisheries. It is perhaps best summed up by the story that Smallwood, whether because of exuberance as new industries were introduced or frustration as measures to revitalize the fisheries failed, advised the Newfoundland fishermen to "burn their boats." While I am fully conscious of the fact that myths, once ingrained in the folk-consciousness of Newfoundlanders, are virtually impossible to destroy — Beothuk genocide by the settlers, British prohibition of settlement, persecution of the Irish in Newfoundland, and others come to mind — I should like to point out the following facts: first, of the fifty cabinet ministers who served under Smallwood not one has any recollection of hearing him utter the invitation, or of reading it in Hansard or any official document; second, of all the matters requiring and receiving cabinet attention (an average of possibly two full-scale meetings a week for twenty-two years) nothing received so much attention as did the Newfoundland fisheries; third, neither roads, hospitals, new industries, electrification, municipal services nor welfare received as much help, both directly and by subsidies, as did the fisheries. Largely because of pressure from the Newfoundland government, Ottawa spent $110 million directly on the Newfoundland fisheries and, indirectly, another $200 million for a total of over $300 million, a figure which excludes the significantly large amounts spent by the province itself.

One interesting aspect of the arguments surrounding Smallwood's attention, or lack of it, to the Newfoundland fisheries is the sharp disagreement that exists between Smallwood critics who are generally in agreement over other matters. In his biography of Smallwood, (*Smallwood: The Unlikely Revolutionary*, McClelland & Stewart, 1968) Richard Gwyn, after referring to the Smallwood administration's lack of attention to the fishery states categorically ". . . right down to the late 1960s it has been the most neglected industry in the Province. For twenty years Smallwood has sought to turn his people away from the sea." But Ralph Matthews, (*The Smallwood Legacy*, McMaster University, 1977) referring to the "widely held belief among Newfoundlanders that the Smallwood Government rejected the fishery," says that "a careful consideration of the available data suggests that this was not the case." Matthews cites both Neary, who felt that Smallwood's twenty-three-year "electoral success" was the result of his generosity to the Newfoundland fishermen, and Copes, who shows to his own satisfaction that the return from the in-shore fishery was actually less than the amount of assistance given it.

With Smallwood's denial of the "burn your boats" proclamation, and with the cabinet also disclaiming it, the matter could have remained a "you did – I didn't" episode. But Smallwood does offer a possible explanation of its origin in his book, *The Time Has Come to Tell*, where he quotes part of a speech he gave in the early 1950s. In it he says, "Newfoundland fishermen are going to have a new chance . . . if Confederation doesn't bring justice . . . a far better chance in life for the man in the boat . . . there will be nothing for the fishermen then but to burn their boats and get as far away from Newfoundland as their last dollar will take them." Notwithstanding the origin of the statement, however, Smallwood's record, from the beginning to the end, is totally inconsistent with the meaning generally attributed to it. In his last speech in the House of Assembly, Smallwood reviewed some of the programmes and achievements for which he and his administration could take credit. These included the building (or help in building) of 63 fish plants, most of them fresh-fish processing, in 58 settlements; the appointment of the Newfoundland Fisheries Development Committee in January 1951, headed by Sir Albert Walsh; the appointment of the South Coast Fishery Commission under John T. Cheeseman; the appointment as minister of fisheries of William J. Keough, C.M. Lane, John T. Cheeseman, Captain Earl Winsor and Aiden Maloney, all men with outstanding experience in various aspects of the fisheries; the calling together of a fishermen's convention — the largest convention ever held in Newfoundland; the formation of the Newfoundland Federation of Fishermen; appealing to Prime Minister Diefenbaker and federal Opposition Leader Lester B. Pearson to treat the fisheries on the same principles as Canada had always treated agriculture; introducing the long-liner to Newfoundland and assisting the fishermen to acquire 722 long-liners, over a period of about 16 years; enabling the fishermen to acquire 1254 additional boats and 3000 boat engines; the introduction of sophisticated gear and equipment such as the Danish seiner and the Larson trawl; the building of the Fisheries College; and, finally, inducing the federal government to provide capital aid for Newfoundland's fisheries.

When Newfoundland joined Canada in 1949, it was already becoming apparent that the affluence of the war years, despite the continued operation of American bases in Newfoundland and Labrador, was gone. Once more, a large number of Newfoundlanders had to resort to the traditional means of sustenance: the fishery and public relief. But it was equally clear that the fishery as it had been known historically could not offer a way of life that would be acceptable to the Newfoundland of the 1950s. Equally obvious was the fact that if Newfoundland was to compete with other countries in world markets, then a revolution had to take place almost overnight. Newfoundland could no longer rely on a few quintals of salt codfish per man to support the average family twelve months a year. New methods of catching and processing had to be devised and emphasis had to be removed from salt cod to other products such as fresh frozen fish of various types.

Following discussions between the federal and provincial governments in 1950, the joint Newfoundland Fisheries Development Committee was set up. The report from this committee, headed by Sir Albert Walsh, was submitted in the spring of 1953. Some of the major recommendations are listed below:

1. Exploration of fishing grounds about which little was known.
2. Biological research.
3. Experimental research.
4. Building and equipment of ships for new fishery methods and conversion of existing schooners to longliners, Danish seiners and other methods of mechanized fishing.
5. Training of fishermen in navigation, diesel engineering and fishing techniques.
6. A joint effort by the two governments and the university to establish a permanent vocational institute.
7. Establishment of dry-docks, repair shops and marine depots.
8. The utilization of other fish in addition to cod, such as flounder and red fish.
9. Centralization of outports whose usefulness had disappeared.
10. Creation of a joint federal-provincial $100-million development programme.
11. Government loans to enable private companies to build fresh-fish plants.

Much of the above presupposed massive aid from the federal government which was not forthcoming, so Newfoundland had to proceed on its own for most of the 1950s. One thing the Fisheries Development Committee stressed was the interdependence of the fisheries with other government programmes, especially municipal, road, and education development. Fresh fish plants needed reliable supplies of clean water, for example; roads were essential if the plants were to be kept supplied with adequate quantities of fresh fish; and, of course, illiteracy could no longer be acceptable for workers handling and repairing sophisticated equipment and machinery, whether in a boat or in a plant. As long-liners and other larger craft were acquired, more and more fishermen were encouraged to venture to the near off-shore banks which had previously been too far and too dangerous for the small boats and skiffs. A second important result of the introduction of long-liners was that they effectively lengthened the fishing season from the traditional six to eight weeks to as much as four or five months. And, as the plants developed, fishermen started moving to larger towns where, in addition to being nearer to buyers, their families would have a better standard of living, as well as access to hospitals and good schools.

Following the Walsh Report, the Newfoundland government set up the Fisheries Loan Board, followed by the Fishery Development Authority. Loans were made to fishermen to enable them to acquire long-liners and other boats, engines and equipment. In all, during the period from 1951 to 1966, 1700 loans were made to individual fishermen. Fish companies were granted a total of $19 million in loans to enable them to enlarge or build fish plants and to acquire draggers and trawlers.

That Smallwood was genuinely anxious to turn the Newfoundland fisheries to good account was manifested not only in the time and money devoted to them, but also by his choice of men to head the fisheries portfolio. Keough had had considerable experience in fisheries co-operatives; Cheeseman had had a vast experience with almost every aspect of Newfoundland fisheries and was especially well-informed on the economics of the industry; Lane was born in a fishing village and spent most of his life in the outports as a teacher and magistrate, and then became general secretary of the Newfoundland Federation of Fishermen, a post he held for ten years.

At the official level, Smallwood was equally zealous in recruiting what he considered to be top-notch men. To attract and hold them he offered salaries considerably in excess of standard scales. To come to Newfoundland as an adviser on fishery economics, he lured Clive Planta from his post at the Fisheries Council of Canada for a salary well in excess of that paid any deputy minister in Newfoundland. An even more dramatic move was his creation of the Fishery Development Authority, made up of H.C. Dustan, a banker; Ross Young, a senior executive with the Crosbie companies; and Harry Winsor, an official with the Fishery Branch of the Food and Agricultural Organization (FAO). To get these men Smallwood had to offer them the then astronomical amount of $25,000 a year, as well as other special considerations. Moreover, he was sufficiently determined that he could shrug off the intense criticism that ensued when the terms of the contract between the government and the three members became known. But the simple fact remained that no matter how hard the Newfoundland government tried, its resources were not strong enough to revitalize the fisheries to the point where they were able to compete with the European fisheries in Newfoundland waters. This would only be achieved if the federal government were to play a bigger role. Consequently, Smallwood stressed repeatedly the need for Ottawa to play an increasingly active role in the fishing industry, to invest more money — in short, to do for the fisheries what Canada had traditionally done for agriculture.

In retrospect, it can be seen that even in the early years of confederation, Canada's contribution to the Newfoundland fisheries was substantial. And, as the years went by, that contribution increased by leaps and bounds. Even if much of it was indirect, it was nonetheless effective. For example, starting from 1949, Canada began building or repairing wharves, breakwaters and slipways. Likewise, in 1958, the Roads to Resources programme under the Diefenbaker administration led to the building of a number of roads designed to link up fishing communities with one another and with centrally situated fish plants. Examples could be found in the roads between Port aux Basques and Rose Blanche, and in the La Scie area, where a large, modern fresh-fish plant had been built.

More directly connected with the fisheries was the federal Fishery Indemnity Plan which, among other things, enabled fishermen to get low-cost insurance for their boats. From its start in 1953, some 1200 vessels, large and small, worth $2 million were insured over the next nine years. In 1956 another major benefit to the fishermen came in the form of a 50-percent rebate on the cost of salt. But the single greatest step forward was when, largely through the efforts of J.W. Pickersgill, unemployment insurance was extended to fishermen. Their happiness was both psychological and practical, since they had deeply resented for years what they considered to be rank discrimination which, merely through accident of occupation, prevented them from enjoying the security and satisfaction that almost everyone else took for granted. Some measure of that satisfaction may be gauged from the official statistics. Between 1958 and 1971 the amount paid to Newfoundland fishermen for unemployment insurance was over $50 million.

In January 1964, at Smallwood's request, a federal-provincial conference on the fisheries was called. Once more, Smallwood had a pulpit from which to stress some of the fundamental issues. Newfoundland's presentation to the conference pointed out that Canada was the only important fishing nation in the world without a national fishery development programme, when, by contrast, its national agricultural programme was one of the finest. Would not Canada start immediately to carry out a national development programme in the fishing industry? Also requested were a review of federal policies respecting the marketing of salt codfish, with particular regard to stabilizing prices; protection of the inshore fisheries from foreign incursions into Newfoundland waters; as well as increased federal aid for "infrastructure" improvements such as more road services for fishing communities.

Following this conference, and perhaps largely as a result of it, Ottawa drastically increased its involvement in Newfoundland fisheries. Federal aid was increased to the Fisheries Household Programme and the Agriculture Rehabilitation and Development Programme (ARDA) was established, later to be followed by the creation of the federal Department of Regional Economic Expansion (DREE). The 1971 DREE agreement between Newfoundland and Canada called for the infusion of $100 million in federal money to the Newfoundland economy, much of it designed to assist the fisheries.

To a large number of inshore fishermen in Newfoundland and Labrador, perhaps the greatest boon was the establishment in 1970 of the Canadian Salt-fish Corporation, a body with the exclusive right to buy, process, package and sell salt codfish. This long-requested corporation has had a stabilizing and reassuring effect on the Newfoundland salt-fish industry, which traditionally left the fisherman a helpless victim of weather, markets and the all-powerful buyers.

Prior to union with Canada the Newfoundland government had a fisheries laboratory which, under the dedicated efforts of Dr. Wilfred Templeman, had done internationally-recognized work in fisheries research, including salmon and herring. With confederation, that laboratory became a part of the national network of laboratories across Canada, which made up the Fisheries Research Board (FRB). The federal research programme which, of course, vitally affected Newfoundland, is too extensive and complicated to consider in detail in this volume. It is sufficient to say that Canada's overall basic research programme, as it relates to the fisheries of Eastern Canada, including Newfoundland, is now recognized and respected worldwide.

AGRICULTURE

For two hundred years, possibly longer, there were two forms of agriculture: commercial, chiefly on the outskirts of St. John's; and subsistence, found in one form or another wherever Newfoundlanders permanently settled.

The accusation has frequently been made that the reason for the backwardness of agriculture in Newfoundland was the harsh and unjust prohibitions made by the British government against those who wanted to develop the land. Yet in the early 1800s, governors were urging and helping the people to grow more. Some actually promoted farming on their own premises, army officers applied for and were given large grants in return for commitments to farming, and the leading political figure in the 1820s and 1830s, Dr. William Carson, developed what was then probably the largest farm in St. John's.

Successive governments aided agriculture in a variety of ways, and individual prime ministers led the way, both by investment in the industry and in experimentation. Bond, Squires and Smallwood each invested relatively large sums in attempts to prove that both vegetable and animal farming were feasible — Bond at Whitbourne, Squires at Midstream near Mount Pearl, and Smallwood at Roache's Line.

The potential hazards inherent in dependence on one industry in Newfoundland have long been recognized. The Commission of Government sought to make agriculture a second major industry, but its attempts at land clearing and settlement proved to be costly failures. It is of interest, however, that these various land-settlement communities, while none have become major farming centres, have nevertheless grown from nothing to become relatively prosperous communities.

Subsistence or supplementary farming cannot be considered a failure. In bad times, vegetables and livestock often spelled the difference between hunger and a full stomach. On occasions, as in the Depression, the supplement was sometimes the difference between life and death.

During World War II and for several years after, there was a decline in agriculture in Newfoundland, especially at the subsistence level. The fact was that with so much employment (virtually 100 percent), and with steady money coming in, no one saw any great need for the back-breaking work involved in producing a bed of potatoes or carrots. But as unemployment returned, interest in growing crops and in raising livestock saw some revival. With confederation and the subsequent establishment of federal-provincial programmes designed to encourage interest, commercial farming took on a new dimension. One of the first measures adapted by the Smallwood administration was the Farmer's Loan Board which permitted loans from $12,000 up to $50,000 to qualified applicants. But the largest programme was set up by the province to provide subsidies for land clearing—perhaps the most difficult aspect of cultivation in Newfoundland.

In 1953 the government took what was to be a long step forward when it created a royal commission on agriculture, headed by A.M. Shaw, Dean of Agriculture at the University of Saskatchewan. The commission, which brought in its report in the spring of 1955, supported the programmes already in existence, recommended certain new programmes, and, as was expected, urged additional federal and provincial help to farmers. No one was more anxious to receive the report and, where possible, to implement it than was Smallwood himself. If there has been one constant thread running through the fabric of his career, it was his interest in every aspect of agriculture — as a boy in St. John's West, as a farmer on Kenmount Road outside St. John's, as a hog raiser in Gander, and as a farming entrepreneur on the Roache's Line. To paraphrase the ancient poet Horace, everything pertaining to agriculture was his concern — cattle, pigs, chicken, mink, horses, and so on.

Another major agricultural enterprise was brought about with the stimulation of the egg, broiler, and hog industries. As a result, Newfoundland ended up producing eight million dozen eggs, one of the few cases where Newfoundland was able to provide enough of something for its own needs. The setting up of a Crown corporation, the Newfoundland Farm Products Corporation, in 1964 had an equally beneficial effect on hog and broiler production — particularly in the building of an abattoir to facilitate the production, slaughtering and marketing of these products. The establishment of the Egg Marketing Board, while opposed by several producers, was considered a necessary procedure if Newfoundland products were to be protected.

Some undertakings, notably mink farming and the land settlement scheme, started off with high hopes but became costly failures, although some benefits ensued from the latter.

Other government programmes which had permanent value were crop insurance, the promotion of blueberry crops, subsidized limestone to combat the excessive acidity of the Newfoundland soil, a sheep breeding station, with subsidies for the purchase of pure-bred breeding stock, and a seed-potato farm. One interesting and highly popular programme in the early years after confederation was the promotion, with government funding, of regional and community fairs and exhibitions. These were not, of course, confined to agricultural exhibits but also included items such as handicrafts and fishery products.

Of deep personal significance to me was the implementation of the campaign against bovine tuberculosis. For some time it had been known that the disease existed in some of

Newfoundland's cattle, and over the years many Newfoundlanders, especially children, contracted the dread illness, usually as a result of drinking contaminated milk. With federal assistance, the government decided to make Newfoundland cattle tuberculosis-free, and to this end, over a period of four years, every cow in Newfoundland was tested. Those reacting positively were sent to New Brunswick to be slaughtered which, in the St. John's area alone, numbered some 200. All farmers concerned were given a cash grant to cover their losses. Another disease in Newfoundland cattle, brucellous, while not so serious to human beings, was the cause of great economic loss to owners of infected cattle. Again with federal help, the Newfoundland government was able to undertake a programme whereby the disease was completely eradicated.

One result of the measures taken collectively by the two governments was that while the number of farms decreased after 1949, the size of the average farm increased. The size of the average commercial farm in 1963 was about 10 acres with only one at 300 acres. In the 1970s, the average farm was 40 acres with more than a dozen over 300 acres.

Newfoundland is never likely to become a great agricultural province relative to the others in Canada. Its scarce and acidic soil, uneven land, uncertain climate, and expensive insularity are certain to remain substantial obstacles to progress. Root farming in itself has seldom been rewarding, but the combination of root with other farming activities such as poultry, hogs, cattle and sheep raising have been shown to be feasible — indeed, in some instances, highly profitable. Moreover, as Clarence Badcock[1], Newfoundland's director of agriculture, has frequently pointed out, in times of economic stress Newfoundlanders can do as they have always done — take advantage of such opportunities as are available from the land.

---

[1] In 1983 Badcock became the fourth Newfoundlander to be admitted to the Atlantic Provinces Agricultural Hall of Fame.

5 TRANSPORTATION AND COMMUNICATION

ROADS

In its last three years of existence, the Commission of Government undertook a programme of building which tried to make up for at least some of the neglect the province's road system had suffered during the years 1934 to 1947. Some of this work consisted of entirely new road, while other projects included the rebuilding of roads that had been started in the 1920s, but which, through lack of maintenance, had become impassable. Although it is sometimes believed that there were no roads in Newfoundland in 1949 (apart from those on the Avalon Peninsula), it should be remembered that there were pockets of local or intercommunity roads throughout the island. Some of these could accommodate motor traffic during the summer season, but most of these roads were unusable during the spring and fall because of softness, and during the winter because of snow. No attempt was made to plough roads during the winter season.

On the Avalon Peninsula, thanks in part to some old railway lines which had been discarded, there was a reasonably good summer network available. From St. John's, short lines ran to such old settlements as Portugal Cove, Petty Harbour, Pouch Cove and St. Phillips. Longer highways went from the capital out to Topsail and then on to Carbonear, Old Perlican and Bay de Verde. The Hodgewater Line to Whitbourne connected this road with the Trinity South Highway which in turn ran the entire length of the south side of Trinity Bay to join the Conception Bay Highway at Old Perlican, thereby completing a circle around the Peninsula which divided the two bays. From Whitbourne, the road was pushed north to join up with a road which ran from Sunnyside to Goobies and along the old railway right of way to Terrenceville in Fortune Bay. From Goobies also, this road went on to Clarenville and out the Bonavista Peninsula to the town of Bonavista to link up with two local networks, the one from Lethbridge to Musgravetown, and beyond; the other connected Catalina to Bonavista. The Cabot Highway, as the road from Whitbourne was called, came into full use in June 1947.

In 1949 the historic Salmonier Line was in full use on the Avalon Peninsula, leading not only to St. Mary's Bay but also to Placentia and to the great American Base at Argentia, as well as to St. Bride's and Branch. From St. John's, also, originated the famous Southern Shore Road which also made use in part of the railway line to Trepassey that had been discontinued in the early 1930s.

From the Terrenceville Highway, a road was constructed down the "leg" of the Burin Peninsula to join up with the network of roads on the "boot" which linked Lamaline, Fortune, Grand Bank, Garnish, Marystown, and a number of other places. This "leg" link was not finished until 1949.

In other parts of the province in 1949, other systems or partial systems served clusters of communities. The largest of these were the road systems joining Grand Falls, Badger, Bishop's Falls and Botwood; the Bonne Bay Road was first put through in the 1920s, then allowed to fall into disuse, and once more made passable in the 1930s so as to connect Lomond, Woody Point and other communities in Bonne Bay with Deer Lake and Corner Brook; the road system serving the farming communities in the Codroy area on the west coast; as well as the Hall's Bay Line which ran from the railway community of Badger north to service South Brook and neighbouring communities in that part of Notre Dame Bay.

These regional road systems were for the most part unpaved. They were narrow, rough, and, since they were not ploughed, were useless in winter. The exceptions were those radiating from St. John's. But in 1949, as can be seen from the preceding summary, the vast majority of settlements off the Avalon

Peninsula were either not connected with one another, or, where local connections did exist, they were not connected by road with other parts of the province. Hundreds of communities, some of them relatively large, had no road connections of any kind — a situation which was aggravated by the fact that many of them were on islands which lacked ferry services. On such roads as did exist, maintenance had been almost entirely of the horse-cart-wheelbarrow type. Most of the bridges were constructed of wood, and therefore subject to frequent damage from ice or floods.

A useful statistical comparison can be made between the fifteen-year period that the Commission of Government was in office, and the fifteen-year period following union with Canada. From 1934 to 1949, the government spent nearly $12 million on road construction and reconstruction. From 1950 to 1965, the expenditure was well over $67 million, excluding any contributions from Ottawa. Maintenance expenditures for the two periods were $11 million and $72 million respectively; and for snowclearing, $300,000 versus $13 million. After totalling these and other road expenditures, even when allowance is made for the fairly modest inflation of the war and postwar years, the figures compare at $25 million and $192 million. If federal contributions after 1949 are added, the total for the second figure rises to $262 million.

Newfoundland's union with Canada almost coincided with the decision of the federal government to assume some responsibility for building a trans-Canada highway, despite the fact that under the Constitution the responsibility for roads rested with the provinces. The original TCH agreement between Newfoundland and Canada was signed in June 1950, and by it Canada agreed to pay half the cost of an approved route across the island of Newfoundland. The route agreed upon was almost identical to that followed by the Newfoundland railway: semi-circular, from St. John's to Port aux Basques, and touching at or near the bottoms of Bonavista and Notre Dame Bay, as well as most other major bays. Although not the shortest possible route across the island, it would serve the most people.

Several clauses in the agreement were designed to protect the public interest, and to ensure value for money spent. Thus, while the province was responsible for calling tenders and seeing that the work was properly done, Ottawa insisted on approving both tenders and tender forms, as well as specifications, before tenders could be called. Also made mandatory was for the provincial minister to certify, and the federal minister had to be satisfied, that the work had been properly completed before Ottawa would make any payment. In practice the following was the basic procedure followed. The Newfoundland government would decide to award a contract for the construction of 15 miles of Trans Canada Highway from A to B. Officials of the Newfoundland Department of Public Works (after 1957, Highways) would draw up the tender forms and specifications, and then submit them to the appropriate department of the Canadian government. If the federal minister was satisfied that everything was in order he would so advise his Newfoundland counterpart who would then order tenders to be called. When the tender date had expired, the Tender Board, made up of Newfoundland's deputy minister and chief highways engineer, as well as the federal engineer representing Ottawa, met to examine the tenders. (Any *bona fide* contractor who wished to sit in on a tender opening was free to do so.) Other things being satisfactory the board would recommend awarding the contract to the lowest tender. The project was then supervised by a resident engineer acting for the province who reported to the chief highways engineer who, in turn, reported to the deputy minister. In the meantime the federal interest was represented by the federal engineer who reported to his superior in Ottawa. If his report was negative or critical of some of the procedures followed, the federal government would refuse to make payment until the matter had been clarified or the mistake rectified.

The building of the Trans Canada Highway in Newfoundland was accompanied on occasions by charges, not always politically motivated, that parts of the highway had been built "below standard." Given the elaborate checking and reporting procedures of the federal-provincial agreement, however, what such charges really amounted to was that the provincial and federal officials concerned had been derelict in their duties. For most of the period when the TCH was being built in Newfoundland, the work was overseen by Deputy Minister C.A. Knight, a Newfoundlander and a professional engineer. Chief Highways Engineer J.A.G. MacDonald, later to become chairman of the Board of Commissioners of Public Utilities, a Nova Scotian by birth, was also a professional engineer. Both men had impeccable records, and were held in the highest respect by their peers across Canada. Since neither had any known political bias, and given the critics' tacit accusation that portions of the TCH were built "below standard" because of haste or other political factors, then both the project engineer as well as Knight and MacDonald would have to have certified improper work as being acceptable, and as conforming to the standards laid down in the agreement. Also, of course, this would reflect on the federal engineer, whose responsibility it was to certify to the minister in Ottawa that the work had been properly done. (Section 12(2) of the agreement stated that a claim [for payment] by the province "shall be accompanied by such statements of accounts certified by the Provincial Auditor General in such . . . form as the Comptroller of the Treasury of Canada may . . . require." Section 13(2) stated further that "no payment would be made . . . that is not properly supported by vouchers and other documents and . . . *certified by a representative of the Minister* [Federal] as satisfactorily performed." Over the years of construction the federal engineers were George Britton, Bert Flatt and Allan Perley — all men of recognized integrity and nationally respected. It seems unlikely, therefore, that at least four professional engineers, each acting independently, would certify shoddy work. They could, of course, have been in collusion, could have broken their oath, or have been seriously delinquent in their work; but no one, not even the most bitter critics would be able to justify making such a charge. What then was the explanation for the charges, some of them made in good faith by highly reputable persons?

The answer to this question lies most probably in the failure of the critics to familiarize themselves with the conditions of the agreement, and the disinclination of the engineers concerned, being civil servants, to make public statements rebutting the charges. Had they made a rebuttal, it is likely they would have pointed out some of the specifications of the agreement:

1. The minimum width of the right of way shall be 100 feet. [Under certain conditions] a minimal initial width of 66 feet will be acceptable.

2. The width of a pavement shall be a maximum of 24 feet and a minimum of 22 feet.
3. The width of the shoulders on each side of the pavement shall be 10 feet. . . . Lesser widths will be acceptable to a minimum of 5 feet where terrain or economy makes this necessary.
4. The curvature of the centre line of pavement shall not exceed 6 degrees except where terrain does not permit this with reasonable economy.
5. The maximum gradient on the highway shall not exceed 6 percent except in cases where this is not economically feasible where 7 or 8 percent will be acceptable for short distances.

Other clauses in the agreement provide for similar flexibility, but the ones I have listed are sufficient to demonstrate the cardinal fact that there was no exact standard. Provinces had the right to vary their standards from a maximum to a minimum, and as long as financial responsibility was shared 50-50, a number of provinces, including Newfoundland, took advantage of the minimum standards. Every inch of Newfoundland's part of the TCH was built to acceptable standards and was recognized by the federal government as such. Newfoundland's portion of the Trans Canada Highway was no more "substandard" than that in Nova Scotia or Prince Edward Island.

In the Terms of Union between Newfoundland and Canada, clause 32(1) stated: "Canada will maintain in accordance with the traffic offering, a freight and passenger steamship service between North Sydney and Port aux Basques which on completion of a motor highway between Corner Brook and Port aux Basques will include suitable provision for the carriage of motor vehicles." The provision of a car ferry was eagerly anticipated in Newfoundland. Apart from the convenience of being able to visit the mainland of Canada or the United States, it was an absolute necessity if Newfoundland was to develop its tourist industry to its maximum potential. It was in the province's best interests, therefore, to do everything possible to expedite the coming of the car ferry, and it was for this reason that the TCH was not started in the St. John's area (as so many had expected), but rather in the vicinity of Port aux Basques.

In 1956 the agreement between Ottawa and the provinces

was revised to permit the federal government to contribute 90 percent to the cost of building one-tenth of the total length of the highway in each province — in Newfoundland's case, around fifty-six miles. This enabled the Newfoundland government to give attention to several stretches of strategic importance, especially that extending from St. John's to Whitbourne, which was sorely needed in order to reduce the intolerable density of traffic on the Conception Bay Highway. As welcome as it was, however, federal generosity did not make it possible for Newfoundland to manage the insurmountable task of completing the highway within a reasonable time. The fact was that by 1964, fourteen years after the signing of the agreement, Newfoundland had only finished half the highway, and most of that built to minimum standards. Everyone wanted the highway finished, but they also wanted new schools, more hospitals, more electricity, more water and sewer systems, and more municipal paving. And the Newfoundland people were not willing to accept reductions in these services for the sake of speeding highway construction.

In 1961, as minister of highways in Newfoundland, I went to Ottawa to present Newfoundland's case for a ratio of financial contribution more favourable than the existing 50:50 split to the Honourable David Walker, of the Diefenbaker cabinet. Using Saskatchewan as a basis for comparison, I made the following points:

1. Newfoundland had only half the population of Saskatchewan, so that with other things equal, the burden of building the highway was twice as heavy on Newfoundlanders as on the people of Saskatchewan. But other things were not equal.

2. The length of the Trans Canada Highway in Saskatchewan was about 300 miles compared with Newfoundland's nearly 600 miles.

3. Because of the route to be followed, the Trans Canada Highway in Newfoundland had to go against the grain, crossing nearly every major river in the province and requiring blasting to build the road over or through ridges and hills. No less difficult was trying to put a solid base on interminable beds of muskeg. I asked that these factors be compared with the vast level plains of Saskatchewan.

59

4. The fact that the average income in Saskatchewan was almost exactly double the average income in Newfoundland needed to be taken into account.

I pointed out to Walker that, adding all these factors together, the per-capita burden of building the TCH in Newfoundland was around sixteen times that in Saskatchewan. For these reasons, I argued, and recognizing the premise that the highway was in the national interest, Ottawa was justified in changing the ratio not only in our favour, but in other provinces, such as New Brunswick for example, where the programme was also lagging far behind. My request was that Ottawa would revise the ratio to 90:10 in our favour, thus giving us a chance to catch up with other pressing needs such as schools and municipal services. But if that was impossible, then 75:25 would be most acceptable. Walker received my presentation with utmost courtesy and sympathy, and agreed to take it to cabinet. Three weeks later, he wrote me to say that cabinet had decided to take no action on the matter.

Perhaps the reluctance of the Diefenbaker administration to revise the TCH Agreement in favour of the provinces arose from the fact that in 1960 a new roads programme under the title of "Roads to Resources" was initiated by the federal government. Under this programme, Ottawa agreed to provide 50 percent of the cost of approved projects, up to a total of $7.5 million, with the province contributing the other $7.5 million. The total of $15 million allocated to this programme seemed small compared with what was to be spent on the Trans Canada Highway. But it must be remembered that specifications and requirements for "resource roads" were considerably less rigid, since the roads were not meant to be trunk highways in the sense that the TCH was and, accordingly, the cost per mile worked out to considerably less than half that for a TCH mile.

The programme emphasized roads to resources, but this was hardly a restriction since it was difficult to build a mile of road in Newfoundland in 1960 that would not be related to resources such as fish, forest products or minerals. One of the first parts of the province to benefit from the new programme was the Baie Verte Peninsula. There the road from the Baie Verte Highway to La Scie opened up forest areas, passed through the famous Rambler Mines area, and went on to La Scie, where a large modern fish plant had recently been built, eventually joining the spur road to the large copper mine at Tilt Cove. Other spur roads to smaller communities on the peninsula facilitated the movement of miners to and from the several mines including the large asbestos mine at Baie Verte. Other road projects embraced by the programme were the road from Gander to Gander Bay, part of the road down the Great Northern Peninsula, and a portion of the road from Lewisporte to New World and Twillingate Islands — "The Road to the Isles."

Our next chance to improve the 50:50 ratio (which looked rather forlorn at the time) was to get the support of Lester Pearson, the leader of the opposition and of the Liberal party. At the national policy convention held in Ottawa in 1961, the strong Newfoundland delegation lobbied for and got the support of a majority of delegates from the other provinces to have a convention vote taken on the matter. In the meantime, Pearson had intimated that if the convention adopted a motion on the 90:10 issue for the Atlantic provinces, he would, if elected to office, feel morally obligated to implement the resolution. At the time, his chances seemed remote, but in 1962 he did win the election and fulfilled his promise. It is of interest to note that in that election the Liberal party won all seven of the Newfoundland seats.

The challenge now confronting Newfoundland was to finish the road by the end of 1965, particularly since the province hoped to celebrate 1966 as "Come-Home Year." Paving was continued until late autumn of 1965 on the two main uncompleted stretches — one between Hall's Bay and Deer Lake, the other between Whitbourne and Clarenville. On at least one occasion in central Newfoundland, the contractors had to contend with snow, thus leading to gloomy predictions that the road would crack up within a year or two. There were indeed some cracks visible elsewhere during the next two or three years, but no damage to these sections. Where problems did occur, as expected by the engineers, was in several parts of the Port aux Basques area and between Glenwood and Bishop's Falls, the two oldest sections of the highway which had been called on to accommodate far more pulpwood and other heavy traffic than the road was originally expected to carry.

Bridges and Causeways

As indicated earlier, one of the big problems in building the TCH, and other Newfoundland roads as well, was the dispro- portionate number of brooks and rivers that had to be bridged. Thus modern concrete bridges were required for the Terra Nova River, as well as the Gambo, the Exploits, Flat Bay, Fis- chell's, Crabbe's, and the Codroy (North and South Branches). Off the TCH, a still larger number of major bridges were re- quired at Gander Bay, Holyrood Pond, Placentia Gut, the Humber, Grand Codroy, Portland Creek, Sop's Arm, Western Brook Pond, and River of Ponds. And in Labrador, the Pinware in the south and the Goose near the airport both required large structures — all, needless to say, at heavy cost.

During the eighteenth and nineteenth centuries, many fish- ermen settled on the islands around Newfoundland, largely to be near the fishing grounds. Following the construction of the railway, however, a centralizing movement started which led to the evacuation of many of the smaller islands — a pro- cess which accelerated during World War II and the follow- ing years. But many of the larger islands continued as viable communities. In fact, some of them had a number of commu- nities on the same island. The problem which had to be faced was of providing transportation to and from such islands, and this was solved in part by building causeways and bridges. Where such construction was made impossible because of deep water or prohibitive distance, ferries were used.

The first major causeway to be built was from Shoal Harbour to Random Island in Trinity Bay. This island, twenty-one miles long, had a half dozen communities, some of them of respect- able size. With the construction of the causeway, the residents of Random Island could continue to occupy their traditional homes, and at the same time enjoy the benefits of the regional capital, Clarenville, less than a half-hour away by car.

The second such project was considerably more complicated and expensive. It involved putting a series of causeways and bridges from the Newfoundland shore to the islands of Dildo Run, and onward to New World Island, where a ferry service provided a link to the large fishing town of Twillingate. Even- tually a causeway and bridge were put across the main tickle — the biggest undertaking of its kind in Newfoundland's history. The result of this causeway-bridge system was that ten thousand people were brought out of their historic isolation, were able to continue their traditional work, and were still within reasonable driving distance of industrial centres like Gander, Lewisporte and Grand Falls. Other causeways were built to the islands of Pilley's Island and Triton in the Green Bay part of Notre Dame Bay.

A ferry service had been in use in Conception Bay to join Bell Island, a town of over 10,000 residents, to Portugal Cove about ten miles from St. John's. The service had long been considered both inadequate and somewhat primitive. During the Diefenbaker regime, however, a large and modern ferry, the *John Guy*, was built for the service. Other ferry services were established to join Fogo Island, with its several thousand residents, to the main island. St. Brendan's and Greenspond[1] in Bonavista Bay were also given ferry services. The remaining services, which were eventually eliminated by the building of bridges, were the one across Placentia Gut and another across Holyrood Pond.

Among the federal programmes which benefitted Newfoundland most was the Department of Regional Economic Expansion (DREE). Instituted in the early years of the Trudeau administration, DREE expedited the building and paving of a number of Newfoundland roads including the Burin Peninsula, St. Barbe, Baie D'Espoir, Cabot, Harbour Arterial and the Trans Canada Highways. The role that DREE played, while some parts of its programme aroused some antagonism, was such that without it, a number of the trunk roads now serving almost every part of the province would not exist.

By 1971 only a handful of communities, most of them either on islands or on the sparsely populated stretch between Bay d'Espoir and Rose Blanche on the south coast were not connected with the rest of the province. Of the 6000 miles of road built or rebuilt by 1971, over 2000 had been paved. The handful of concrete and steel bridges existing in 1949 had grown to include almost every river and large brook in 1971. The historic curse of isolation had become just a bad memory for over 95 percent of the Newfoundland people who lived on the island.

---

[1] A causeway has since been built to give Greenspond a road connection with the mainland.

Labrador

For the Labrador part of the province, however, the story was not so happy. At the time of confederation the 3000 or so *Livyeres*, or permanent settlers, were settled in coves and islands stretching from L'Anse Éclair at the Quebec border, along the Strait of Belle Isle up to Hebron near Saglac Bay—a distance, following the main indentations, of several thousand miles. No one ever gave serious consideration to the idea that a coastal highway should be constructed to serve this small group, since the per-capita cost would probably have been the highest in the history of road building. There was, however, one fifty-mile stretch, where the communities were sufficiently close to one another to justify a road service, from L'Anse Éclair along the strait to Red Bay. The project began in the early 1950s, but progress was slow and it was not until the 1960s that it was completed. As this road progressed, it was decided to establish a car ferry service from Newfoundland across the strait to Labrador.

The only sizable pocket of population in Labrador in 1949 was at and around Goose Bay where the airport was situated, and from which the military had built a five-mile road to its growing satellite town of Happy Valley. The next nearest community was North West River on the far side of the river of that name, situated some twenty miles from Goose. The town had a hospital, operated by the International Grenfell Association, churches, day and boarding schools, as well as other services. Putting a road from Goose to North West River, however, was made difficult not so much by distance as by the fact that en route there were two major rivers, the Goose and the North West, the bridging of which would cost several million dollars. A compromise was reached by deciding to put a bridge over the Goose and a cable car over the wider North West — a plan which worked reasonably well until the Newfoundland government was in a position to span this formidable waterway.

By 1954 the Iron Ore Company of Canada had developed the mines in northwest Labrador, but since the main community was on the Quebec side of the border, the need for roads was not a problem for Newfoundland. Within a few years, however, the giant ore deposits were developed on the New-

foundland side, and two towns — Labrador City and Wabush
— came into existence only five miles apart. Unfortunately
these large prosperous towns were 200 miles from their nearest neighbours at Goose Airport, and about the same distance
from Sept Isles/Seven Islands in Quebec. The result was that
the more than ten thousand people of these two towns had to
rely on airplanes or the railway to reach the outside world.

Another agent which had served to remove some of the isolation and encourage mobility of residents was the start of the
trans-insular railway in the 1880s. Completed around the turn
of the century, the railway was deliberately semi-circular in
design, enabling it to tap the great bays where the bulk of the
population was to be found. At the time of union with Canada
the Newfoundland railway, together with the coastal fleet
which served most of the coastline of Newfoundland and all
of coastal Labrador, was taken over by the Canadian National
Railway which, as part of its obligations, had to pour many
millions of dollars into improvements, both of the line itself
and of the equipment. As a result, nodal points like Port aux
Basques and Lewisporte benefitted enormously; in fact, it was
largely CN activity which was responsible for their almost
meteoric population growth and modernization.

The existing Newfoundland railway suffered from two main
defects. First, it was narrow gauge, thus making it less efficient;
second, the line had been constructed fifty years earlier with
little attention to grades and curves. Many Newfoundlanders
felt that both from a constitutional and a practical standpoint,
CN should have changed to a wide gauge, as this would have
facilitated improving the route in other ways. However, both
CN and the federal government resisted the idea of putting in
a wide gauge, and inevitably, with increasing competition from
highways, fewer people used the railway, and CN losses were
correspondingly greater. Rightly or wrongly, many Newfoundlanders felt that CN was deliberately down playing the passenger service to arm itself with arguments for eventually eliminating the passenger service altogether. Finally, in 1969, the
CN closed down its trans-island passenger service.

Air Travel

The first regular air service to Newfoundland was started in
1942 when Air Canada established a service from Montreal to

65

St. John's, calling at other cities en route. In 1949 Air Canada carried just over 13,000 passengers who boarded at Newfoundland airports. In 1964 the number was 100,000. In 1971 it was 115,000. A local company, Eastern Provincial Airways, was formed in 1949, principally to carry on "bush" services. Its growth was rapid. In 1963 it absorbed Maritime Central Airways and by 1971 it had become the largest regional carrier in Atlantic Canada.

Telegraph and Telephone

While physical separation meant that most Newfoundlanders in 1949 were prevented or, at best, restricted from contact with other communities, it should not be inferred that their isolation was absolute. In fact, the great majority of Newfoundland communities were linked by telegraph land lines which had been strung between them in the previous century and which, by the time of confederation, stretched to over 9000 miles, with central telegraph stations in 246 communities. From these centres, land telephones radiated out to smaller places. To take an example, Woody Point in Bonne Bay had a central telegraph line connected with the main line. Some seven smaller communities were connected by telephone with Woody Point and, through that community, with the outside world. Following Marconi's invention of wireless, radio stations were set up at strategic points on the Labrador coast where land lines, because of distance and other factors, had been impractical.

After 1949, Canadian National Telecommunications took over the responsibility formerly held by the Newfoundland Department of Posts and Telegraphs. Almost immediately, expansion followed: the 8000 miles of telegraph channels grew to over 78,000 by 1964 and there was a corresponding increase in telegraph circuits to the mainland.

Telephone services on the island were divided between the Avalon (later Newfoundland) Telephone Company and CN Telecommunications, with continuous growth in the services provided.

Radio and Television

From its earliest days, radio represented a real blessing to the Newfoundland people, especially to those in the outports. It was also a very powerful medium: in 1949, it was thought that radio had played a decisive role in bringing about confederation. Whether true or not, the succeeding years were marked by a phenomenal increase in the number of receiving sets around Newfoundland. By 1971 almost 100 percent of the households had at least one radio.

Television did not reach Newfoundland until 1954, when a local radio company, CJON, acquired a licence. Its growth, too, was phenomenal. National television service did not extend to Newfoundland until 1964 — to the exasperation of many Newfoundlanders. Soon afterwards, however, with the two networks rapidly expanding, virtually every part of the island was being reached by at least one and usually the two services.

6 EDUCATION

THE DENOMINATIONAL SYSTEM

When Newfoundland became a part of Canada in 1949, the educational system was essentially that which had been set up in 1874 and 1876. Under that legislation, those churches recognized for educational purposes were entitled to own and administer their own schools and to receive, on a per capita allocation, grants voted for education by the legislature. The major denominations in Newfoundland in 1874 were the Roman Catholic, Anglican, and Methodist (now United) Church. The Catholics and Anglicans each made up about one-third of the population and the Methodists about one-quarter. The 1876 Act authorized the appointment of three denominational superintendents whose salaries would be provided by the government, but who were responsible to their respective churches for their actions. When the Department of Education was created in 1920, the superintendents became officers within the department, with two primary responsibilities: one, to look after the educational needs of their respective churches; and two, to recommend policy to the government and to assist in the implementation of policy adopted by the legislature.

Inevitably, with churches and church boards not only owning and operating schools but selecting and training teachers, charges were made that education in Newfoundland was church-ridden, that there was wasteful duplication and that governments lacked the courage to take from the churches the educative powers which, according to the critics, were being used not to advance education but to guarantee church control. A disturbing number of examples were cited where several one- and two-room church schools existed with improperly or inadequately trained teachers, when the same population could have been served by a single larger school with, perhaps, four or five classrooms, and reasonably well trained teachers each looking after two or three grades.

In general, the Roman Catholics favoured the system as it existed in 1949, the Anglicans were divided (although probably with a majority in favour), while those in the United Church sustained the opposition to the system which they had first expressed in the 1870s when a full denominational system had been adopted.

One of the chief reasons advanced by those who opposed confederation was that by joining Canada the traditional link between the churches and education would be loosened and, in time, abolished. To reassure those who feared such a development, the authors of the Terms of Union devised Term 17 which, because of its importance to so many Newfoundlanders, especially Roman Catholics, is given in full below:

17.

EDUCATION

In lieu of section ninety-three of the British North America Act, 1867, the following Term shall apply in respect of the Province of Newfoundland:

In and for the Province of Newfoundland the Legislature shall have exclusive authority to make laws in relation to education, but the Legislature will not have authority to make laws prejudicially affecting any right or privilege with respect to denominational schools, common (amalgamated) schools, or denominational colleges, that any class or classes of persons have by law in Newfoundland at the date of Union, and out of public funds of the Province of Newfoundland provided for education,

(a) all such schools shall receive their share of such funds in accordance with scales determined on a non-discriminatory basis from time to time by the Legislature for all schools then being conducted under authority of the Legislature; and

(b) all such colleges shall receive their share of any grant from time to time voted for all colleges then being conducted under authority of the Legislature, such grant being distributed on a non-discriminatory basis.

In reality, all Term 17 accomplished was to reaffirm what was already a part of Newfoundland's body of law: namely, the right of the churches to own and operate their own schools for their own children. This did not mean, however, that there were as many systems of education as there were churches. Since the churches had their own superintendents in the Department of Education and the Council of Education, a great deal of co-operative action could be taken in such matters as curriculum, teacher training, grading regulations — in fact, in all matters which did not impinge on the basic principle of church control.

The need for consolidation of boards within the denominational system had become apparent early in the 1950s, particularly when the regional and central high school programmes were introduced. The new schools called for large-scale financing and managerial and administrative expertise — something which the small, loosely organized, traditional board was unlikely to be able to supply.

In St. John's the overlapping of school boards was more obvious than in the outports, as each of the major churches in the city had two school boards, one to administer the "Colleges," schools based on the English tradition and designed to look after the educational needs of the "upper" or well-to-do classes, and the other to administer the ordinary schools. Between 1954 and 1962 the major churches all consolidated their internal educational services in St. John's so that the one church board looked after the needs of that particular church. Significantly, during that period the Anglican and United Church boards started discussions to determine whether there were educational areas in which the two churches might act co-operatively. In the meantime the churches started a deliberate policy of reducing the number of boards by a simple process of consolidation. The Roman Catholic Church, for example, had eighty boards in 1962; within a relatively short time that number was reduced to twelve.

The Anglican and United Churches found themselves in a somewhat different situation, since there was more overlapping between the Protestant churches than between the Protestant and Roman Catholic, partly because of the geographical segregation of Catholics and also because a larger proportion of Catholics were in large centres such as St. John's and Grand Falls. Consequently, after the Anglican and United Churches had each consolidated their respective boards, there was still a good deal of overlap remaining.

In spite of the relatively enormous strides that Newfoundland had made in the fifteen years following confederation, there were still many areas of educational discontent. Standards of education continued to be the lowest in Canada and, if anything, the gains that had been made had only served to whet the appetites of the Newfoundland people. In the late fall of 1964, the government announced the creation of a royal commission on education and youth, under the chairmanship of Dr. P.J. Warren, a professor at Memorial University.

The composition of the commission presented some anomalies, however, as half its members were from the United Church, although that church represented only 20 percent of the population; there was no one from the Salvation Army or Pentecostal churches, despite their making up 10 percent of Newfoundland's population; only one member, the Chairman, was an acknowledged Anglican; and the Roman Catholic Church, which represented 36 percent of the population, had only three members out of the total of twelve.[1] Also curious to many observers was that the six United Church members had, for the most part, been as vociferous in their criticism of the denominational system as their church had traditionally been. At the time of its institution, however, very few publicly criticized the composition of the commission, probably because the commission's terms of reference enjoined the members, tacitly if not directly, to proceed on the solid fact of a denominational system and to exclude any recommendations which could be considered an attack on that system.

The commission had not been long in existence before two things became apparent: first, that a large proportion of the people insisted on discussing the denominational system cri-

---

[1] The secretary of the commission was Fred Kirby, an Anglican educator who had spent his entire working life in the field of education.

tically, and second, that terms of reference or not, the commission had decided that it could not make a report that ignored denominational factors. When the report was submitted in January 1967, the first recommendation was essentially an attack on the church system. It recommended that the Department of Education be reorganized on a functional basis. Translated, this meant that the churches should move out of the Department of Education, leaving the department to concentrate on instruction, administration and other services. The churches could still play a role through the medium of advisory bodies outside the department.

The Roman Catholic members of the commission disagreed with the majority recommendations, and submitted a minority report in which they argued that the commission had no business to make such a recommendation since it contravened the mandated terms of reference and, in any case, it was *ultra vires* the Terms of Union. So while the Protestants generally did not allow constitutional niceties to deter them from supporting the commission's report, the Roman Catholics, as the largest church in the province, and with the complete support of the small but highly organized Pentecostal Church, opposed the commission's majority position that church representatives should be moved out of the department. The likelihood of a confrontation between the two groups was rapidly reaching a crisis stage, threatening to undo the harmonious relations between Catholics and Protestants that had been built up over the previous eighty years. Moreover, the government stood to find itself in the hopeless political position of trying to survive with one-half of the electorate opposed to it on one fundamental issue. With everyone aware of the serious possible consequences, leaders in both groups and the government itself were determined to head off a public confrontation. Discussions were held privately in order to discourage extremists from actions which could aggravate the situation; the Roman Catholic Church accepted an invitation to join with the Protestant churches in a series of discussions; the premier and key members of the cabinet met with church leaders to stress the dangers inherent in the situation and to urge a compromise that would be acceptable to both groups. Eventually one was worked out whereby the churches agreed to move out of the department, and the posts of departmental church superintendents were abolished. In return for this concession the government agreed to sponsor legislation setting up two committees, one a denominational educational committee for each church and the other a joint denominational policy committee with the right to advise the government on educational matters. The necessary legislation was adopted in the 1968 *Department of Education Act.* As a result of this agreement — which, incidentally, went far beyond what the commission had recommended — the Department of Education was completely reorganized on a functional basis. In the meantime the churches, through their education committees, retained their rights regarding school district boundaries, training and certification of teachers, and a number of other stated matters, including, of course, religious education in the schools.

Another of the royal commission's recommendations was that the consolidation of school boards and of schools within a denomination be accelerated. Furthermore, it argued, the churches had a practical and moral duty, where complete church control was not a matter of faith, to integrate their school systems — especially in isolated areas where there were problems of transportation — with a view to eliminating the totally inadequate small schools wherever they existed. But the three largest Protestant churches, with the almost unanimous approval of their people, went further. In March 1969, the Anglican, United Church and Salvation Army churches signed a "Document of Integration," whereby each church relinquished the right to operate its own schools in favour of a completely integrated system. Within a short period the Presbyterian Church was also accepted into the integration, and it was not long before the 229 Protestant school boards were reduced to 22.

The Schools

The great problems of Newfoundland education did not result solely from multiple schools, however, although there was enough duplication to give opponents of the system a potent weapon. The really serious concerns resulted from isolation, scattered settlements, lack of roads, small pockets of population, and the historic poverty which had been a concomitant of the Newfoundland fisheries for three centuries. Here, if proper comparisons are to be made, it is difficult to avoid figures. The number of schools in Newfoundland in 1949 was 1187, of which 778 had only one room. Of the 778 teachers in these schools, over 700 had not spent a year at university. Of the total of 2375 then teaching in Newfoundland only 57 were university graduates. The median salary for teachers was $981 a year, a figure which was chiefly responsible for the steady drift of potential educators away from teaching into private business, the civil service and other professions.

In theory, any child could complete his or her high school education and, once having earned a matriculation diploma, could go on to Memorial University College in St. John's for two or, in some cases, three years. If he or she wanted to obtain a degree or complete professional studies, it was necessary to go outside Newfoundland. In practice, the great majority of pupils outside of St. John's and a few larger centres did not complete their high school courses. Of the thousands of pupils in the one-room schools referred to above, only 1 in 700 ever obtained a Grade 11 matriculation. And of those who did obtain a matriculation in the larger schools outside St. John's, few had the means to go on to Memorial or to any other post-secondary educational institution.

In 1949 there was little to distinguish the average Newfoundland school from its predecessor of fifty or sixty years earlier. There was no electricity and therefore no lighting except in the very rare instance when kerosene lamps were used. The schools were almost invariably constructed of wood, and were heated by wood or coal stoves. There was no water supply either for drinking or sanitation. Proper ventilation was non-existent, as were school libraries, gymnasiums and laboratory facilities. The only concession to sanitation was the decrepit and obnoxious out-house. Again, in theory, pupils who wished to could come into St. John's and attend one of the denominational "colleges" — large, well-built high schools, for the most part well-staffed and with those basic facilities lacking in most of the outport schools. In practice, it was usually only the child of the doctor, merchant or, perhaps, the clergyman who could undertake this expense, and that rarely for more than Grade 11.

The traditional tendency for Newfoundland boys and girls to leave school around the age of fourteen, or even less, still prevailed in the Newfoundland of 1949. Even for those who registered, attendance, despite having been made compulsory a few years earlier, was abysmally low, averaging 73 percent. Since the compulsory attendance went only to the age of fourteen, that legislation probably encouraged school-leaving once pupils reached that age. Once more, some figures: the total number in school in 1949 was 75,000. Of this number only 2400 were 16 years old. In Grade 11 (the high-school-leaving and matriculation grade) the number was 1600 and, of these, only a fraction would receive a matriculation diploma. In other words, the pool of 300-odd matriculants had to shoulder the impossible responsibility of fulfilling the needs of teacher recruitment, nursing, medicine, law and all other professional studies. Even as late as 1957, the number of matriculants had risen to only 502.

Of all the problems confronting the government and the churches in 1949, the lack of trained teachers was the greatest. This deficiency manifested itself in a number of ways. Many of the schools had no choice but to employ either untrained teachers, teachers whose training consisted of only a few weeks at summer school or, in many cases, who did not even possess a Grade 11 certificate. For those teachers who could be found, even with an isolation bonus, it was difficult to keep them in lonely hamlets where communications with the outside world were rare. Often teachers left after a few weeks, or at the Christmas break, leaving their positions unfilled for the rest of the year. Under such circumstances, many children never learned to read or write in school, thus helping to swell the ranks of the illiterate when they reached adulthood. In the year 1949 to 1950, despite strenuous efforts by the boards and by the Department of Education, forty classrooms were closed, leaving 1000 pupils untaught. Many other schools operated for only four or five months of the year. An already difficult situation was compounded by a student population which increased at the rate of 5000 a year, as well as the effect of recruitment from the ranks of teachers for both the federal and the provincial civil service, where salaries were almost astronomical by comparison. Finally, the lack of space and facilities at Memorial to increase its output of teachers, became more apparent each year.

The beginning of the problem could be traced to kindergarten, since successful high school work was dependent on a firm grounding in primary and elementary work. But this was impossible in one- and two-room schools, even if staffed by competent teachers. And so the established pattern became one of repeating grades, and leaving school at thirteen or fourteen, often without having acquired even the basic skills of the three R's.

In the early 1950s the best that the government and churches appeared capable of doing was to run as fast as possible in order to stay in the same place. But with an increasing student population it was clear that without heroic measures, disaster lay ahead. Accordingly, in late 1956, the minister of education announced on behalf of the government that a conference on the issue of teacher shortages would be called early in the new year. Delegates to the conference represented the Department of Education, the Newfoundland Teachers Association, the various churches, the university, boards of education, home and school groups, the Federation of Fishermen, and the municipalities. Of the forty-one resolutions adopted, many were implemented within the next year. Indeed, the Teacher Shortage Conference was so successful, it was decided to call a general conference on education later in that same year. This conference, with over 100 delegates, was considerably larger than the earlier one and, of course, covered much more ground, passing in all, 71 resolutions. Since the two were closely related both in content and in time, it will save space to treat them as one in this summary.

Since many students who reached Grade 11 had only a limited chance to matriculate, a special "academic" summer school was created where students were able to complete their matriculation requirements. The first school held that year drew nearly 200 students who picked up the sciences or foreign languages or mathematics subjects they lacked. To encourage better-trained teachers to remain in the profession, bonuses were paid for the first time to those teachers doing university studies beyond four years. Loan funds were established for teachers' residences and to enable teachers to return to university to advance their studies. Educational legislation was amended in the House of Assembly to remove some of the penalties which had traditionally deterred those who had left the profession and wished to return. The difficulties and frustrations experienced by both teachers and high school students in the small schools were recognized by instituting a radio-correspondence course to be integrated with their classroom work. In its first year, this course was taken by 256 high school students attending 94 schools around the province.

A recommendation that the five-year regional high school programme be extended to a total of 15 years, to enable boards to undertake long-term financing, was implemented by the government—with an immediate effect on the number of projects undertaken. The government also accepted the recommendation that more temporary buildings be erected on the university campus to accommodate the increasing number of students of education, as well as one advocating higher indenture grants to encourage untrained teachers to register in the education faculty. Other resolutions (not listed in any order of priority) were the implementation of Grade 12[2] in the schools; the continuation of the government's centralization policy; and that the government should "proceed with the erection of the new university buildings [the new campus] with the least possible delay." One other resolution debated at some length, and receiving exactly 50 percent of the delegates' votes, was that the government appoint a royal commission "to enquire into the existing state of education in this province and to make recommendations with regard to its future organization and development at all levels." As noted earlier in this chapter, the government decided to adopt this recommendation six years later.

Vocational and Technical Schools

For a full century before 1949, it had been customary for both government and the public to decry the lack of vocational education and the over-emphasis on academic studies in a country where the need for the former was so obvious and opportunities to apply the latter were so scarce. From time to time, faint-hearted attempts were made to cope with the problem, but at no time did Newfoundland possess either the financial means or the trained personnel to implement a substantial programme on a comprehensive scale. The situation changed slightly as World War II came to an end and the government

---

[2] This recommendation had to wait over twenty years before being acted on.

found itself with discharged veterans filling the ranks of the unemployed. In 1946 the tentative steps of the latter war years were brought together by the establishment of a vocational institute where courses such as diesel and motor mechanics, electrical work and plumbing were made available. By 1948, with some 600 veterans trained, it was decided to terminate the institute's activities as a school for veterans. At the time of confederation, the institute was operating with a skeleton staff for civilians needing training in a limited number of areas. The success of this exploratory year encouraged the government to take advantage of federal legislation designed to enable Ottawa to give help to the provinces in the vocational field. In 1950 the provincial and federal governments signed the *Vocational Schools Agreement Act*, by which Ottawa pledged half the cost of approved capital projects. This was followed in 1951 by complementary apprenticeship legislation.

In spite of the federal assistance available for capital projects, the Newfoundland government was not in a position to take advantage of it, largely because of the increasing demands for ordinary schools. But the vocational institute increased its role considerably as space and new equipment became available. Five courses available in 1950 had become eighteen courses by 1960, embracing such highly practical work as navigation, barbering and marine engineering. In 1960 the Diefenbaker government upped its contribution to the programme from 50 to 75 percent. And with the problem of elementary and high schools by then at least partially solved, the Newfoundland government decided to take full advantage of this generosity. By 1963, eleven modern trade schools had been built. Located in Corner Brook, Grand Falls, Gander, Burin, Bell Island, Carbonear, Port aux Basques, Stephenville Crossing, Lewisporte, Clarenville and Seal Cover (Conception Bay), these schools varied in size, with accommodation ranging from 150 to 350 students. Where necessary, of course, the schools could be used for teaching night courses. The impact of these well-equipped and competently staffed schools may be appreciated by the fact that by 1966 well over 5000 students were registered — a figure which does not include those registered at the new College of Trades and Technology.

The college was built under the 75:25 financing agreement and was completed by 1963. With an area of 262,000 square feet it was the largest building in the province. Four years later it was filled to capacity with 1150 daytime students and 1000 in evening classes. Thereafter, qualified applicants were being rejected in growing numbers, despite putting other buildings to use and attaching sixteen portable classrooms to the college building. By 1971 the full- and part-time student population had topped the 4000 mark. The enormous demand for admission was almost beyond belief. In 1971, for every qualified student registered, four were rejected; also that year, the pharmacy class, designed for 25 students, received 200 applications.

The overcrowding which, from the beginning, had troubled the technical college was not as much of a problem for the trade schools. But by 1970 it had become so widespread, and the demands from areas lacking vocational services had become so vociferous, that a second programme was introduced. That year the minister of education announced that the capacity of the Seal Cove school would be doubled, substantial enlargements were forthcoming for the Burin and Gander schools, additional portable units would be set up at five other schools, and that new schools would be constructed at Happy Valley in Labrador, St. Anthony, Baie Verte, Bonavista, Springdale and Placentia, bringing the total number of schools to seventeen.

An important innovation was tried out at the vocational school at Seal Cove: because several academic high schools were located nearby the vocational school, the two boards responsible for them set up a trial system whereby high school students could participate in vocational and technical studies while still carrying on their "home" school studies. This experiment proved so successful and popular that the second group of vocational schools scheduled to be built were designed to handle the double programme.

As valuable and necessary as the vocational and technical measures were, they still left virtually untouched the largest single occupational group in the province — specifically, its 20,000 fishermen. Again, notwithstanding the beliefs of his critics, Smallwood never underestimated the continuing importance of the fishery to Newfoundland, nor was his attitude to its future as fatalistic as indicated by the mythical exhortation to fishermen to "burn their boats." Perhaps nowhere was his real concern manifested more strongly than in his conception and creation of the College of Fisheries, Navigation, Marine Engineering and Electronics. Here two facts dominated his thinking: first, that while fishing in all its forms was one of the great industries of Canada, the federal government had never shown the same practical interest in and concern for the fisheries as it had for agriculture (for example, there were a number of agricultural colleges strung across Canada, all of them depending on federal funding in one way or another; but there was not one institution devoted to fisheries); second, that with the modernization going on in the fisheries of other countries — notably the Soviet Union, Japan and Western European countries — either the Newfoundland fishery had to keep pace or it would perish. In the latter case, the fishermen would indeed have no choice but to burn their boats.

In spite of the formidable problems confronting the project, particularly the problem of staffing it, the College of Fisheries became a reality in 1963. Several pieces of good fortune attended the announcement. Memorial University had moved to its new campus, thus releasing the old university building on Parade Street, as well as several adjoining buildings. In addition, the premier had been successful in obtaining the services, as a fisheries consultant, of a well-known Canadian scientist, Dr. O.T. Cooper, who had assisted the Nova Scotia government in the creation of their Department of Fisheries.

The difficulty in obtaining staff was overcome, in part, by recruiting qualified specialists from various countries in Europe. (As time went on, of course, more and more Newfoundlanders were drawn into what many regarded as one of the most important undertakings of the era.) Financial help came too when, as with the university and technical college, Ottawa was able to support the new institution, by including it under the Technical and Vocational Agreement and by agreeing to have senior technical federal personnel seconded to the new project. At the beginning of 1964, only 146 students were registered. Two years later, the total registration had climbed to 3000. Almost 10 percent of these students were from outside Canada — an indication of the respect with which the college was regarded by other fishing countries.

Memorial University

In 1949 the only post-secondary institution in Newfoundland was Memorial University College, which had been opened in 1925 and had offered two-year courses in arts and science and three years in engineering. One of the first acts of the Smallwood administration was to legislate the college into a university. That in itself meant little change at first, apart from the offering of a few additional courses and awarding a handful of degrees. The old campus became the new university with essentially the same staff. By 1952, however, Memorial was growing. Each year saw increased enrollment, additional courses, and increased pressure on accommodation. This was met, at first, by temporary buildings on the Parade Street campus, but by 1957 the university had to restrict enrollment —a situation which continued for three years. In the meantime, the government had acquired land to the rear of old St. John's, and a planning committee had been set up to make recommendations for the new campus. The blueprint called for four main buildings — Arts-Administration, Science and Engineering, Physical Education, and the Library — on a campus of approximately 100 acres. These buildings, together with the residences, occupied most of the space on the new campus, and by the fall of 1961 when the new campus was officially opened, it was clear that the university was growing faster than most observers had anticipated. Fortunately, there was a large stretch of land to the north which was only sparsely occupied. The problem of how to obtain this needed land was solved by the beneficence of a St. John's businessman, C.A. Pippy, who provided a million dollars for the acquisition of the 500 acres. Since one reason for building the new university was to help solve the problem of training teachers, the Arts-Education building was constructed with no delay, followed by the Chemistry-Physics building. Others followed in quick succession: a student centre, three church residential colleges, and other residences. Yet so rapid was the increase in student population, a number of temporary buildings had to be built on the new campus to take care of the surplus. In 1971 degrees were conferred on 850 students, compared with only 30 in 1952.

The lack of teachers was not the only shortage plaguing the

province in the years following confederation. Newfoundland had the lowest per-capita number of medical practitioners in Canada, and few of those doctors (or nurses) were willing to serve in remote Newfoundland outports. A variety of expedients were adopted to try to make the shortages less acute: recruitment in the British Isles, provision of special inducements to keep young Newfoundland doctors from leaving the province, and full government assistance towards university expenses. But these and other measures all fell short of the mark, with the result that people in remote communities suffered and, in many cases, died for want of medical attention.

After nearly two decades of attempted incentives, and after consulting with world-renowned medical authorities, the government decided in 1967 to undertake the momentous step of establishing a medical school at the university. This was accompanied by a decision to turn the old St. John's General Hospital into a chronic care institution and build a new general hospital on the campus as an adjunct to, and teaching facility for its medical school. One indication of the need for a medical school in Newfoundland may be gauged by figures given by the dean in 1971: to fill the 60 first- and second-year places in the medical school, 2000 applications were received.

Other developments which helped to establish Newfoundland's university in the academic and scientific world were: the founding of the School of Engineering in 1967; the creation in 1959 of the University Extension Service to sponsor glee clubs, choirs, drama, art, electronic activities, films, and a host of other projects affecting life styles in various parts of Newfoundland and Labrador; as well as the establishment in 1967 of the Marine Sciences Research Laboratory at Logy Bay, about five miles from St. John's. This marine laboratory has done pioneer work in cold water research and, in particular, has attracted world attention in studies involving the giant squid. Also notable for pathfinding work in new areas are the Institute of Social and Economic Research, set up in 1961, and the Institute for Research in Human Abilities created in 1968. The net result of activities in these and other disciplines was that within twenty years of its founding, Memorial had become the largest and most modern university in eastern Canada, was held in the highest esteem by sister universities and, more important, was having a revolutionary effect on the province it was created to serve.

Educational Funding

Newfoundlanders, possibly because of their economic background, had always shied away from direct taxation — a fact which made it extremely difficult for boards of education to finance a proper school system. As a result, they had to rely on the modest fees and help in kind (such as free work, wood and other items.) The system worked reasonably well with a primitive one- or two-room school, but with large, well-equipped schools requiring sophisticated equipment and apparatus, more reliable methods of long-term financing had to be devised. The problem was further aggravated by the almost total lack of municipal taxation, outside of St. John's, in 1949.

The first attempt to impose direct local educational taxation was made in 1954 at Corner Brook, in the face of strong opposition, through legislation which was known as the *School Tax Act*. This authorized the government to declare any municipality or portion thereof to be a school tax area and, for that purpose, to create a school tax authority for such an area. Opponents of the measure fought it through the courts but were overruled on most of the important issues involved. This encouraged other municipalities, especially industrial centres, to follow Corner Brook's example.

Under the Constitution, responsibility for education falls on the provinces, and Ottawa had always been most particular in making sure that no precedents were set that would embroil the federal government in provincial education. Yet the simple fact remained that Newfoundland's standards for basic education were the lowest in Canada, and could not be elevated without additional federal help. We have already seen the methods by which Ottawa assumed the major cost for vocational and technical education. In 1967, however, an important breakthrough took place when Ottawa agreed to a formula whereby the federal government would pay 50 percent of the approved cost of post-secondary (i.e., university) education or, at its option, a province could choose to accept an escalating per-capita grant. Newfoundland chose the latter and, as noted earlier in the chapter, it was Ottawa's coverage of half or more than half the cost of post-secondary education which made possible major developments, first in vocational and technical and later in university activity. Of course, Newfoundland still faced problems with its elementary and high schools, but here too a partial breakthrough was imminent.

Ottawa was apprehensive about getting involved in the provincial affairs of basic education, but particularly so in Newfoundland's case. Given the province's denominational system of education, the federal government shuddered at the prospect of accusations pouring in from the rest of Canada that it was helping to finance church schools. But Ottawa nevertheless found another way to begin helping Newfoundland solve at least part of its prodigious education problems. In northern Labrador there were about 2000 Inuit, part Inuit, and Indian residents. And while it is true they did not enjoy the same status as their relatives in the Territories, Ottawa felt, following a federal-provincial conference in the early 1950s, that both logic and humanity dictated the necessity of helping Newfoundland in its responsibilities to these aboriginal citizens. Accordingly, a package deal was arranged which included federal help for educating the two groups — help which has been sustained through the years.

Federal assistance for basic education stemmed from two philosophical concepts which had grown and crystalized chiefly as a result of the federal-provincial conferences that dotted the period. The first was the belief that the federal government had a responsibility for helping to offset the effect of regional disparities; the second was a recognition by all concerned that schools were fundamental to any process of social adjustment or economic expansion in the underdeveloped, underprivileged or depressed parts of Canada. These two concepts found expression in the Department of Regional Economic Expansion (DREE) programme.

Thus it was that by 1970 the two governments were able to sign a far-reaching agreement whereby Ottawa would pay 75 percent of the cost of approved projects, included among which were eight elementary and high schools. The remaining 25 percent of the cost was also advanced by Ottawa in the form of long-term loans. These new schools were not typical of the ordinary schools of Newfoundland: built to give pupils an education as modern as any available, they contained provision for athletics, music, art and other activities now accepted as being part of every child's educational birthright. A subsequent agreement called for the building of nine additional schools — all as large as the first group, and designed to serve children who had to be transported daily from small isolated communities.

Starting from an educational expenditure of $4.5 million in 1949, representing an eighth of the total provincial budget, the expenditure for 1971 had grown to $115 million, or about one-quarter of the total budget. Also significant was the development of the scholarship and bursary programme which, starting with less than a dozen scholarships in 1949, rose to a grand total of nearly 1200 scholarships and bursaries by 1971, all funded by the Newfoundland government. (There were, of course, a substantial number of private scholarships and bursaries.) In sum, by 1971, Newfoundland had the most comprehensive and most generous student aid programme in Canada. Added to the above measures were provincial allowances and free or partly free university tuition, 50- to 75-percent subsidies for textbooks in elementary and high schools, and at the university level, Canada student loans. The student aid amounting to a few thousand dollars annually in 1949 had become well over $11 million in 1971.

7 HEALTH AND WELFARE

T he Commission of Government was often criticized for the inadequacy of its efforts to provide such basic services as roads, municipal development, welfare, electrification and education. But the one area of which criticism was either muted or non-existent was in medical health. During its tenure the Commission had built a number of strategically located "cottage" hospitals, had enlarged the general hospital in St. John's, and tripled the number of beds at the tuberculosis sanitorium. At the time of confederation in 1949 a new 270-bed tuberculosis sanitorium and a new hospital (Western Memorial), both at Corner Brook, were under construction. In total, there were twenty-eight hospitals and eleven nursing stations which, counting the mental hospital and the T.B. "San," housed 2600 beds. Compared with conditions in Newfoundland fifteen years previously, this was a gratifying improvement; but relative to the rest of Canada, medical services were still woefully inadequate.

One of the first actions of the government, following the first provincial election in 1949, was to divide what had been known as the Department of Public Health and Welfare into two completely independent parts. With this change it could no longer be said — as it had been — that welfare had always taken second place to public health in the government's thinking and planning. Whether this charge was true or not, the separation of departments made it possible for the government to give individual attention to each of what were bound to become two of the largest and most active sectors in public affairs, health and welfare.

When the new Department of Health was able to assess its position it was clear that some progress had already taken place: a large wing which had been added to the St. John's General Hospital in 1945; a joint campaign had been launched by both the government and Tuberculosis Association against the province's traditional historic scourge, tuberculosis, with recently acquired additional X-ray equipment; a wartime hospital in St. John's had been made available for T.B. patients after the end of World War II; new anti-tuberculosis drugs, and the X-ray equipped vessel, the *Christmas Seal*, had been acquired; a 120-bed nurses residence at the hospital for mental and nervous diseases had been completed in 1949; a second RCAF Hospital near the general hospital in St. John's had been turned into an orthopedic hospital; two wartime hospitals at Gander and Botwood had been given over to the province and were being operated as general hospitals; and, finally, a group, albeit small, of highly trained and experienced medical personnel headed by Doctors Leonard Miller, James McGrath[1] and Edward Peters who led the fight which only a few years earlier had seemed so hopeless.

But despite the positive steps that had been taken, Newfoundland was still beset by serious problems. Doctors and nurses were in chronically short supply, and few of those available were willing to serve in remote parts of the province. The number of tuberculosis cases per capita was still higher than anywhere else in the western world. Periodic onslaughts of childhood diseases such as enteritis and polio ravaged the population, and there was an ongoing need for more hospitals, nursing stations and, in particular, for a children's hospital. Finally, there was a shortage of dentists in the outports and a lack of dental care for large numbers of the public, especially children.

These health and medical problems were so interlinked that to find a solution to one required an assault on one or several issues, not all of which were strictly medical. The shortage of

---

[1] McGrath later entered the Smallwood cabinet as minister of health.

Newfoundland nurses, for example, could be attributed to the inadequate number of matriculants which, in turn, could only be remedied by bringing in more and better teachers, and more central high schools. But this meant more roads, and so on, in an unending spiral.

The problem of doctor and nurse shortages was probably more a matter of psychology than arithmetic. Before road link-ups, a doctor or nurse had to contemplate living in a small outport, often with only five or six hundred residents in the immediate vicinity, having to do a lot of travelling by boat, cut off from contact with his or her medical peers for lengthy periods, and often having to live and practise primitively without electricity or water and sewage facilities. Indeed, many Newfoundland-born doctors and nurses refused outright, after graduation, to go back to serve in makeshift surgeries or nursing stations in their own homes or nearby communities. I remember once asking a man about the possibility of his daughter, then nursing in one of the St. John's hospitals, returning to serve in her home-town, where the nursing station had closed down for want of a nurse. He replied rather sharply: "I educated her so that she wouldn't have to live in a small Newfoundland outport like this." Indeed, during the ten years that I represented White Bay South, no Newfoundland-born nurse served in any one of the four nursing centres in the district. It was not until road connections were made, modern facilities constructed and a central hospital was established at Baie Verte that it was possible to recruit Newfoundland nurses for that area.

Similarly with doctors: for three medical posts vacant in the district at La Scie, Baie Verte and Hampden in the late 1950s, Dr. McGrath, the minister of health, and I had to go to Britain to recruit doctors. We were successful, but only because special inducements were offered. Almost invariably, once the recruits had fulfilled their contractual obligations — as a rule, two or three years service in a designated Newfoundland area — they left the province for greener fields in Canada or the United States. And so the frustrating process was repeated year after year. The minister or some senior official of the department would go to Europe, successfully recruiting some doctors and nurses, only to be confronted a year later by another crisis. Newfoundland's own young doctors were usually not anxious to go anywhere in Newfoundland, unless these places happened to be Corner Brook, Grand Falls or a similarly large and modern town. Of those who had gone abroad to complete their training, some simply refused to return to Newfoundland. And so, during the two decades following confederation, medical authorities were sometimes forced to close down nursing stations for lengthy periods, and were unable to operate some of the hospitals at full potential. What was true of medical services was even more evident and difficult in respect of dental services. For decades only St. John's and two or three other centres had practising dentists, and these were in private practice. The residents of hundreds of other communities simply had no dental services available, unless the patient was prepared to undertake considerable travelling and other expenses. It was clear that drastic measures were required, if the Newfoundland people were to enjoy medical and dental standards equal to those of rural areas in other parts of Canada.

The possibility of building a medical school at the university had been raised in government circles on several occasions, but had usually been discarded as being little more than a fantasy. Nevertheless, there were those who believed that the choice came down to either a medical school in Newfoundland or a continuation of the lowest medical standards in Canada. Pending a decision on this question, two other steps were taken in 1963 to ease the situation. One was the establishment of a school of nursing at the university, a step which yielded almost immediate benefits on both the quality and quantity of nursing supply. The second measure was equally effective. The government announced that fifty registrants in pre-medical, pre-dental, medical and dental faculties would be given annual grants of $800 if they lived in St. John's, and $1200 if they came from the outports, if they attended Memorial. The offer was extended to $2000 for medical students at universities outside Newfoundland. The programme was to run for six years. In return for this help prospective practitioners had to sign an agreement to practise at a place and for a term designated by the Department of Health.

In 1964–65 a report by the Hall Commission, set up to examine Canada's medical services, stated that Canada needed several additional medical schools and suggested that Newfoundland might be the logical place for one of them. Two subsequent commissions, one set up by the university and the other by the Newfoundland government, both recommended a medical school at Memorial. But even with this formidable support, progress was made slowly. Still another committee, this time made up of representatives of the university regents and senate, the Newfoundland Medical Association and the Newfoundland Department of Health, studied the matter further and, with the approval of the Newfoundland government, the decision to go ahead was made in April, 1967. But the project was not yet out of the woods, and for a time there was some doubt about the ability of the Newfoundland government to carry out the financing. Help came, however, when the federal government promised to undertake two-thirds of the capital cost of both the School of Medicine and of the new 380-bed facility that would serve as its teaching hospital.

The ongoing struggle to find enough doctors and nurses for the population of Newfoundland was only one of the campaigns of the 1950s and 1960s. For over two centuries, tuberculosis had consistently ravaged the Newfoundland people, to the point where many Newfoundlanders had come to accept it fatalistically. No community was free from it, and there were repeated examples of families being decimated and sometimes wiped out by it. This tremendous struggle ended in virtually complete success, however, and the story of how this was accomplished deserves more attention than it usually receives.

For several decades Newfoundland possessed only one sanitorium, situated on the Topsail Highway just outside St. John's. This was expanded, however, at the end of World War II when the Royal Canadian Naval Hospital, adjoining the old sanitorium, was passed over to the government in 1947. That same year, the Newfoundland Tuberculosis Association began operation of the *Christmas Seal*, a 148-ton vessel carrying a BCG[2] team from the Department of Health and equipped to do x-ray work. In 1950 a new 270-bed sanitorium was opened at Corner Brook, and the following year the T.B. Association acquired two new mobile x-ray units — a railway car and a bus. But the attack on T.B. was not confined to the two cities. In 1953 a 53-bed T.B. wing was opened at St. Anthony as part of the International Grenfell Association's medical complex in that

[2] The name came from the bacillus discovered by French scientists Calmette and Guerin.

town. The need for such a facility had been felt for some time since, apart from the normal incidence of T.B. in northern New-foundland and in Labrador, the aboriginal groups — both Inuit and Indians — seemed to be even more susceptible to the dis-ease than were the whites. This addition, when coupled with the surgical skills of Dr. Curtis, Dr. Thomas and their associ-ates in the International Grenfell Association, served to bring down the T.B. incidence in Labrador from one of the highest in the world to controllable levels.

By 1954 the St. John's Sanitorium, consisting of 460 beds, had been strengthened by the provision of a major operating room. The following year, for the first time in its history, New-foundland found itself with substantially more sanitorium beds than it needed, to the point where it was considered advis-able to give one of the former RCN buildings to the Hospital for Mental and Nervous Diseases. Happily, the trend continued: 1956 saw still more empty beds both in St. John's and Corner Brook, and in 1957 the original St. John's "San" was allocat-ed to the Mental Hospital. By 1963, the number of empty beds had become so great that the government was able to transfer the Corner Brook Sanitorium to the general hospital corpora-tion in that city, and the few remaining patients were treated as outpatients. The Tuberculosis Annex to the Curtis Memori-al Hospital in St. Anthony was phased out in 1968. Then, in 1972, it was decided to close down the one remaining sanito-rium in the province, located in St. John's West. Tuberculosis in Newfoundland had finally been brought under control. If it had not been completely conquered, it was no longer the deadly enemy we had known for decades. It was just another disease, still insidious, still needing to be watched, but avoid-able and capable of being cured when caught in time.

In view of the historic devastation T.B. had caused to the Newfoundland people, bringing it under control must be regarded as one of the greatest victories of the era and, indeed, of any era in our history. The victory was an example of the achievements possible when all the resources of the commu-nity were brought to bear. The work of the Newfoundland Tuberculosis Association, dedicated medical specialists, mass X-ray screenings, enlarged facilities at St. John's, Corner Brook and St. Anthony, thoracic surgery, BCG vaccine, new drugs, better diet, more attention to hygiene and a generally higher standard of living, all combined to bring a death rate of 100 per 100,000 in 1949 to almost zero by 1971.

Tuberculosis was not, of course, the only mass killer in Newfoundland. Early in the century, outbreaks of smallpox and diphtheria had brought tragedy to Newfoundland households. The former had been virtually eliminated during the 1920s by mass vaccination programmes, but diphtheria lasted longer, with cases appearing as recently as the 1950s and 1960s. In 1957, for example, eleven cases were reported, of which three were fatal. Control was achieved only gradually by means of anti-toxin in the 1920s and then, after the first part of the 1940s, by means of the diphtheria toxoid. Periodically, there were also outbreaks of polio, the last of any significance being in 1953 and in 1959–60. Here, too, the new vaccines proved their worth, first with the Salk vaccine in 1953 and then the Sabin vaccine of 1962. Interestingly, Newfoundland was the first province to make use of the vaccine on a wide scale, with the result that, practically speaking, there was no polio in Newfoundland after the first year it was administered.

Early in 1966 the health minister announced the introduction of a vaccination programme against measles for children between the ages of two and nine years, thus putting a curb for the first time on a childhood disease which, in addition to being intrinsically dangerous, often left its victims with permanent physical or mental damage. Here again, Newfoundland was the first province to adopt an organized measles vaccination programme.

A fact not always recognized is that whooping cough was often a bigger killer of Newfoundland's children than polio, the high mortality being due to the subsequent effects of pneumonia that ravaged young bodies weakened by the whooping cough itself. From the 1940s to the 1960s the disease was brought under control, both by means of vaccine and the rising standards of general hygiene and sanitation. But the greatest killer of very young children was not one of the above, devastating as they were. It was gastroenteritis — a disease which always seemed to be lurking in the shadows and which, year after year, carried off its grisly quota of the very young. And, while it was no respecter of persons, the disease was particularly destructive among the Inuit and Indian children of Labrador. As late as 1963 there was a major resurgence of this disease, with around 1100 cases and 79 deaths reported province-wide. But even then, compared with the first four decades of this century, remarkable progress had been made in the 1950s and 1960s — again, largely due to improvements in nutrition, hygiene and general health standards. Control in all of these childhood diseases was made easier by the increasing spread of hospitals and nursing stations and the comparative ease with which stricken children could be carried to hospitals.

Roads, while by far the most usual routes of transportation, were not the only ones. As early as 1949, the government made the first moves towards establishing an "air ambulance" and, by 1955, an aircraft was based at St. Anthony and at North West River to facilitate medical services to the isolated parts of Labrador and of White Bay and St. Barbe. In time, the air ambulance covered the whole province, proving particularly valuable as a means to get critical patients, such as the victims of car accidents, to one of the general hospitals where advanced treatment and surgical techniques were possible. This service was supplemented by a four-boat service for the more isolated parts of the province, thus enabling even the most remote outports to receive routine medical and nursing attention.

Another governmental policy affecting the welfare of Newfoundland's children was the first-stage implementation in 1957 of the Children's Health Service. Under the programme, all children up to sixteen years of age received free hospitalization and out-patient diagnostic services. This was followed the following year by the provision of free medical care in addition to the free hospitalization. Apart from the Children's Health Service, probably the most valuable step taken by the government in the field of child health was the decision to build a modern children's hospital on the site of the American base hospital at Pepperrell. The facility was several years in the planning and implementation stages. Several of the world's leading medical practitioners were consulted and advised the government to go ahead. Subsequently the hospital was named after Charles A. Janeway, one of the consultants and a world authority in the field of child health. At the local level leadership and advice were provided by Dr. C.J. Joy, a St. John's pediatrician.

The hospital was opened in August 1966, with a rated bed capacity of 280. Some idea of its impact on the health of the Newfoundland children may be gauged by the fact that in the five-year period from 1966 to 1971, over 55,000 children were given in-patient or out-patient treatment. In one year, 1971, nearly 7000 patients were admitted to the hospital.

Hospitals were one essential to the implementation of any effective health plan. In 1949, despite the efforts of the Commission of Government, there was a shortage of hospital beds — a shortage which was aggravated by the rapid increase in population and the fact that such large proportions of the total population consisted of the old and the young. To meet this growing need, a number of hospitals were built during the period 1949–71, among which were those at Channel, Fogo, Springdale, Stephenville Crossing, Labrador City, Gander, Baie Verte, Pleasantville, Grand Falls, Happy Valley, and among the nursing stations were those at Lamaline, Trepassey, Jackson's Arm, and La Scie. In addition, hospitals were replaced at Twillingate, St. Anthony, and North West River and, in St. John's, the two church hospitals — St. Clare's and the Grace — were able, with government backing, to make major additions to existing facilities. Accommodation and nurse training at the St. John's General were greatly increased when, in 1964, the fourteen-story nurses' residence and training school, Southcott Hall, was opened for use.

Starting in 1949, with Newfoundland as a part of Canada, it qualified for federal health grants. These grants not only relieved Newfoundland of some of the inevitable financial strain of carrying out essential programmes, but also made possible the undertaking of projects which would not otherwise have been possible. The agreement signed with Ottawa in 1956 served notice of Newfoundland's willingness to participate in the federal-provincial hospital insurance programme. The programme became a reality in July, 1958. By it Newfoundlanders became eligible for free hospitalization at ward levels, together with drugs, physiotherapy and necessary diagnostic and nursing services provided while in hospital. As well, out-patient diagnostic services and physiotherapy were included in the programme.

Since Newfoundland had never denied hospitalization or medical services to those unable to pay (a sizeable segment in view of the large number on social welfare), the additional services and programmes that came with confederation meant that by 1968, Newfoundland, both on her own and with various federal grants, was approaching the point when everyone in the province would enjoy free health care. The only concern was whether Newfoundland would be able to carry its share of the programme's financial burden indefinitely. But this was obviated in 1968 and 1969 when Canada introduced its famous universal Medical Care Plan (MCP). This plan gave free medical attention to all Newfoundlanders, irrespective of their ability to pay. Of all the provinces, none benefitted more from this programme than did Newfoundland.

During the Commission of Government regime, public health and social welfare had been joined together in the one Department of Public Health and Welfare. In the minds of many, Welfare was the Cinderella of the union, with Health receiving both the money and the kudos. The proof of this allegation would seem to lie in the fact that for most of the Commission period, welfare was largely able-bodied relief — small amounts of relief in-kind, paid out grudgingly and only after stringent means tests, to persons without jobs or resources. Traditionally such persons had been eyed askance by those who, because of good luck or superior ability, either could not or would not apply for such assistance. In the minds of the more fortunate, many of those on relief were there because they were too lazy to work. This attitude helps to explain why those who have to support able-bodied recipients of relief occasionally demand that the latter be made to work for their assistance.

Even in the Commission of Government's latter years, from 1945 to 1949, the attitude of the government could only be described as parsimonious when compared with that of other western countries. In Canada, for example, those reaching seventy years qualified for old age pensions and received thirty dollars a month; in Newfoundland the payment was six dollars a month, and that only after the applicant had reached the age of seventy-five and had passed the means test to show that he was destitute. In Canada there were family allowances, payments to mothers for the support of all dependent children; in Newfoundland there were none. Canada had unemployment insurance; Newfoundland, with its hosts of unemployed, could not even dream of taking on such a responsibility. Many factors helped to bring about confederation, but most observers feel that the one predominant factor was Canada's great social welfare programme. Over and over, Smallwood and his lieutenants stressed the beneficial effects these social programmes would have, not only on Newfoundland's economy overall, but on every individual family, especially where there were children or old persons.

To appreciate the real significance of these social measures in 1948, one must be reminded of certain basic facts which characterized Newfoundland's culture and economy at the time. Family life was very strong in Newfoundland. Large families were the rule and a surprising number of people reached an advanced age. The average Newfoundland family never ignored its responsibility to parents and grandparents, and old people were as much a part of the family as the youngest child. But with large families and limited incomes, the elderly nevertheless represented a burden on the breadwinner. No matter how economical they were, one person could not live indefinitely on six dollars a month. In any case, the majority of older people were in the 65-to-75 age bracket and could not qualify for any assistance, small as it was.

Assistance for widows and their dependents was, if anything, more meagre than for old age pensioners. And given the hazardous occupations of many Newfoundlanders in the Labrador fishery, the Grand Bank fishery and the seal fishery, there were a large number of fatalities. The net result was that Newfoundland had the highest percentage of widows and orphans in Canada, none of whom could survive on government assistance.

The federal benefits which came in April, 1949 were of great help to both the elderly and widows. But the biggest benefit was the family allowances. For thousands of Newfoundland mothers, cash was a rarity — if they saw it at all. Now for the first time the mother had money to use for food, clothing, and school expenses. Then, too, hundreds of elderly persons living with their children found themselves with real money. Sixty dollars a month spelled luxury not only for the couple themselves but, when added to other benefits such as family allowances, unemployment insurance and possibly, a veteran's pension, for the whole family as well. Within a few years after

1949, a transformation had taken place in the children of Newfoundland. They were more alert, more interested, looked better, were better clothed and fed — in short, for many, especially in remote communities, a brave new world had emerged.

In one area of welfare substantial progress was made in the latter years of Commission of Government. The war had increased the problem of neglected and delinquent children many of whom were born out of wedlock and often lacked the stability of home life. Several of the churches had done yeoman work in looking after orphans and those who came from broken homes. But the orphanages were geared, for the most part, to providing a home atmosphere for what could otherwise be called normal children. In 1944, the Division of Child Welfare was set up, followed by the creation of the *Welfare of Children Act*. The basic purpose behind the legislation was to protect children who would otherwise be neglected or allowed to engage in undesirable activities. Such children could be made wards of the division and placed either in foster homes or in welfare institutions. In 1949 over 300 children were in the care of the division. The first director was Dr. H.L. Pottle, later a Newfoundland member of the Commission of Government and, in 1949, a member of the Smallwood cabinet as minister of public welfare.

The new Department of Public Welfare took over the entire Child Welfare Division as well as those areas which had been identified with relief, old age pensions and other welfare activities. What the department lacked was a cadre of professional or semi-professional men and women, capable of being trained in the professional aspects of welfare. Administration of welfare outside of St. John's came under the "relieving officers," men who had been appointed to these posts without having any special qualifications. Their duty was largely concerned with investigating applications for relief ("dole") and deciding whether to give the assistance or not. In those districts where members of the Ranger force were stationed, they included relief in their duties, but with the advent of the RCMP, the Ranger force was disbanded.

In the early days of confederation, the government of Canada was glad to employ Newfoundland's existing welfare services in processing applications for federal assistance, until such time as the federal welfare structure in Newfoundland was in place.

But it soon became clear that the Newfoundland structure was inadequate to the task and that the department would have to be rebuilt—both professionally and structurally. A board was set up with the deputy minister as chairman and with senior officials of the department as members, to invite and examine applications for the newly created posts of welfare officers. Applications came in by the hundreds, giving the department a wide selection from which to choose. By late 1950, some 25 had been appointed; by late 1960, a total of 100 had been appointed and, by 1966, the province had been divided into 53 districts, staffed by a total of 146 welfare supervisors and staff. The welfare officers, for the most part, had had experience in fields related to social welfare — in teaching, nursing, and co-operatives — but it was clear that specialized training was necessary in view of the various measures that had to be co-ordinated and integrated, and the impact these new measures were having on the people generally. Accordingly, a system of in-service training was devised, much of it under the benevolent supervision of Toronto's School of Social Work. Several nationally known figures in social welfare came to Newfoundland during summer periods to assist in the training, while Dr. Cassidy, head of the Toronto school, and probably Canada's leading sociologist, undertook to set up at the Toronto school special summer classes for the training of Newfoundland social workers. Although Dr. Cassidy died prematurely a short while later, within four or five years Newfoundland's social welfare programme and the machinery for administering it were regarded by impartial observers as being on a level with most of the rest of Canada.

Family allowances, old age and blind pensions had an immediate effect on Newfoundland, since all those eligible qualified from the moment that the province became part of Canada. There were, however, other areas where Canada had no specific responsibility and where, therefore, the new provincial government felt obligated to take immediate action. The first of these was to provide assistance for mothers who were widows with children under sixteen years of age, or whose husbands were institutionalized or physically or mentally disabled, or had deserted the family, or where the mothers were unmarried or had foster children. In all such cases, the *Mothers' Allowances Act*, passed in 1949, gave help in the form of cash allowances for the mother and additional amounts for each child. Within two years well over 3000 families had qualified for help under this legislation. The second area of need was for widows (without dependent children) as well as adults who were physically or mentally disabled. To look after this large number, who in the past had usually been heavy burdens on the family, or objects of haphazard charity from their neighbours, the *Dependents' Allowances Act* was adopted, also in 1949. By 1951 nearly 6000 persons had qualified for these allowances.

Except for two or three artificially prosperous periods during major wars, Newfoundland had never been without the problem of able-bodied and sick relief, traditionally called the dole. During the latter years of World War II, however, there was no able-bodied relief. But as soon as the war was over, there was a gradual reversion of the economy and by the spring of 1949, nearly 8000 families were receiving relief at a cost to the Newfoundland government of nearly 2.5 million dollars — an ominously high figure given the province's annual revenue. As had happened so often in Newfoundland's past — and, indeed, in the history of most countries where taxpayers have had to support persons not working — the cry was raised that the community or the province should get some return from the sums being handed out. This had been tried before in Newfoundland, especially in the nineteenth century when many of the primitive roads were built by pick, shovel and wheelbarrow by men who, in return for their work, received a meal of indian meal and molasses. But all these efforts proved ineffective and were ultimately abandoned. Such was the fate of the experiment of 1949. And once more the question was asked: "Why wasn't it successful?" The answer to this question, as with many others, can best be understood in the context of Newfoundland's history.

A disproportionate number of people in Newfoundland have always known the ravages of poverty. Among those who were poor there were two distinct groups: those who regarded relief as a right, applied for it and usually got it, and another group who, while qualified for relief, would rather go hungry than endure the stigma of being "on the dole." Indeed, for thousands of families in Newfoundland their proudest boast was that, in spite of the periodic "hard times," they had never gone to the government for help. Often it was a matter of luck that such families did not starve. Some could make up for what they could not afford by cutting their own firewood, picking the wild berries, growing their own potatoes, jigging codfish, catching caplin, keeping a few hens, raising a few sheep for wool and mutton, even keeping a cow for milk and beef. Obviously most of these things could only be done where the environment permitted. A few families scattered in a rocky hamlet or isolated on some barren island were not likely to have much opportunity to do such things, apart from the catching of fish and caplin.

There was one unwritten law, however, which was applied consistently throughout Newfoundland's history. If any amount of government money was made available, then every unemployed man in the town, whether on dole or not, had the right to share in that money. For example if $500 was given to the local board to repair the roads or bridges, and if there were 60 unemployed men in the village then all 60 expected — in fact demanded — that they be employed (and paid) to do their share of that work. Such demands where never turned down. In fact, it was traditional that money granted for roads or other public works was not worked out in the summer, since some of the men were fishing on the Labrador or were in the lumber woods. The money was held until all the men had returned home and could participate.

In 1949 as the unemployment rate rose and demands for relief increased, the government decided to make another attempt at getting a return on the relatively large sums it was handing out in relief payments. The plan was fairly simple. The local road board or some community organization would identify certain public projects needing attention — the rebuilding of a dangerous bridge, laying down a road to the cemetery or improving a community playground, for example. All those who had qualified for able-bodied relief were to be taken on. But instead of being given food (as their ancestors had been), they were to be paid in cash at one-half the standard rate for labour. Unfortunately, however, this meant that dole recipients were perceived by their self-supporting neighbours as being rewarded for their improvidence and opportunism, while those who had elected not to accept dole and had supported their families at no expense to the government were penalized for their industry and independence. Consequently the cry was raised once again for an equitable share of this government money, and once more the age-old tradition asserted itself. If the government had persisted in trying to restrict this money to those on or needing relief, the result would have been strife, probably to the point of violence. Consequently, even after allowing for any benefits accruing to the community, the net effect of the programme was that the number receiving government help was far higher, perhaps twice as high, as the number who would have been on ordinary relief. And, of course, the government found itself having to provide far more money than it would have had to do otherwise. Moreover, if one extrapolated from the present effects of the programme to its logical conclusion, the government would have soon found itself being held responsible for finding work, even if at only half the regular rate, for every unemployed man in Newfoundland. Faced with these horrendous financial and political considerations, the government cancelled the programme in 1950 and reverted to the traditional system of able-bodied relief. During the few months it had been in operation, however, the expenditure had come to nearly $2 million in direct payments and considerably more in indirect costs.

The cost to Newfoundland of its own provincial welfare programme increased yearly and effectively hampered the government's attempts to deal with other ongoing needs such as education, roads and health. The advent of the Canada Assistance Plan in April 1966 brought great relief to both the government and the people, and brought together most of the services hitherto provided only by the Newfoundland government — social assistance (able-bodied and sick relief), child welfare, adoptions and the enlargement and operation of welfare institutions. Of the total cost, the Government of Canada paid about half. In its first year, the cost to both governments was just over $23 million, and in 1970–71, almost $47 million.

It is a truism to say that one of Canada's greatest social programmes was the institution of unemployment insurance. In theory, Newfoundland became qualified to participate in the programme from the first day of its union with Canada. In practice, however, Newfoundlanders would have to wait two years, since the original legislation stated that coverage depended on the contributions paid for the two-year period prior to the claim. Newfoundland, of course, had not paid any, and would not have enjoyed any benefits whatsoever had not Parliament passed special legislation, known as Unemployment Assistance, which covered the two-year hiatus until Newfoundland would normally qualify. On March 31, 1951, Newfoundlanders became qualified in their own right. In the meantime, however, thanks to the generosity and co-operation of the federal government, Newfoundland received nearly $7 million in benefits.

Some of the other generous benefits accruing to Newfoundland following confederation were the Blind Pensions, and Old Age *Assistance* (as distinct from Old Age *Security*). The Assistance was designed to look after the needs of those between the ages of sixty-five and seventy years, although it could only be given following a means test. But in 1966, Assistance began its five-year evolution to becoming universal Old Age Security. That is, in the first year coverage of sixty-nine-year-olds was transferred to Old Age Security, the second of sixty-eight-year-olds, and so on until everyone sixty-five years and over could qualify.

At the time of union the government was operating several welfare institutions, of which the best known (and most notorious) was the century-old building known variously as the Infirmary, the Home for the Aged and Infirm, or the Poor House. It was a wooden building, a fire-trap, overcrowded and lacking almost every requirement for a modern institution. That it was able to function as well as it did spoke very highly of the dedicated staff. In 1965 the patients were transferred to the just-completed Hoyles Home, an institution which provided everything that its predecessor had lacked.

Another institution operating in 1949 was the Waterford Hall for Infants. It cared for a wide variety of children aged from a few months to two years, many of whom had been born to unmarried mothers. The building could accommodate no more than forty children, however, so in 1954 the Home was transferred to a larger building. Subsequently, and thanks to the striking increase in the number of foster homes, it was possible to convert the building to a home for severely handicapped children. Other institutions included a boys' home and training school located first at Whitbourne and then, following a fire, at Bell Island; then, in 1953, at Whitbourne again, where a modern institution had been built following the acquisition of the Bond estate by the government. A girls' home and training school was opened in St. John's in 1947 and continued to operate there until a larger building was found in 1963.

As early as the nineteenth century the Newfoundland government was giving modest help to enable blind as well as deaf and dumb children to obtain special training. This help consisted for the most part in sending blind children to the School for the Blind in Halifax and deaf children to the two schools for the deaf — one in Halifax, the other in Montreal. By 1949 twenty blind children were being sent to Halifax and forty deaf children to the other two schools. This help was expanded until, in effect, the government of Newfoundland had assumed responsibility for training all such handicapped children. In 1964, with the closing of the American base at Pepperrell and of the Canadian bases at Torbay, the Newfoundland government utilized some of the property to establish a school for the deaf. By 1971, one hundred and ten deaf students were being educated at the school. Blind children continued to be sent to the Halifax School which Newfoundland had helped to renovate. In its assistance to the visually handicapped the government continued to work in close collaboration with the Canadian National Institute for the Blind.

Following confederation there was a steady increase in the assistance being given other physically or mentally handicapped children. For this purpose two institutions were established in St. John's. In summary then, the government assumed responsibility during the period for the education and training of all blind and deaf, as well as a large number of physically and mentally handicapped and a still larger number of neglected, deserted and delinquent children.

When the Smallwood era began, Newfoundland's health and welfare programmes were deficient and primitive. When it ended they compared well with those in other parts of Canada. In the fight for confederation Smallwood had promised things which, on the surface, appeared difficult (if not impossible) to fulfill. By 1971, however, not even his severest critics took issue with the claim that in these particular fields the Newfoundland people enjoyed benefits and services which no one thought attainable in 1949. Part of the credit for this happy state of affairs had to go to the federal government for its contribution. But even here the province was entitled to share in that credit since at no time did the Newfoundland government and legislature relax its pressure on Ottawa to assume greater responsibility for both welfare and health measures. A few cynics argued that Smallwood's efforts in these matters were motivated by his overriding desire to survive politically. That, of course, is a charge that could be made against any member of any legislature, whether Liberal or Conservative. In any case, what is certain is that all members derived satisfaction from being able to participate in measures which did so much to improve the lives of the Newfoundland people.

8 RESETTLEMENT AND CENTRALIZATION

L ike so many aspects of Newfoundland's history, resettlement and centralization during the Smallwood era can be analysed and interpreted only by reference to what went before — in this case, to the earliest European settlements in Newfoundland. This examination of early settlement practices is particularly necessary if we are to deal with the mythology that has attached itself over the years to this aspect of Newfoundland's history, and which is still a part of its present-day folklore.

Although nobody knows when the first permanent settlement occurred in Newfoundland, it is probable that the temporary Portuguese settlements on the Avalon Peninsula were among the earliest. Evidence of this still remains in the prevalence of Portuguese names on the southeast and east coasts, right up to Notre Dame Bay. We know that the Basque whalers were wintering in Newfoundland during the 1500s and, this being so, it would follow that the English were doing the same on the "English Shore" — that part of the coast from Cape Race north to Cape Bonavista — and without doubt some French vessels followed the same pattern. Some of this may have been intentional, whether to protect fishing property left behind in Newfoundland, or to have preference for favoured harbour sites and fishing grounds in the spring. Also, with so many hundreds of English and western European vessels involved, it may have been simply a case that at least a few of them were bound to fall prey to shipwrecks, or early freeze-up in the late fall which prevented the crew from returning home. What we do know is that Guy founded the first formal colony in 1610, and there is no indisputable record of others having preceded him. Significantly, however, neither at the time of founding, nor in the voluminous correspondence between the colony and England, was there any claim advanced to indicate that Guy's colonists were the first to winter in Newfoundland.

Other attempts to establish permanent colonies followed, and several met, at least temporarily, with some measure of success. In the meantime some of the colonists moved from these formal colonies into neighbouring harbours, while other West Country fishermen increasingly adopted the practice of staying over the winter for one or more years. Eventually, some of these became permanent settlers. We know from the accounts of the French invasions in the King William and the Queen Anne's wars that, by the late 1600s, several dozen harbours were settled — although some of them with only one or two families.

The eighteenth century was largely a period of growth for the English settlements on the "English Shore." The famous fishing harbours of St. John's, Harbour Grace, Renews, Bay Bulls, Trinity, Heart's Content and several dozen others, gradually filled up to the point where newcomers, or young men reaching adulthood found there was no more room. The same thing held for mooring space within the harbour. The number of skiffs, schooners, and other vessels that could swing clear in the harbour was strictly limited. If fifty boats was the limit, then newcomers wanting to start a boat fishery of their own had to confront the simple physical problem of finding room.

Over time, still a third problem presented itself. Fish had to be netted or jigged on the fishing grounds near the harbour, usually not more than two to five miles away, since longer distances required too great an expenditure of time. Fishing grounds or banks could accommodate a certain number of boats and nets and no more. When these limits were reached the would-be fisherman had two choices: he could watch for a chance to get out of Newfoundland altogether and go to New England or he could go to some other part of the eastern seaboard along what is now Canada and the United States. Many Newfoundlanders did this, often to the dismay of the planters or merchants to whom they owed money. But probably the majority simply moved on to another harbour where there was room available. As nearby harbours filled up the fishermen went further afield, and as available harbour space diminished they settled in coves and inlets, and on islands which, while not good harbours, offered a measure of protection from the elements.

This process of population dispersal, rapid as it was in the later decades of the eighteenth century, intensified in the 1800s and spread right around the island to include the French Shore. This tendency followed a geographical progression. Thus Trinity, in Trinity Bay, was a well-settled harbour by the middle of the seventeenth century; Bonavista was a comparatively large community by 1700 long before Fogo and Twillingate were settled. The populating of Notre Dame Bay took place largely from 1700 on, a process that continued well into the next century. Thus Seldom-Come-By on Fogo Island was settled by migrants from Conception and Trinity Bays around the end of the eighteenth and the early part of the nineteenth centuries. The family names of Holmes, Rowe, Boone, Anthony, Penney, Dawe, and Harnett, all could be traced to families who had been among the early settlers of Trinity and Conception Bays. Contrary to popular mythology, the vast majority of settlers in the more remote parts of Newfoundland were not men trying to escape the anti-settlement laws regarding land; nor were they escapees from justice or from naval and fishing ships. No doubt some would have fit these descriptions, but they were extremely rare.

Recent studies by Keith Matthews, Chesley Sanger and others have confirmed what many Newfoundlanders, in rejecting the Prowse school of thought on these matters, have always believed. The spread of population in more than a thousand villages scattered in various hamlets and on islands, resulted neither from British persecution, nor anti-settlement laws, nor oppression by West Country fishermen, nor the misdeeds of the fishing admirals, persons escaping justice, nor a dozen other alleged reasons. Indeed, as much as they may appeal to our sentimentality or enhance our pride, these reasons were considerably less valid than factors which were purely geographic and economic. Settlers spread out from the historic settlements of the Avalon and Bonavista peninsulas to Bonavista North and to the islands of Notre Dame Bay because they wanted more room to fish, and to net or kill seals which came down the northeast coast every spring. In addition, they needed to catch the salmon run at the mouths of the large rivers like the Terra Nova, the Gambo, the Gander and the Exploits, as well as to benefit from the increasing European demand for furs, which meant that they had to be nearer to the fur-bearing animals than was possible when living in, say, Conception Bay. It was not a coincidence that the development of the salmon fishery and the growth of the seal hunt took place during and following the settlement of the myriad small communities in Bonavista Bay, the Straight Shore and Notre Dame Bay.

This process of decentralization continued uninterrupted right through the nineteenth century. By 1890 there were between 1200 and 1300 communities, the great majority of which had only a handful of families. When the dispersal trend which had characterized Newfoundland population patterns for several hundred years was eventually reversed, however, it was not by the Smallwood administration in the 1950s, but by several earlier factors usually ignored when resettlement is discussed.

At one time most of Newfoundland was covered by trees down to the water's edge. This applied even to the headlands which today, with one or two notable exceptions, are nothing but exposed rock. Examples of this can be seen at Cape Freels, Cape Spear and other places. An exception is Cape St. John, the highest and one of the most exposed headlands in the province: unless it has been recently destroyed by "clear" cutting or by fire, it still has trees of lumber size growing almost to the edge of the cliff — a clear indication that until burnt or otherwise destroyed, most of Newfoundland's present-day rocks and "barrens" were covered by trees. Consequently, the early settlers on the Avalon Peninsula resorted to the illegal practice of deliberately setting fire to the forest in order to clear the land for building and farming purposes and also to provide a source of dry wood for fuel.

For the early settlers, wood was the most indispensable item apart from food. Wood was needed to build wharves, stages, sheds, dwellings, boats and schooners. Above all, it was needed for fuel. This presented no problem so long as the wood was next door, or even when it was only two or three miles away. But as cutting, fire and disease took their toll, wood became increasingly scarce, with the result that longer and longer expeditions were required solely to obtain firewood or saw-logs. In time the practice developed of leaving the harbours and headlands in the fall, and moving into the sheltered bottoms of the bays for the winters. This had two advantages: a winter's fuel was close at hand, and boats or schooners could be built with nearby materials "in the bay." As the demand for lumber grew, so did the use of mills, powered by steam or brook water. By the late 1800s bigger mill operations were developing, so that a number of places on the northeast coast such as Gambo, Gander Bay, Burnt Bay (Lewisporte), Norris Arm and Botwood gradually changed from being winter "tilt" sites to year-round communities, with work available for cutting and sawing lumber. There was, therefore, a tendency in the second half of the nineteenth century for families to desert their original homes and become domiciled around the river mouths or bottoms of the bays in places like Kite Cove, Scissors Cove, Bird Cove, Big Burnt Bay, Salt Pond and Indian Arm, which older people will recall as being the original names of such well-known towns as Lawrenceton, Stanhope, Botwood, Lewisporte, Embree and Campbellton.

Although the availability of wood was usually the most important, the new sites had several other advantages. The long arms and fiords in the big bays facilitated access to the interior for the hunting and trapping of wildlife. Also, since most of the islands and exposed communities had little soil for cultivation, the land "in the bay" was usually suitable and available for cultivation. In fact, many of the new communities in Notre Dame Bay were, for some time, largely based on agriculture rather than on fishing or logging. By 1890 it was clear that resettling further in the bays provided the best of two worlds: summer fishing on the outlying coast or at Labrador, and logging, saw milling, hunting and trapping in the fall and winter.

Somewhere, then, during the second half of the nineteenth century, the spread of settlement to uninhabited coves and islands slowly came to a halt and the process of centralization gathered momentum. With the building of the trans-insular railway in the late 1890s it accelerated, since wherever the railway went it attracted people to the communities it served. The railway line went as near as possible to the centres of population, which meant touching the bottoms of the bays at such places as Clarenville, Gambo and Humbermouth. Where that was not feasible, branch lines were built to communities such as Placentia and Lewisporte. Most of these "touch" points were already small villages by 1900, but within a few years these hamlets had increased their population several times over, and had become the relatively large communities of Whitbourne, Clarenville, Gambo, Lewisporte, Norris Arm, Humbermouth, Curling, St. George's, Channel and Port aux Basques. And these increases consisted almost wholly of Newfoundlanders. But still another factor was to enter the picture.

The completion of the railway soon resulted in the smaller saw-mills giving way to larger operations. For example, Lewis Miller established a white pine lumber operation at Glenwood and Millertown and shipped his board through Lewisporte over the newly built railway. Early in the new century the Grand Falls enterprise got under way and by 1909 was shipping paper. This huge project created a number of new towns — such as Grand Falls, Windsor, Badger and Terra Nova — and caused rapid growth in other neighbouring communities such as Norris Arm, Lewisporte, and above all, Botwood — the shipping port for Grand Falls paper.

In the 1920s another great paper mill, this time at Corner Brook, went into operation and once again there was a surge in centralization as hundreds of families moved into the new centres. Concurrently during the early decades of the 1900s there was an upsurge of mining activity, typified by the expansion at Bell Island, as well as the creation of a new town, Buchans, with a population of nearly 3000 in the wilderness of Red Indian Lake, and new mines at St. Lawrence on the Burin Peninsula. But perhaps the peak of resettlement took place in World War II when the permanent population of St. John's doubled in just a few years; when a new town of Gander grew to three to four thousand inhabitants almost overnight; and when towns like Lewisporte, Clarenville, Springdale, Deer Lake, Glovertown, Corner Brook, the Placentia complex, Stephenville, Goose, Happy Valley, doubled, tripled and in some cases quadrupled their populations over a period of only five to ten years. This was resettlement on a major scale, raising immediately the question as to where the new settlers had all come from. One thing was certain: they were not from other countries; they were Newfoundlanders.

The following example will serve to show the origins of some of the newcomers. In the year 1900, the Sceviours, Birchy, Knight, Long, Swan, Dunnage, Dildo and Wadam's islands all had families living on them. In 1949 — in fact, long before 1949 — they still had one thing in common: they were completely uninhabited. The people had moved into Lewisporte, Botwood, Springdale, and several other large places — on their own, and without help or encouragement from the government or from any other agent. Between 1946 and 1954, forty communities disappeared simply as a result of the families deciding to move to larger more centralized places. This movement, for the most part, was not planned or organized in any formal way. Out of, say, ten families, one or two moved one year, two or three the next year, and so on until the place was empty. In a few cases, all the families in a community would meet and decide it was in their economic, educational or medical interests (for themselves and their children) to move to some large place where better facilities could be found. It was precisely because of such community decisions that the government eventually got involved in the resettlement process. It is important to remember, however, that resettlement and centralization had been underway for sixty years before 1954 and that the continuous, and in some cases unexpected, almost overnight growth of twenty-five or thirty of the largest towns in Newfoundland and Labrador was the result of that migration.

The government became involved in two ways. An example of the first was when residents on one of the islands in Bonavista Bay had decided to move their homes to the main land so that they would be nearer to forestry operations, and would not have the ongoing problem of transportation back and forth. After floating their homes to the main island they ran into unforeseen difficulties (e.g. need for heavy equipment, terrain problems) which were too expensive to solve on their own. Accordingly they appealed to the premier, who was also their representative in the House of Assembly. Around the same time, I was visited by a fisherman from a small isolated place called the Drook, a few miles from Cape Race. He told me that the residents were all fishermen and normally would have no desire to leave the Drook, but since it was impossible to get a teacher to come to their community, or if one did come, to get him or her to stay there even for a few months, they had decided that they should move to Trepassey or St. Mary's Bay. In those places there were convents and schools, and the Drook men could still carry on the fishery. The problem, in their case, was that unlike their counterparts in Bonavista Bay, they had to float their homes across the open ocean. Would it be possible for the government to give them some help towards getting homes in those places?

At the time there was no government policy offering help in such cases as the Bonavista Bay islands or isolated hamlets like the Drook. But I undertook to have the Drook problem brought to the attention of the government where, as it happened, the Bonavista Bay request was already being considered. Soon there were other requests and within months there was a deluge of inquiries about receiving assistance in transporting homes by water or overland, and where this was not feasible, then in finding housing accommodation in the larger or newer centres. At first the government tried providing help-in-kind, (bulldozers, scows, etc.), but when this proved unsatisfactory, modest cash grants were offered — at first $150 a family and then gradually rising to $600 a family. The main condition for receiving help was that all the residents of the community would move — a condition regarded by some as being too stringent. The rationale for this condition was that if a community with, say, fifteen families had experienced difficulty in finding and retaining a teacher for its twenty-five school children, the plight of that place would be worsened if the number of families was reduced, say, to eight families.

At first, families moving with government help could go anywhere they wished, which did not always result in improved conditions. However, under the first plan, between 1954 and 1964, a total of 115 families, involving 7500 persons, moved to larger centres, usually to places where hospital or medical services were available, where there were road connections, and, most important of all, where there were good schools staffed by competent teachers. This first phase of formal resettlement involved only the government of Newfoundland. People were helped because they had requested help to move to other places. No pressure, direct or indirect was ever applied. Personal experience in my district of White Bay South and elsewhere will help to illustrate the conditions that many members of the House of Assembly faced in the early years following confederation.

In 1956 there were twenty-six communities in the district. In the period from 1949 to 1954, six communities, three of them on islands, had moved to the mainland — to Hampden and to what was later known as Pollards Point in Sops Arm — of their own volition. Most of them had floated their homes to the new sites. In fact, on my first visit I found that a couple of fairly large houses were stranded on the beach and the owners were desperately looking for assistance to get the houses on higher and more solid ground. With one exception, the places evacuated had fewer than ten families each. The district still had twenty-six settlements, two of them on islands. Of the twenty-six, La Scie, Baie Verte, Jackson's Arm, and five or six others were big enough to support three-to seven-room schools, three could support nursing stations and, periodically, three had doctors. (Eventually a forty-bed hospital was established at Baie Verte and larger regional and central high schools were built at strategic points.) Until the mines at Baie Verte, Rambler and Tilt Cove got working in the late 1950s, practically all the workers were fishermen-loggers.

On October 1, 1956, I visited the little community of Coney Arm, scenically one of the most attractive in all Newfoundland. It had five families, with eleven children of school age. Since it was my first visit, and as it appeared very likely that I would be elected the next day as their member in the House of Assembly, I asked them what their special needs were. They had two. First was a road to link them with Jackson's Arm, ten miles to the south, where a nursing station was just being started and where there was a Grenfell nurse; second, they wanted a teacher, since the ungraded one sent them a month before had stayed only two weeks before leaving.

After hearing them out, I was forced to give them the facts of life regarding roads and teachers. The terrain between Coney Arm and Jackson's Arm was among the most difficult to be found anywhere in all Newfoundland. In fact, with its series of mountainous ridges separated by deep valleys, the ten-mile stretch would probably have cost half a million dollars — the equivalent of several million today. There was simply no way the government could incur such an expense for five or six families and I did not hesitate to tell them so. On the matter of the teacher I had to explain that teachers were engaged by boards of education. All the government could do was to facilitate their training and pay their salaries. Only a day or two before, I had heard one of the officials of my department (of education) say on radio that some eighty classrooms, almost all of them sole-charge schools, were without teachers. There were just not enough trained teachers to go around, and even though we were offering both graded and ungraded teachers special bonuses to go to isolated places, the boards were unable to fill the vacancies. I explained that neither the boards nor the government could force teachers to stay if they wanted to leave, and that the best I could do was, upon my return to St. John's, to discuss their particular teacher problem with the appropriate superintendent of education. In fact, I was most anxious to do this, since I had discovered from our conversations that none of the children could read or write. The lack of a teacher there was nothing new and, in any case, because of their small number, they were entitled only to a five-month school year. In view of these facts, I felt it my duty to point out to them that their fishing activities put them in the same waters, or in close proximity to the waters fished by men from Jackson's Arm and Sops Arm; that they worked in the same logging camps as did the men from those places, and, in fact, to get to the camps they had to go through or pass by large communities like Hampden and Jackson's Arm. If they lived in Jackson's Arm their children would attend a four-room school where staffing was not a problem, and the community nurse would be available in minutes, instead of the days and sometimes weeks otherwise required. I did not press the matter further, however, since I was aware of their sentimental attachment to this unique spot with its glassy lagoon inside the bar, and with a spectacular waterfall jetting down in the heart of the village. I did assure them, when questioned, that if they decided at any time to move to one of the larger centres discussed, I would see to it that they got the maximum amount of help available. I left them that night fully expecting to receive no votes from them the next (election) day. To my utter surprise, when the electoral officer sent me the results a few days later, I found that every voter in the community (my recollection is fourteen) had voted for me. That following winter, in February, one of the men in the community became ill. The nurse at Jackson's Arm and Dr. Thomas at St. Anthony (who kept in contact with each other and with Coney Arm by radio telephone) were unable to fly in because of heavy blizzards. In the meantime Dr. Thomas diagnosed the illness as pneumonia and knew that the situation was critical. Eventually the Grenfell plane carrying Dr. Thomas and a nurse undertook the considerable risk of flying the over 200-mile round trip to Coney Arm and back, using a marsh as a landing strip. The patient died the same day. But it must have occurred to the residents that if their unfortunate friend and relative had been living in Jackson's Arm he most probably would not have died. Perhaps it was that experience which triggered their decision, the following summer, to move to Jackson's Arm and Sops Arm. (There is a happy epilogue: a few years ago, I was informed that one of the former Coney Arm children had graduated from Memorial with an honours degree, having won a scholarship on the way.)

Another incident involved a fifteen-year-old boy living on the Horse Islands — surely one of the most idyllic summer spots in Canada, although savagely inhospitable in the fall and winter. There was also no harbour apart from a small space for motor boats. The boy had fallen off a cliff and broken his arm — a compound fracture. The family immediately contacted me, as their member, and I got in touch with Dr. Thomas at St. Anthony, who could contact the Horse Islands by radio telephone. Since it was January, it was two weeks before a plane could land on the island. But again risking their lives the doctor, nurse and pilot made the trip because Dr. Thomas had diagnosed gangrene and knew the boy's life would soon be in danger. The boy's life was saved but only after two weeks of pain and worry. Fifteen miles away were three doctors, but to people on the Horse Islands in January, they could have been in China. As with the people of Coney Arm, I was forced to tell the Horse Island residents that there was no way we could get a nurse to live amongst them simply to look after the twenty families there. Once more it must have occurred to them that with a great fish plant at La Scie and large mines at Rambler

117

and Baie Verte, none more than about fifteen to eighteen miles from the Horse Islands, most of their medical, educational, and to some extent economic troubles could be solved by moving into La Scie, where there were water and sewage systems, a nursing station with a doctor or nurse, electricity, a hospital only forty minutes away, large schools and opportunities for alternative work in the mines. In the meantime, while living in La Scie or Baie Verte, there was nothing to prevent their returning to the Horse Islands every summer to fish if they so desired. Eventually, with what I am sure was some regret at the time, they did move to La Scie and other places on the peninsula.

A somewhat similar incident occurred when I was Member for Labrador. At that time the most northerly, and therefore the most remote and isolated community in the province was Hebron. And it was there, in the middle of winter, that one of the Inuit residents of the community broke his leg — again, a compound fracture. For over two weeks the Grenfell plane at North West River tried to fly north but was prevented from doing so by wind and snow. Finally, after a dangerous journey, Dr. Paddon, the nurse and pilot reached Hebron, only to find that the leg had become gangrenous and that it had to be amputated.

But isolation was only one of the factors that Hebron and its nearest neighbour, Nutak (almost equally remote), had to contend with. Because Hebron was north of the tree line, firewood was so scarce that teams would have to travel increasingly longer distances merely to get enough to try to keep warm. Looking for and hauling scrub wood became almost an obsession, certainly during the winter, and in the last years before the residents moved south, getting a dog-team load of wood became a three-day operation.

The first phase of resettlement assistance lasted until 1965, when the governments of Canada and Newfoundland instituted a programme of assistance far more generous than the original set up by the province had been, under the rather formidable title of the Fisheries Household Resettlement Programme. By it, 80 percent of the people in a community had to express a desire to move, in which case each household wishing to relocate was given a basic amount of $1000 plus $200 for each member of the household. In addition, removal and travelling expenses were paid and a grant to a block of land was made. Under the plan, the departments concerned had to approve the "receiving" centres. Also, as time went on, supplementary grants were provided. Under the new formula, a total of 3876 householders, involving 19,197 persons were assisted in moving during the period from 1965 to 1972. The total cost to the two governments was just over $9.5 million, of which Ottawa provided over $6.5 million.

Because the programme caused some of the larger, older fishing communities to disappear, it was inevitable that there would be a minority — merchants, for example, or local office holders such as the postmistress — who were resentful. Consequently, of course, it became a political issue, with its usual complement of charges and counter-charges. The governments were accused of ignoring the idyllic life of the small, isolated hamlets; of bribing or coercing the simple, hard-working residents; of depriving these communities of essential services when they resisted government blandishments and threats; of dumping the unsuspecting Newfoundlanders in the alien surroundings of large urban centres where they spent their time on dole, lamenting their lost paradise. Farley Mowat, in *The Rock Within the Sea*, for example, invoked the image of the anonymous fisherman who, over his pipe, ponders the wrongs done under resettlement and then pronounces "we was drove." Pottle in *Newfoundland: Down Without Light*, states categorically that the programme was "humanly and socially misconceived," while Iverson and Matthews in *Communities in Decline* state, somewhat surprisingly, that " One of the strongest grounds for opposition to the Newfoundland resettlement programme is that it tended to eliminate traditional ways of making a living before there were sufficient jobs available for those already unemployed."

One is curious as to what is implied in "traditional ways of making a living." For hundreds of men living on islands and in isolated hamlets, the traditional ways of "making a living" were to fish for six or eight weeks in the summer (if the fish "came in") and then apply to the government for able-bodied relief during the fall, winter and spring. Here, while on the subject of relief, two points should be made: first, historically and consistently, the per-capita number of relief recipients has been higher in the small and isolated communities than in the

119

larger ones; second, the charge that those moving to larger places had little to do except go on relief is not borne out by the figures supplied by the Department of Public Welfare. Of the 3234 families who moved in the five-year period from 1965 to 1970, 11.7 percent were on able-bodied relief at the time of moving. When the situation was reviewed in 1970, the proportion of people on relief for the same group was 6.9 percent. It is significant to note, too, that the difference was under-estimated, since the moving was done in the summer months when relief rolls are lowest, and the second review was done in February and March when relief rolls are highest — usually several times higher than in the summer.

The "lack of humanity" charge, before anything else, begs to be defined. Here one wonders what the word "humanity" entails. Presumably it is meant to suggest things like medical and hospital care in case of illness, periodic dental and visual examinations, a chance to attend a half-decent school (a large minority of those who attended the one-room schools during the period under review were and are unable to read or write), a chance for householders to enjoy the benefits of electricity, for all involved to have water and sewer services in place of the uncertain and back-breaking necessity of dragging water by the bucket, and to have indoor plumbing instead of being forced to use unsanitary wells, brooks, and outhouses. But apparently we are to believe that those responsible for development of resettlement assistance were labouring under the false impression that things like health, education, dental and eye care, and relief from the historic impossibility of trying to maintain acceptable standards without the basic amenities of modern life were indeed "human" considerations. Yet we are told, the whole thing was based on "socially unsound considerations."

Two aspects of the criticism raise intriguing questions. First, was there nothing good at all about the role of the two governments in the matter? Did it not matter that thousands of children now enjoying a high school education—and, in hundreds of cases, going on to university — were doomed to illiteracy or semi-literacy if the several hundred hamlets and villages that were evacuated had continued to exist? Did the critics have any alternatives or options to offer? Apparently not, unless one regards seriously the vague references to local industries

— presumably home-crafts of one kind or another — and one wonders if they remembered that, for nearly three-quarters of a century, the International Grenfell Association promoted home industries. And what of the efforts of NONIA, established in 1924, or the Jubilee Guilds, established in 1935? Valuable as these efforts were, no one familiar with them would see them as an alternative to the need for economic development involving tens of thousands of persons, nor would they solve the basic problems inherent in the smallness and isolation of communities.

The criticisms made of the centralization programme, while no doubt warranted in certain specific areas (such as, the question of "social capital"), have been so extreme and grossly unfair that one wonders at the motives behind them — whether malice, political ideology, or, in some cases, simple ignorance.

In 1956 the government called a conference to study problems on the south coast of Newfoundland. The conference was attended by fishermen, clergymen, doctors, nurses, merchants, tradesmen and others representing all facets of life on the coast. Among the comments and recommendations were the following:

> A large percentage of the problems are associated with isolation, and to these there appears to be no immediate solution short of resettlement.
> The consensus of opinion was that centralization of the [fishing] industry, and consequently of the fishing population in selected areas is the key to the solution of most of the problems of the South Coast.

The convention ended with the following resolution:

> Be it resolved that this Convention request the Government of Newfoundland to appoint a Committee of the South Coast with powers to investigate and to make recommendations to the Government as to the steps to be taken to remedy adverse conditions.

The government set up its commission of inquiry the following year to examine conditions on the south coast of Newfoundland where, from the Burin Peninsula west to Port aux Basques there was a preponderance of small communities

121

depending entirely on the fishery. The chairman, J.T. Cheeseman, born in the small village of Port au Bras, had the grounding of a life-long experience with the Newfoundland fisheries and with the outports. The other two members were both native-born Newfoundlanders, also raised in the outports. After visiting every community on the coast and meeting with hundreds of residents, they included the following among their recommendations:

> Some relocation of population is desirable and essential. The Government of Newfoundland should give financial support for resettlement and rehabilitation.
> The recommendation of the Gordon Commission that financial assistance be provided by the Federal Government for people who wish to move to areas showing greater prospects is part of the solution which we see for the South Coast.

In his "Economic Survey of Newfoundland," Parzival Copes recommends that "the Government of Newfoundland be encouraged to continue its programme of community centralization." S.J.R. Noel, in his widely acclaimed *Politics of Newfoundland*, written in 1971, after the household resettlement programme had been in force for over five years, wrote that with the island's population so scattered, the Newfoundland government could not hope to raise the standard of public services to a level approaching even that of the Maritimes.

Iverson and Matthews, cited earlier for their criticisms of some aspects of the programme, nevertheless felt impelled to make a basic concession:

> In many respects resettlement is an absolute necessity if future generations of Newfoundlanders are to keep pace with the changing employment requirements of the Province. Unless their parents move to larger centres, many children will, one day, find it difficult to earn a living for they will almost certainly lack the necessary education and skills.

Iverson and Matthews seem to fall back on economic factors to justify the programme. Others, especially mothers, were inclined to give first place to the humanitarian factors involved. Thus Copes reported that a majority of those surveyed were glad for the children's sake that they had moved.

Typical outport fishing village.
Newfoundland & Labrador Tourist Development Office

Anglican church and school at St. Anthony, circa 1930; codfish drying on flake in foreground.

Grand (or Hamilton) Falls, 1954, later renamed Churchill Falls.
C.K. Howse

**Fishing off the rugged
Newfoundland coast.**
Newfoundland & Labrador Tourist
Development Office

Sealing ship on the coastal ice.
Newfoundland & Labrador Tourist Development Office

Car ferry, the *William Carson*, built by the Canadian government, in accordance with the Terms of Union, to operate between Port aux Basques and North Sydney. The ship was lost in 1977 after hitting ice off the Labrador coast.

Newfoundland & Labrador Tourist Development Office

Bulldozer stuck in mud during construction of road from Melrose to Port Union.

Gander International Airport.
Newfoundland & Labrador Tourist Development Office

Isolated one-room school, pre-1949.

Typical small outport school, pre-1949.

F.G. Bursey Memorial Collegiate (Pentecostal), Grand Falls, 1968.

Memorial University College, 1925. Construction marked the advent of
university-level education in Newfoundland. When the new campus
(below) was completed in 1961, the building became the nucleus of the
College of Fisheries and Marine Technology.

Memorial University

Air Ambulance. After a modest beginning in 1949, this service gradually expanded to cover almost all of Newfoundland.
Newfoundland & Labrador Tourist Development Office

The hospital ship *Lady Anderson*, one of several operated by the government of Newfoundland.
Newfoundland & Labrador Tourist Development Office

Nurses' Residence, St. John's General Hospital.
Newfoundland & Labrador Tourist Development Office

The Arts & Culture Centre, St. John's.
Richard Stoker

Skiing in Labrador West.

Conference in Northern Labrador, 1956, first of the regional conferences. Seated (l. to r.): Rev. Lester Burry, United Church missionary; Magistrate H. Noseworthy; Dr. W.A. Paddon, Medical Supervisor, Grenfell Services in Northern Labrador. Standing (l. to r.): Roy Rowsell, Welfare Officer; Rev. Fathers Cyr and Tessier, Oblate Mission; the Author, Chairman of Conference; Dr. Gordon Thomas, Superintendent, Grenfell Association; Ronald Roberts, Chairman Happy Valley Community Council; Rev. F.W. Peacock, Superintendent, Moravian Mission.

St. John's Daily News

Smallwood Cabinet, 1959, (l. to r.): B.J. Abbot, M.P. Murray, the Author, J.R. Chalker, S.J. Hepperton, W.J. Keough, Premier Smallwood, L.R. Curtis, C.H. Ballam, E.S. Spencer, Dr. J.W. McGrath, P.J. Lewis, J.T. Cheeseman. (J.G. Channing, Clerk of the Council, seated in right corner).

Smallwood Cabinet, 1966. Clockwise from Premier Smallwood: L.R. Curtis, G.A. Frecker, Eric S. Jones, H.R.V. Earle, A. Maloney, C.M. Lane, B.J. Abbot, the Author, J.R. Chalker, W.J. Keough.

Constitutional Conference, February 1968. Seated (l. to r.): Premiers Smallwood, Thatcher, Bennett, Robichaud, Johnson; Prime Minister Pearson, Governor General Michener; Premiers Robarts, Smith, Weir, Campbell and Manning. Standing at extreme left, Justice Minister P.E. Trudeau.

National Film Board

Joseph Roberts Smallwood

Other factors besides the economic had to be considered: compound fractures, gastroenteritis, rotten teeth by the thousands in children who had never seen a dentist in their lives; scores of one-room schools where in nearly one hundred years not a single child had reached Grade 9, and where a student's chance of attaining matriculation was one in seven hundred; the pregnant women on the Horse Islands and other islands due to give birth in January, February or even March, who were removed from the islands in December by the Grenfell medical authorities and were looked after in St. Anthony in the event of difficult deliveries; the nine children of John Anstey who, living on a remote island in Notre Dame Bay, all died of diphtheria within the space of five weeks; the deranged father who, for three weeks, had to be tied hand and foot, to prevent his killing himself and his family; the pregnant woman who, unable to achieve a normal delivery, kept the little community awake for three days amidst her cries and convulsions until a blessed death terminated her agony; the twenty-three-year-old vigorous young logger whose abdominal pains turned out to be acute appendicitis, and who did not reach a hospital for three days by which time peritonitis had set in. Since most of the critics do not include these factors in their human and social equation, we must assume that they either knew nothing about them (extremely doubtful in some cases) or that they were deemed inconsequential. Critics will, of course, cite cases of epidemics in large centres, or that of good teeth in this hamlet, or of Grade 11 matriculants in the one-room schools on Random Island. Of course there were exceptions, but it would be patently unfair to take a hamlet like Flat Rock, two or three miles from medical attention in Carbonear and only two or three hours, normally, from a St. John's Hospital, and compare it with the Gray Islands, twenty miles out in the roughest ocean in the world, and surrounded by Arctic ice for as much as four or five months of the year.

But the charges of resettlement by bribery and coercion linger on and have probably become a permanent part of Newfoundland folklore. Allied to it is the myth of the peaceful contented idyllic community that was cajoled or pressured into leaving. My own experience in the districts of Labrador (at that time one district) and of White Bay South, have, in some mysterious way, been utterly at variance with those who report meeting numbers of persons who resettled but who pine to go back to become permanent residents again of their now deserted hamlet. So far I have not met one person, young or old, who longs to return. Nostalgia, yes. Summer visits, yes. Leaving Springdale, or Lewisporte or Clarenville with small children to take up permanent residence again on one of the small islands in Bonavista Bay or Notre Dame Bay, no. Perhaps I can do no better here than to plagiarize from my own writing of several years ago:

> Life in a small isolated Newfoundland outport was never idyllic; it was, for most concerned, one long history of poverty, deprivation, and hardship. One basic fact to be found in the records is illuminating. The majority of residents in such communities were never independent or self-sufficient. Regularly, for half the year or more they had to resort to government relief of "dole." With no indoor plumbing, uncertain water supply, no electricity, for most of the women everyday life was continuous drudgery; for most of the children it meant a life sentence of total or near illiteracy; and for all it meant inadequate, if any, medical attention. Those who bewail the disappearance of the isolated hamlets of Newfoundland quite obviously never lived in them, and even more obviously, in an age of television and motor cars, did not have to face the grim prospect of raising a family under the primitive, indeed almost medieval, conditions which with a few exceptions characterized life in those coves and on these islands. We may, therefore, forget the fictional and proceed to the more realistic.

Smallwood himself was besieged by critics of the resettlement program, who seized on it as a heaven-sent weapon. Repeatedly he was accused of arrogantly forcing the people to move, of creating urbanized ghettos which, according to Mowat, were designed by Smallwood to supply cheap labour to the new mercantile oligarchy. The truth was that, apart from giving his overall blessing to the idea, Smallwood was quite happy to leave the details of resettlement assistance to the appropriate ministers, who were, in chronological order, myself, Lane, Maloney, and William Rowe and to the highly qualified officials. Apart from one or two, all were outport Newfoundlanders. At no time did Smallwood express any apprehension about the programme, since he knew that it represented the desires of the vast majority of the people living in these hamlets and on the islands. These desires had been made known to him in scores of public meetings, in innumerable letters, and in unending visits to his office by individuals and delegations. The fact that he received so few complaints and so few, if any, accusations of injustice, unfairness and arrogance, illustrates another fact: namely, that most if not all of those moving, while experiencing some trauma, some regret and nostalgia, were willing to accept these things in the interests of their children and grandchildren. The complaints and accusations came not from the people who moved, so much as from the few who did not want to move, or, in a few cases, who stayed behind. I referred above to the charges levelled against Smallwood by his critics in this matter. The Memorial University periodical *Decks Awash* of February, 1977, carries a letter from Smallwood in which he deals with the charges directly. While this letter will not change the minds of his more intransigent critics, those who want to judge the whole matter impartially will find this letter both informative and interesting:

> Your Volume 5 Number 6 issue contains some statements or insinuations that are completely wrong, and if for no better reason than historical truth these total inaccuracies should be rectified. I, perhaps, am better qualified than any to do so.
>
> On page 40, referring to Lumsden, your magazine says: 'The Government had talked several times with people of both of the communities about moving to Newtown, about ten miles away to the south, but the residents had firmly rejected that idea.' I was at that time the leader of the Government.
>
> Regarding centralization or resettlement of population, the Government of Newfoundland during the twenty-three years when I was responsible for its administration had no policy of centralizing or resettling population. What it had was a policy of giving financial and other help to people who expressed a positive and sincere wish to resettle or centralize. Not only was there the strict condition that the Government would help only if the people themselves wished to move, and made their wish absolutely clear, but the Government still would not help unless 90% of the people of a place wished to make the move — in short, if the people were unanimous in their decision, and if that decision were taken publicly at a public meeting, and if a civil servant of the Government were present

at the meeting to certify that it was genuinely the wish of the people, and if the Government approved the place or places to which the people wish to move, and if a number of other terms and conditions were agreed to, then and only then would the Government help financially or otherwise. The initiative had to come from the people themselves. I know of no case of the Government suggesting, or proposing, to the people of any settlement that they should move, or that they would be wise to move, or that the Government wanted them to move. I know of no such case. I dare say an occasional civil servant might have expressed an opinion along those lines; I know of no such case, and if I had known of such a case, I would very quickly have sent for that civil servant and given him unmistakable orders never again to commit the offence. It was my Administration's policy to get the people of a settlement to move if, and only if, they themselves wished to move under the terms and conditions clearly set forth. Those terms and conditions were given in a printed pamphlet written by a man then on the staff in the Premier's office, the present Mr. Robert Wells, M.H.A. The pamphlet was sent to anybody who wrote in about resettlement, and we always sent an official to attend the public meeting to explain the terms and conditions and to explain how the help would be given.

My Administration's reason, and my reason, for being willing to help people who wished to move was primarily a powerful wish to help the children. As our programme of upgrading the standards of excellence of the teachers came into successful play, it became increasingly difficult, and ultimately all but impossible, to get qualified teachers to teach in small settlements, especially small islands, or in any remote or isolated settlement. The same was (and is) true of doctors and nurses.

I am proud of our accomplishments in the resettlement developments that we helped people in hundreds of settlements to bring about. It was one of the truly great accomplishments of my Administration.

One of Newfoundland's most experienced civil servants is C.W. Powell, former outport magistrate, deputy minister of municipal affairs, and chairman of the board of public utilities, now retired. His recent comments on the resettlement programme are most worthy of note:

I believe the resettlement programme should be explained in the light of the circumstances that existed at the time. These included isolated settlements completely cut off from the principal public services except by sea; one room schools with a few pupils in each of grades one to six or eight taught by teachers whose qualifications were high school graduation and a willingness to work in isolated places because nothing else was available to them; everyday health services, provided by local midwives, whose skills consisted mainly of folklore; persons with serious injuries or in labour who could not be moved for days because of bad weather and in the end moved in small boats in hurricane weather at great risk to all involved, to the nearest cottage hospital 20 miles or more distant. The younger people were moving away as fast as they could find employment elsewhere leaving behind the old, the sick and the romantics. It was in these circumstances that the governments offered help to any who wanted to relocate to approved communities. To provide any acceptable level of public services to these isolated places would have been impossible from both financial and staffing points of view. In my opinion, resettlement was inevitable without government support. Government recognized the inevitable and promoted it. Government could not have stopped it any more than it could stop the mechanization of wood harvesting or fish catching.

My own assessment of the resettlement that took place in the 1950s and 1960s is that large numbers of our people on islands and in isolated hamlets wanted to move, but that few could move without some degree of help. Once it saw the need, the government decided to help.

Undoubtedly there was some degree of bureaucratic blundering, some lack of planning, and not full appreciation of the traumatic effect, especially on the old, of tearing up roots to settle elsewhere. Perhaps some of the larger and older communities should have been encouraged not to resettle. Having conceded this, it is my opinion, based on a lifetime knowledge of outport life, that, overall, resettlement was a good thing, bringing as it did, untold blessings in health, education and in living standards to people generally, but especially to the thousands of children involved.

9 CULTURE, RECREATION AND TOURISM

T he great majority of the Newfoundlanders are descended from the English (mostly West Country), Irish and Welsh. The early settlers had little to encourage cultural pursuits but did preserve old songs, ballads, tunes and melodies, often accompanied by mouth organ, accordion or violin. This oral tradition has become one of the richest in the western world and has been the basis, in part, for the province's cultural revival which started in 1949 and has continued at an accelerating pace ever since.

There was, of course, evidence of cultural talent in Newfoundland long before 1949: E.J. Pratt was writing poetry; Pilot, Cullen and Vincent were painting; John Murray Anderson was producing on Broadway; and Georgina Stirling (Madame Toulinget) was starring in grand opera. Indeed, for more than a century St. John's could boast of a deep interest in drama, music and the fine arts. It was one of the first parts of North America to produce the light opera of Gilbert and Sullivan.

One reason for the early emergence of artistic interest and talent may have been the large Irish and Welsh element in the city (probably as much as 65 percent), but even more influential was the fact that Catholic girls received a first-class indoctrination in art and music and related matters from the Presentation Sisters and the Sisters of Mercy. All the denominational colleges assumed responsibility for giving their students some training in choral music and in music appreciation, and most of them were able to engage specialists who taught piano and voice to individual students who could pay the fees. For most of the schools in Newfoundland, however, no such opportunities existed. But the interest remained and found expression in church services — where congregational singing, especially among the evangelical churches, was always emphasized — and in the Sunday night sing-song, grouped around the cottage organ, or the "come all ye's" sung lustily on week nights to the tunes of an old accordion.

In the early days following 1949, the majority of schools were still too small and too poor to pay attention to music or, for that matter, anything else relating to the arts. But with the beginning of central and regional high schools, and the large consolidated elementary schools, the situation changed. The ten-room central high school almost certainly would have an auditorium, a piano, and a full- or part-time music teacher. Many schools were large enough to have school orchestras and choirs. By the end of the Smallwood period there were 250 glee clubs and choirs, 16 school bands and orchestras, and over 100 full-time qualified music teachers, a goodly proportion of whom were graduates of some of the world's leading conservatories. In 1970 much of the work in music was coordinated by the creation of a division of music within the Department of Education. The consultant appointed to this post was Sister Paschal of the Presentation Order, who immediately devoted her outstanding talents to drawing up a musical programme for Newfoundland schools.

Not all progress in developing musical talent was the result of government sponsorship, however, and the role of volunteers was an important one. Probably the most far-reaching of these was the establishment of the Kiwanis Music Festival Association in 1951, followed by its first festival in 1952, attracting 1400 entrants. By 1971 nearly 12,000 were participating in St. John's, and an equal number in the centres of Grand Falls, Corner Brook and Carbonear. (The Corner Brook Festival was sponsored by the town's Rotary Club.)

At the university, under the auspices of the Extension Department, the Extension choir and the St. John's Symphony Orchestra added to the musical life of the province and, over the years, achieved some measure of national acclaim. At the same time other choral groups were formed, several of which also received national attention. In addition to these, several school choirs, after winning trophies at home, were invited to perform in a number of Canadian cities, including the nation's capital.

While drawing or painting had always been encouraged (it was an accredited course for high school students), Newfoundland's lack of teachers and proper facilities made it difficult to develop artistic talent, apart from some notable exceptions, and little came of it. There were, however, several private art schools set up at various times prior to 1949, chiefly in St. John's, which did have the effect of keeping some interest alive. In 1949 two talented Newfoundland artists — Reginald Shepherd and his wife Helen Parsons Shepherd — founded the Newfoundland Academy of Art which grew to a point where 120 pupils a year were enrolled. The Shepherds operated their academy for twelve years, during which time a number of art teachers, as well as students, improved their artistic competence. Those familiar with the work of the school were convinced that the Shepherds were at least partly responsible for the growth of interest in art which characterized the period following 1949. In addition to the Shepherds, other Newfoundland artists blossomed during the period, some to the point of being considered among the leading artists of Canada. Among them were Christopher and Mary Pratt, and David Blackwood.

Drama was always an integral part of life in a Newfoundland outport, even as far back as the early nineteenth century. It was a rare community that did not have its school concert, made up of dialogues, recitations, solos, and so on. Many undertook to put on a play at least once a year, usually at Christmas or Easter. With the building of arts centres, as well as the auditoriums in the consolidated schools, opportunities for more elaborate productions became common. In 1950 the interest in amateur dramatics was manifested in the creation of a Newfoundland Drama Festival Society, which the following year became part of the national organization. The annual Dominion Drama Festival soon became one of the most popular entertainment items of the year with groups from St. John's, Labrador City, Grand Falls, Corner Brook and Gander competing.

131

One interesting aspect of the period was the emergence of a number of talented local, or locally born, playwrights. This list included the late Ted Russell, Al Pittman, Grace Butt, Tom Cahil, Cassie Brown and Helen Porter.

In prose and verse there were concurrent developments with the other arts. Gordon Pinsent, Harold Horwood, Percey Janes built up large followings as novelists and, in the field of Newfoundland history, Peter Neary, S.R. Noel and Patrick O'Flaherty did pioneer work. Ray Guy became nationally known as a humourist. Arthur Scammel, who in the early 1930s had composed what is now one of Newfoundland's best known folk songs, "The Squid Jigging Ground," returned to the province in the 1960s to continue his writing and to give lectures. J.R. Smallwood continued his monumental task by creating Volumes 3 and 4 of the *Book of Newfoundland*, to follow the two earlier volumes done in the 1930s. In poetry, R.A. Parsons (now deceased), Tom Dawe, Paul O'Neil and Al Pittman became increasingly well known as they developed poetical themes with a Newfoundland motif.

The development of drama, painting, sculpture and music require space and facilities if they are to become part of the community's heritage. But apart from the high school auditoriums, valuable as they were when compared to what had gone before, Newfoundland still lacked the kind of professionally designed arts and culture centres, that could be found elsewhere in Canada, where maximum interest and benefit could be derived from local talent and where visiting troupes, choirs, orchestras, and related groups could bring to regional centres outside St. John's entertainment which they would otherwise have never enjoyed.

In 1964 the premier and I went to Portugal where he was the guest of Prime Minister Salazar. While in Lisbon we were taken to see the University of Lisbon where, we were told, there was a splendid auditorium. Smallwood was completely fascinated by every aspect of the magnificent structure and repeatedly vowed that if there was any way to do it, Newfoundland would have one as nearly identical as its different climatic conditions would allow. The opportunity to satisfy his ambition soon presented itself. In 1967, Canada was to celebrate its centennial year and, as part of that great event, the federal government agreed to pay two-thirds of the cost of a provincial project mutually agreed on by the federal and the provincial government concerned. Newfoundland decided that its project would be an arts and culture centre modelled on the one at Lisbon. While not so large as some of its counterparts across Canada, it is generally agreed by knowledgeable authorities that it is one of the best in the country. It is worth recording that when the project was first announced by Smallwood, there was strong resistance from a number of critics (most of them well-to-do) on the grounds that Newfoundland could not afford such an extravagance; that with other needs so apparent it would be a "frill," and would simply be an ivory tower for a small group of "long-hairs." This opinion was not shared by the majority, however. In fact, families in the lower and middle income ranges were among its strongest supporters. This was understandable, given that it was their children, unable to visit Toronto or London or New York periodically, who would derive the greatest benefit from the eight-million-dollar edifice. In the last year of the Smallwood era, attendance at the centre reached the unbelievable figure of 600,000. Many of these patrons were not residents of St. John's, but from all parts of the province.

The St. John's Arts and Culture Centre features a fully-equipped proscenium theatre, seating comfortably over one thousand, a stage large enough to accommodate the largest symphony orchestra, two orchestra pits, three public libraries (one a Newfoundland reference library, one for children and one for adults), three art galleries, the provincial library headquarters, a large lecture room and two meeting rooms, a drama rehearsal room, a studio theatre, a craft training division, as well as a public restaurant and a snack bar.

The St. John's Centre was not even completed before there were demands from other large communities for similar facilities. The first to receive one outside St. John's was Corner Brook. It contained a theatre able to seat 400, an exhibition area, meeting and rehearsal rooms and an olympic-size swimming pool.

Many visitors to Montreal's Expo 67 were agreed that the most attractive building on the grounds was the two-part Czechoslovakian structure. Following discussions between the Czech and Newfoundland governments it was agreed that Newfoundland could have the building — provided that the province did the dismantling and removal. The larger part was re-erected at Grand Falls and the smaller part at Gander. The Grand Falls building had a 400-seat theatre, two lending libraries, an exhibition area, and the usual meeting and rehearsal rooms. The Gander building was converted to an olympic-size swimming pool, a classroom and an area for women's institutes.[1]

The first Newfoundland public library of which there is any record was established in St. John's in the early 1800s. In the 1820s there was a well-stocked reading room much frequented by visitors. In the 1920s, with the assistance of the Carnegie Corporation, a small travelling library of 7000 volumes was established. Then in 1935 the Commission of Government passed the *Public Libraries Act* and set up a public libraries board for St. John's. The library which followed was essentially the product of several gifts — one from the former Mayor Gosling (whose name was given to the new library), another from Lord Rothermere, head of the Grand Falls enterprise, and one from the government, consisting of the remnants of the old legislative library damaged in the 1932 riot. In 1940 the government approved the founding of twenty-five libraries over a five-year period to serve as distribution centres throughout the island. By 1945 that task had been completed.

With the advent of confederation no dramatic increase in library services occurred. The government grant for libraries in 1949 was $80,000; in 1954 it rose to $125,000, an amount which the government guaranteed for four additional years, thus enabling the board to plan its operations systematically and with assurance. In 1956 the libraries had catalogued a total of over 250,000 volumes, compared with 17,000 in 1937. By 1967 the government had raised its annual grant to over half a million dollars, and by the end of the Smallwood era to one million dollars which, by coincidence, was the same amount the government spent for all education in the country some forty years earlier. In 1965 there were sixty public libraries in the province. This basic expansion was accompanied by complementary developments of various kinds, including a film service (started in 1960) and a music library which was added in 1970 to the adult library in the Arts and Culture Centre. A

[1] Subsequently this building was enlarged to provide a regular theatre, an appropriate meeting room and a library.

bookmobile service was started in 1968 and grew to the point where seven specially built vehicles were in use.

These developments had no direct impact on school and other institutional libraries, however. For most schools in Newfoundland there were no library services at all before 1949. The denominational colleges and a few other St. John's schools had small libraries, as did three or four of the larger schools in the outports. The occasional school had a few rarely touched books sitting in a corner. But until the building of the regional high schools, school libraries were almost as rare as the Great Auk. The new large schools usually had a special room provided for libraries and related services.

In 1958, following the educational conferences described earlier, the government introduced a system of library grants for schools — $50 a year for each school with less than four rooms and $100 a year for schools with more than four rooms. (This modest amount was later raised to $200 a year for schools with more than ten rooms.) Many schools used these grants as the basis on which to build substantial library services, but, incredibly, 37 percent of the schools had not applied for their grants — a curious oversight given that in the larger Newfoundland schools the average number of books per student was 1.47 compared to an average of 5.02 for similar schools across Canada. By 1971, however, great improvements had taken place. The statistics showed that the 1958 average had risen to 4.6 books per student and that the total number of volumes in the school libraries had risen to a quarter of a million.

Attempts to establish a museum in Newfoundland started in the early 1800s, but did not succeed until 1849. The devastating fires of 1842 and 1892 twice destroyed the museum. In 1907 the present building was erected and a creditable number of artifacts were assembled. But in the first year of its administration, the Commission of Government took over the building for offices, allegedly in the interests of space and economy, and the museum's contents were scattered to the four winds, a goodly portion eventually being destroyed by fire. Consequently, one of the first acts of the Smallwood administration was to search for and reassemble the remaining artifacts. In 1957 it was again possible to reopen the museum.

The contents of the present museum can be divided into

two categories: first, artifacts relating to Newfoundland's pre-history, for the most part to the Maritime Archaic, Dorset Eskimo and Beothuk cultures; and, second, artifacts relating to the European settlement of Newfoundland. Other museums also established during the period included the Naval and Military Museum in St. John's and a number of smaller ones at Trinity, Twillingate, Hibbs Cove and Harbour Grace, largely set up by local initiative. Those at Gander Airport, Quidi Vidi, Cape Bonavista Lighthouse and the Seaman's Museum at Grand Bank were preserved and developed largely by federal aid. These institutions did more than give Newfoundlanders information. They have helped to create an appreciation for and pride in the rich historical fabric which had, for a period, stood in danger of being permanently lost and forgotten. As was to be expected, the building or preserving of the local museums led to enormous tourist interest in the towns concerned.

Closely allied to the museums are the archives, although the latter did not formally exist until 1956. Attempts had been made from time to time to preserve documents, but in the absence of any responsible body, these spasmodic and haphazard attempts were bound to fail. For more than a century, irreplaceable papers floated around from government department to department or were kept by individuals, or remained in the legislative library. The credit for establishing public archives must go to Premier Smallwood and to Memorial University, which undertook the task of assembling and cataloguing documents in 1956. In 1960, with the Colonial Building vacated by the legislature, the archives were formally taken over by the government. The first archivist was the late Allan Fraser, a former professor of history at Memorial, and for several years a member of Parliament. He was succeeded by Burhman Gill in 1970.

The archives have done a remarkable job, not just in looking after the records that were passed over to it by the university, but also in soliciting private donations, and in purchasing rare and otherwise historic documents, especially church, court and mercantile records. Britain, too, has proved to be a particularly valuable source of Newfoundland documents, many of which have been microfilmed and stored in the archives, where they are available to all interested persons.

RECREATION AND PHYSICAL EDUCATION

When Newfoundland joined Canada in 1949, the province was far below the national standard of recreational services. The great majority of schools had no gym or playrooms, no playing fields or playgrounds. The denominational colleges and several other schools in St. John's were exceptions, as were, to some extent, several company-supported schools in Grand Falls, Corner Brook and Buchans. Memorial University had a small gym and a small makeshift playing field used occasionally for soccer. Neither the university nor any of the high schools possessed a swimming pool. No public recreational or physical education programme existed.

Reasons for the neglect of recreation and physical education before 1949 were manifold. To begin with, the average outport teenager in those days (and before) had no need for exercise since performing morning and afternoon chores around the house were invariably taxing enough. These consisted of the mundane tasks of hauling or carrying water in buckets from the brook or well, of tending to the garden crops in season, of sawing and cleaving wood, of looking after the poultry and domestic animals, of caring for the family's horse or cow (if they had one), of picking seasonal berries, and, in fishing villages, of helping to process salt fish. Obviously, not all these tasks would be at every single house, but a goodly portion would. And for thousands of outport boys (and girls) there was no time for sport, even if the money to buy sports equipment was available. Geography, too, was an impediment, since much of Newfoundland is rocky or boggy, and a majority of outport villages simply did not have enough level ground to play soccer or other outdoor sports; needless to say, neither the money nor the heavy machinery was available to level the rocky ground or to dig the trenches necessary to drain a bog or swamp.

Obstacles also existed at the few schools which had sports facilities, since many teachers persisted in their belief that games or exercise was not an integral part of the education process. Rather, they tended to regard it as a kind of lollipop given to (or taken from) the students according to their progress in their academic subjects or their general behaviour. A

137

poor arithmetic or English assignment, or misconduct in the history class could carry with it a suspension from basketball or another sports programme for that day or week. A second impediment to a successful physical education programme was the tendency of suitably equipped schools to concentrate on the athletic elite, with a view to producing a winning team in field hockey or ice hockey, thus reducing the opportunity to participate for the mediocre or clumsy would-be athlete.

In order to change the picture for the better, the government instituted a policy to provide funds to the churches for the building of central and regional high schools, most of which would have a gymnasium or playroom space. Almost overnight hundreds of students were participating in sports such as basketball, badminton and volleyball, many for the first time in their lives. What the students needed now, however, were trained teachers capable of instructing and supervising them in these new undertakings.

The university set up its department of Physical Education in 1956, and by 1961 was awarding degrees in that discipline. The move to the new campus in 1961 provided the department with a large building devoted entirely to physical education and related studies. By the end of the Smallwood period, over 300 Memorial students were registered in the physical education faculty.

The royal commission on sports and youth activities, under the chairmanship of well-known hockey player and broadcaster Howie Meeker, was set up in 1958 and made its report in the following year. Unfortunately, a temporary financial recession meant that the government was unable to implement many of the recommendations immediately. But the delay was not permanent. Leading from the report, a physical fitness division was established in 1964, under the direction of Graham Snow, a former physical instructor in several of the province's larger schools. This division became both a clearing house and a liaison agency in respect of the educational programmes and the federal activities connected with the Canada Winter and Summer Games. Another recommendation of the commission was implemented in 1970 when the division became a single co-ordinating youth agency for the province. During the critical period of athletic and recreational expansion in the 1960s, school boards, schools and recreational agencies had the advantage of being able to go to the division for guidance and, where necessary, professional help in the construction of facilities, the purchase of equipment, and the countless details relating to what had become for Newfoundland a vast programme of recreation and physical education.

One great deficiency in recreational sport in the early 1950s was in the lack of stadiums, both in St. John's and all over the province. St. John's had lost its stadium by fire in the 1940s and efforts to provide a replacement had repeatedly broken down. Eventually, the Newfoundland government, on the condition that the building would be used for government-sponsored agricultural exhibitions, undertook the major financing of the project, resulting in the St. John's Memorial Stadium. This action opened the flood gates to massive pressure from other communities demanding equal treatment. Various formulae for government help were tried out, leading to a capital grants programme which enabled the government to fund 75 percent of the capital cost of approved projects up to $150,000. These projects consisted of facilities such as indoor and outdoor natural rinks, softball and soccer fields, swimming pools and athletic centres. As a result of this programme, thousands of children and adults at the community level were able to enjoy facilities which would not have been otherwise available.

When the Canadian National Defence units that had occupied Torbay Airport from the time of its construction in World War II moved out in the middle 1960s, its recreational and athletic facilities, including an indoor swimming pool, a double gymnasium and a youth hostel, were passed over to the Newfoundland government. This gave the government a chance to create a recreational and provincial training centre for the whole province, located only four miles from St. John's. The facilities were renovated and a comprehensive programme involving physical training, leadership, coaching seminars and conferences was implemented. And although this centre, as its name implies, serves the province as a whole, since most of such government institutions as the schools for the deaf are in the St. John's area, the centre was able to play a special role in their training and rehabilitation. At the end of the era the centre was serving 80,000 people a year.

A few comparative figures will help to underscore the trans-

139

formation that has taken place in Newfoundland's recreation services since 1949. During confederation year there were ten gyms and five physical education teachers in all Newfoundland. At the end of the Smallwood era in 1972, there were 300 gyms in use, served by a corresponding number of trained teachers, most of them physical education specialists. In 1949, high school teams had a combined roster of under 800 boys and girls; at the end of the period there were 4600.

TOURISM

At least as far back as the early years of the nineteenth century people talked hopefully of the great potential for tourism in Newfoundland. Much of the scenery was unusual, some of it was unique. The streams were full of trout and salmon; caribou in their thousands roamed the barrens. But few tourists came. Things would be better, it was argued, when the trans-insular railway was built, as this would make it possible for both visitors and local citizens to reach rivers like the Humber and the Gander without too much difficulty, and to reach the hitherto inaccessible barrens in the heart of the island. So, with the railway, more tourists came. But generally these were restricted to sportsmen who were affluent enough to afford the expensive safari, including guides and equipment. Not surprisingly, this did not translate into a healthy tourist industry.

Another category of tourists which developed following the construction of the railway was the expatriate Newfoundlander or the Canadian or American with Newfoundland roots. Year after year, large numbers left Toronto, Boston or New York to take the long train ride to Sydney, crossing the gulf (Cabot Strait) by steamer, and on to the family home by train again, often having to finish the trip by boat. What the value of this tourism was to Newfoundland's economy was difficult to assess, since there were few accurate or competent records kept. Overall, however, it was probably fairly substantial.

With confederation in 1949, there was an upsurge in expectations for tourism, for it seemed certain that thousands of Canadians would want to visit the new province. (The converse, of course, was that many Newfoundlanders would want to visit their new country — especially if, as was likely, they had relatives living abroad.) But, as in the 1800s, expectations were ahead of reality. First, there was the problem of transportation: while the railway still operated, and there was now a daily air service between St. John's, Gander, Stephenville and the mainland, people in the 1950s had gotten used to the car and were inclined to postpone visiting Newfoundland until it was accessible by road. Moreover, the ferries used to cross the Cabot Strait were not car ferries, and in the early years of confederation a person who managed to get his car across was not going to get very far in western Newfoundland, or in any other part except the Avalon Peninsula. The Terms of Union obligated Canada to set up a suitable car ferry service across the "Gulf" as soon as a road had been built from Port aux Basques to Corner Brook, a distance of about 140 miles. Unfortunately, this condition was not met until 1958.

The absence of roads and adequate car ferry service were not the only problems inhibiting the growth of tourism. Outside of St. John's there was scarcely anything that could be classified as modern hotel accommodation. There were a few reasonably acceptable wooden hotels or boarding houses with indoor plumbing, but the remaining types of accommodation could only be considered primitive. In St. John's there was the relatively small Newfoundland Hotel, built in the 1920s, with acceptable standards apart from its size. The hotel was unable to meet even the local demands, however, and for a period had the highest occupancy rate in Canada. Periodically the Canadian National Railway, to whom the hotel was transferred following union, announced that it was going to enlarge the premises or even, they hinted, replace it. These announcements or rumours always seemed to surface wherever it was rumoured that a mainland hotel chain was going to move into Newfoundland, and seemed to dissipate into thin air when negotiations between the entrepreneurs and Newfoundland had broken down. In the meantime, the province was losing millions of dollars in possible tourist business and millions more from national organizations of every kind which would have scheduled a convention in Newfoundland were it not for the fact that there was no hotel accommodation available.

An important step forward was taken in 1953 when the government set up the Tourist Development Loan Board, to assist those with limited capital who were willing to invest in tourist enterprises of one kind or another — especially hotels, motels and restaurants. The growth that occurred between 1949 and 1966 — "Come Home Year" — was from a 1949 total of 33 hotel or motel establishments capable of accommodating fewer then 1300 people, to 251 tourist establishments able to handle nearly 7000 guests. These figures do not include the 100 hunting and fishing camps, nor the 9 boats with tourist accommodation, nor the increase in the number of Newfoundland's restaurants — 143 in 1949 and 523 in 1966.

In 1964, when I was minister of highways, it became apparent that, largely as a result of the 90:10 deal with Ottawa on financing the building of the Trans Canada Highway, there was every prospect that by the late fall of 1965 we would have a paved road from St. John's to Port aux Basques. It occurred to me that Newfoundland might well capitalize on this great achievement by declaring 1966 "Come Home Year" and inviting tens of thousands of former Newfoundlanders or descendants of Newfoundlanders to come back to Newfoundland during the summer of that year. I raised this matter with Premier Smallwood who agreed wholeheartedly with the idea and submitted it to the cabinet. Cabinet agreed with the suggestion and also with the premier's proposal that I should be chairman of the governing committee.

The tasks ahead of us were formidable — particularly the old bugbear of accommodation, for while there had been gratifying developments in this field in the previous three or four years (new modern hotels and motels in Gander, St. John's, Grand Falls and Corner Brook), we were still unable to cope with normal tourist traffic. A well-publicized Come Home Year would magnify the problem several times over. Then, too, there was the all-important matter of car ferry service across the Gulf. Already the *William Carson*, carrying about fifty vehicles and 250 passengers on the daily round trip, was overtaxed. Clearly, even though some extra use would be made of trains, and Air Canada would undoubtedly expand its frequency of service to Newfoundland, without substantial increase in the gulf car ferry service, Come Home Year could degenerate into a fiasco.

The first task was organization. As our executive officer we were fortunate to obtain the services of a George Giannou, newly retired after a very successful career as a businessman in St. John's. From there we set up a number of master committees each headed by Newfoundlanders of recognized ability and dedication.[2] From the beginning it was recognized that the eventual success or failure of Come Home Year would depend on the degree of local involvement. With this in mind, 205 local committees were set up all over the province. Each committee devised a programme of entertainment which would be of interest to visitors. In addition, the committees arranged for accommodation in private homes whenever commercial accommodation became overtaxed. The problem of hotel accommodation in larger centres was solved, for all practical purposes, when, following negotiations with Holiday Inns of Canada, a chain of inns was established at St. John's, Clarenville, Gander and Corner Brook. Also, with government support, existing hotel facilities were renovated or enlarged. In all, hotel accommodation was increased by 1000 rooms. Thus, in spite of the big influx of tourists in 1966 no serious accommodation crisis developed. The problem of car ferry service evaporated when the Canadian government purchased for the gulf service a large European car ferry, later named the *Lief Eriksson*. With this large ship added to the service it was possible to transport back and forth across the gulf 1000 passengers and 200 cars daily. This number, added to a greatly expanded Air Canada service to Newfoundland, meant that all those who wished to visit Newfoundland were able to do so. Many of the vehicles were trailers or vehicles with camping equipment, taking advantage of the large increase in the number of parks and picnic sites in the province.

Picnic and camping grounds had been started in the early 1950s and, as the road system expanded, so too did the need and the demand for more camping sites and park services. In 1958 a federal-provincial agreement was signed under which Ottawa contributed one-half the cost of thirteen picnic parks and seven camping parks. The year 1965 saw a big increase in park development as the government prepared for the influx of visitors almost certain to come in 1966. This anticipation was justified, for during Come Home Year the number of park visitors increased by 218,000 over the previous year. This was

---

[2] Among the chairmen of committees were Frank Moores, then a businessman and later to become premier of Newfoundland; also Donald Jamieson, who was later to become a senior minister in the Trudeau cabinet, and still later, Canadian high commissioner to Britain.

reflected, too, in the gross value of tourism to Newfoundland for the 1966 year, calculated to be $13 million over the previous year, more than doubling the largest increase previously recorded.

But in addition to its immediate benefits, Come Home Year had other far-reaching effects on Newfoundland's economy. It is true that a large percentage of visitors to Newfoundland that year stayed with relatives and friends, making it difficult to compute the material value of their visits to Newfoundland. But that it was substantial was obvious. More important, however, was that the thousands who came home that summer (which was blessed with some of the best weather in many years) carried back with them glowing accounts of the vast changes that had taken place in Newfoundland. They became, in effect, ambassadors of goodwill and inevitably were instrumental in persuading their friends, relatives and even casual acquaintances to visit Newfoundland. Since then, the tourist industry has never looked back. By the end of the Smallwood era it had become one of the major industries of the province.

10 LABRADOR

T he Province of Newfoundland is made up of two parts, the island of Newfoundland and the mainland territory of Labrador, the latter measuring about two and a half times the area of the former, but with a permanent population in 1949 of only between four and five thousand. This figure increased rapidly between 1949 and 1971, however, due chiefly to the mining developments in Labrador West and to continuing growth in the Happy Valley-Goose Bay area. By 1971 the total population of Labrador was around 32,000, of whom the two Indian groups made up about 700 and the Inuit something over 2000.

For several decades prior to 1949 there had been a dispute as to whether Quebec (and therefore Canada) owned the territory or whether it belonged to Newfoundland. The matter had been referred to the judicial committee of the Imperial Privy Council in the early 1900s, and in 1927 that body handed down a decision which substantially confirmed Newfoundland's claim. It was a matter of great relief to those who favoured union between Newfoundland and Canada (as well as to those Newfoundlanders who had had some misgivings about the venture) that the Terms of Union, which became part of the *British North America Act* (and, therefore, of the Constitution of Canada) clearly spelled out the boundaries of the new province. That the Province of Quebec did not accept the decision was a fact which some Newfoundlanders found irritating, but for all practical purposes, it had no significance whatever. Term 2 of the Terms of Union states:

> The Province of Newfoundland shall comprise the same territory as at the date of Union, that is to say, the island of Newfoundland and the islands adjacent thereto, the Coast of Labrador as delimited in the report delivered by the Judicial Committee of His Majesty's Privy Council on the first day of March, 1927, and the islands adjacent to the said Coast of Labrador.

To understand the conditions that existed in Labrador in 1949, it is necessary to go back some 200 years to the time when ships from Britain, France, New England, and other countries gradually pushed north from the Strait of Belle Isle to take advantage of the rich fishery resources along the Labrador coast. At the time there were two aboriginal groups, the Eskimo — now generally known as the Inuit — and the Montagnais-Nascopie Indians. The Inuit exploited the northern coastal resources, particularly the seals, while the Indians tended to depend on inland resources, especially caribou for food and clothing, and other game for trapping. The two groups generally regarded one another with hostility and had little contact. In addition, following the early European discoveries, the Inuit were fiercely antagonistic to white explorers and settlers. By the eighteenth century, however, some commercial establishments had been set up as far north as Sandwich Bay while, still further north, the Moravians (a religious organization from central Europe) gradually overcame the fears and suspicions that the brutal treatment from other European and North American adventurers had engendered among the Inuit.

Many of the white settlers in Labrador came directly from Europe rather than by way of Newfoundland. Generally this occurred where "servants," indentured fishermen or semi-skilled labourers, after fulfilling their obligation, decided to stay on in Labrador rather than go back home; often this happened as a result of marriage to an Inuit or part-Inuit, or with another white settler in Labrador. There were thus three main groups in Labrador prior to World War II: the Inuit and part-Inuit of the North; the Indians whose permanent homes were in Davis Inlet and North West River, but who lived a seminomadic life; and the white settlers, concentrated in the southern half of Labrador but with a sprinkling of clergymen, clerks, police and the like scattered all along the coast. The great majority of whites in southern Labrador were inshore fishermen; the settlers in the Lake Melville area were also trappers as were the Indians. The Inuit relied chiefly on seal and fish. This remained the pattern for several centuries until a change in lifestyle began to develop during World War II.

Once war had been declared it became evident that the Allies would need another air base in eastern North America, both as a taking-off point for the thousands of planes to be ferried to Britain, and as a base for anti-submarine patrols in the North Atlantic. The site, near Goose River at the end of Lake Melville, became known as Goose Airport. During the latter part of the war and during the subsequent Cold War of the 1950s, it was the second busiest airport in the world. The huge American and Canadian installations, with their ongoing construction and maintenance requirements, meant that Goose needed a steady supply of semi-skilled and unskilled labour, with the result that hundreds of people from Labrador and Newfoundland found work there. And while some of the personnel and their families were given living accommodation on the base, others were not so fortunate. Consequently, hundreds of men from the coastal villages of Labrador and Newfoundland outports were deprived of family life for months, living in barracks and seeing their wives and children for only a few days or weeks during the year.

The reservation which had been given to Canada by the government of Newfoundland for Goose Airport was a large stretch of land far in excess of that normally needed and provided for such a purpose. Part of the reservation included the north bank of the Hamilton (later Churchill) River, about five miles from the base. In a short time, civilian workers began to squat on a Hamilton River site to which someone had given the name of Happy Valley. It appears likely, too, that some of the squatters received the tacit approval[1] of the base authorities to remain there, conditional on their good behaviour, with the base reserving the right to remove the settlers at short notice. This, in fact, did happen on occasion when workers

---

[1] The base authorities found it convenient to have a reservoir of manpower on which to draw for construction and other projects.

became redundant or because of drunkenness or other misbehaviour. But despite its unsettled status, the community continued to grow until, by 1952, when I became member of the House of Assembly for all Labrador, the population had reached nearly one thousand.

In the months following my election to the constituency, I visited Goose Airport and Happy Valley. In the latter place I found an unbelievable situation. The residents who had settled there had no rights whatever — except, presumably, the right to leave. They had no title to land and could, therefore, be ordered to demolish their living premises and move off the base reservation completely. They were not permitted to own or operate vehicles for private or commercial use. No commercial establishments of any kind were permitted, and since the residents had no title to the land and water and sewer facilities were not available, the tendency was to build to a minimum standard. In other words, I was witnessing the creation of one of the largest slum areas in the province. The military authorities had made some concessions, however. Since the Happy Valley residents needed food and clothing, they were permitted to purchase their needs at the large Hudson's Bay store on the airport property. This required transportation, however, and here again the authorities co-operated: from time to time open trucks used by the workers were allowed to carry prospective shoppers the ten miles back and forth over a gravel road. This journey was somewhat unpleasant in winter, especially for women and children, when the temperature ranged between $-20°$ and $-40°$ F, but that was all the authorities were prepared to do.

Once I had seen conditions at first hand I sought an interview with the base commanders. Their position was very simple: Happy Valley was an "illegitimate" community existing only on sufferance. Since it was only five miles from the airport itself, and since the nearest other community, North West River, was not connected by road and was some twenty-five miles away by water, evacuating hundreds of civilians from Happy Valley in the event of another war would present a logistical problem for which the Department of Defence did not want the responsibility. Hence their deliberate policy of discouraging permanent settlement. What I had to consider as well, they said, was that Goose Airport had seen its heyday

(1952) and was therefore in decline; thus, far from encouraging further settlement, the department should be thinking of removing some of those already settled. Also was the fact that Happy Valley contained some undesirable elements which, added to the ever-present security problem, would simply make the burden of administering such a large base unnecessarily heavy.

For my part I reminded the commanders that on the island of Newfoundland there were three large bases — Pepperrell, surrounded by a hundred thousand civilians; Argentia, with at least five communities surrounding it; and Harmon Air Force Base surrounded by the town of Stephenville and several other communities — with a total population of over ten thousand. No one would seriously suggest removing the people of St. John's because it would be vulnerable in case of war. Quite apart from the reality that in an atomic age nobody is free from danger, however, there was still the one more important fact that a thousand Canadian citizens were being denied rights available to all other Canadians. Furthermore, there was no justification for denying these citizens such simple amenities as food and clothing stores, taxis, motor cars and movies. I pointed out, too, that there were no community problems involving alcohol or the like that a simple community organization and the police officers in the area could not control; that similar problems had confronted the other bases without their ever having argued that the St. John's residents should be deprived of basic rights because security problems existed. My arguments proved to be unacceptable to the base authorities, however, and in 1953 I was left with no alternative, after consulting with Premier Smallwood, but to go to Ottawa to discuss the matter with the minister of national defence, the Honourable Brooke Claxton. Claxton was one of the most capable, as well as one of the most popular members of the St. Laurent cabinet. I described to him the deprivations and discrimination being suffered by the residents, the great majority of whom were hard-working, law-abiding citizens. At the close of my remarks I made it clear to the minister that if nothing were done to give the Happy Valley people the same basic rights enjoyed by people living near the other bases in Newfoundland, I would have no choice, as member for the area, but to make a public statement which would, of necessity, be

149

highly critical of the Department of National Defence and, by association, of the Liberal government. (My feeling was, subsequently, that Claxton would have done what he did next without my veiled threats.) After hearing me out, Claxton informed me that he was flying to London to attend a Commonwealth conference the following week and would fly by way of Goose Airport rather than through Gander, to give himself a chance to spend a day there and see the situation for himself. When he got back to Ottawa he contacted me to say that he agreed something should be done at once, and asked for my recommendations. Since the base had no apparent plans for the Happy Valley site, I suggested that the land being used, together with a reasonable amount for expansion, should be passed back to the Government of Newfoundland, who would then be able to survey and make available building sites already occupied by the squatters, as well as additional land for others wanting to move there. This suggestion was accepted by both governments, and the result was a relatively large, affluent community, with a hospital, schools and community facilities. The town was incorporated and water, sewer, telephone and electrical services were provided. In 1974 it joined with its sister town of Goose Bay to form one of the largest municipalities in the province, with high standards of living, as well as the facilities which it inherited from the military bases that eventually closed down operations.

Until the building of Goose Airport, Labrador had experienced little change from what it had been a hundred or even two hundred years before. The summer season saw hundreds of schooners and thousands of Newfoundland fishermen go "down" to Labrador and either fish from their schooners ("floaters"), or establish themselves on land for two or three months and fish with small boats from the shore ("stationers"). Those "whites" who lived year-round in Labrador were called "Liveyeres,"[2] while the Indian and Inuit were usually referred to as Natives.

The whole of Labrador as well as northern Newfoundland was under the medical supervision of the International Grenfell Association. One of the great problems confronting the Grenfell doctors was the natives' lack of resistance to white men's diseases, notably influenza and tuberculosis. In the world-wide

[2] There are various spellings.

150

influenza epidemic of 1918, few parts of the world suffered so much as did the Eskimo settlements in Northern Labrador. A particularly tragic example was Okkak, one of the larger settlements which lost 300 of its 365 Native people, including every adult male in the community. Several smaller settlements were virtually wiped out.

In 1952 when I first visited the Indians of Davis Inlet it was obvious to even the most untrained eye that many of the adult Indians were seriously ill. From discussions with Dr. Gordon Thomas, superintendent of the association, and with Dr. Anthony Paddon, Grenfell Supervisor of the northern medical operations, it became clear that extraordinary measures were needed if the extinction of two more Indian groups, in addition to the Beothuks, was to be avoided. Because the Indians lived crowded together in tents, once one member in the group developed tuberculosis, the others, with their known susceptibility to T.B., were bound to become infected. Dr. Thomas gave figures which showed that the incidence of tuberculosis for all Labrador in 1951 was 300 per 10,000, the highest in all Canada. Furthermore, of the 1064 cases treated at the Grenfell hospital during the twenty-year period from 1927 to 1947, only 25 percent were alive in 1952. One must remember, too, that these figures represented all groups in Labrador during that period; those for the Indians or Eskimos alone were still more disturbing. In fact, probably one-half of all the Indians at Davis Inlet in 1952 had tuberculosis. Clearly it would not be very long before the group would disappear completely, especially with infant mortality so high.

In the case of the Indians, as distinct from the Eskimos, the problem confronting the authorities was a complex one. The Indians did not speak English; they were suspicious of white people and avoided them where possible; and they were most reluctant to go to hospitals or sanitoriums. But two fortunate developments helped the situation. First, the Indians were all Roman Catholics, and after they were placed under Quebec jurisdiction, members of the Oblate Order were sent to Labrador to live with the Indians. These highly intelligent and dedicated priests co-operated to the fullest with the civil and medical authorities to bring the disease under control. The second development was the discovery and introduction of BCG vaccine and of "miracle drugs" such as streptomycin to help fight the scourge. The combined results of segregating infected persons, improved medical treatment, the success of the Oblate priests in getting patients to go to hospital or sanitorium, the building of houses to eliminate the tent syndrome, and the institution of basic hygiene all combined to save the Nascopi Indians of Labrador from extinction. The 272 Indians living in Labrador in 1945 had probably fallen to less than 250 by 1949. But by the 1960s and 1970s the Indian population had increased by several hundred despite the ravages of gastroenteritis among the small children.

Even before 1949, plans were afoot to develop the great iron ore deposits known to exist in northwest Labrador, straddling the presumed border of Quebec and Labrador. To summarize (since this development was mentioned in some detail in an earlier chapter), the greatest benefit of this mining activity to the province, apart from the royalties paid on the ore, was the immense amount of labour required in the building of the 365 miles of railway and the other installations, as well as the creation of two of the most modern towns in Canada — Labrador City and Wabush. For nearly twenty years the mines operated at capacity, but world-wide market depressions after those early decades reduced the levels of activity thereafter. Despite this setback, however, full-time employees in the two communities enjoyed standards of living which, whether in athletic and recreational facilities, well-equipped schools, highly trained teachers, or cultural activities, were generally considered to be among the highest in Canada.

By the time the Smallwood era ended in early 1972, Labrador was made up of several distinct areas with highly contrasting economies and cultural backgrounds. As we have seen, Labrador West boasted the two ultra-modern towns of Labrador City and Wabush, with their lovely homes, golf course, swimming pool, ski slope, gymnasiums, stadium, supermarkets and first-class hotel. (Only one facility was lacking — a highway to link it with the outside world.) Also in the wilderness, was the smaller but equally modern town of Churchill Falls. At the head of Lake Melville, over 100 miles from the open ocean, was the joint town of Happy Valley-Goose Bay and, some 20 miles away, the community of North West River — a religious, commercial, educational, medical, fur-trapping centre. Out on the coast north of Lake Melville were the communities of Makkovic, Postville, Hopedale, Davis Inlet and Nain (the most northern community in Labrador), all existing on seals, codfish, char, salmon and caribou. On the southern coastal area, from Cartwright south to the Strait of Belle Isle, dozens of fishing villages continued much as they had a century before. Taken all together, Labrador was unique for the extraordinary range of living standards in its various communities — from among the highest to the lowest in Canada.

In 1949 the communities north of Cape Harrison, apart from Davis Inlet, were populated mainly by part or full Inuit. Hebron was above the tree line and the nearest source of wood was a grove forty-five miles south. Since this meant a two- to four-day round trip in order to get a few hundred pounds of wood, much of the winter had to be spent simply going back and forth. With wood so scarce the utmost economy had to be exercised, which meant that the wooden houses and the sod huts were at times unbearably cold.

As stated earlier, the medical supervisor for Grenfell Services in northern Labrador was Dr. Anthony Paddon,[3] who had his headquarters at North West River at the head of Lake Melville. In one of his public speeches in St. John's, Dr. Paddon described the difficulty of providing medical services for Hebron. With Dr. Paddon's permission, a portion of his speech is given hereunder:

> I visited Hebron twice each summer in a small hospital ship on regular medical patrols, going on north as far as Saglak or further. In the winter I visited only once, using a combination of aircraft hitch-hiking and dogteam — 3 hours of one, 6 weeks of the other. By the end of the 1940s annual mass X-rays by ship became possible, and the first hundred Hebron Inuuks I X-rayed produced 35 cases of open cavitary tuberculosis. Treating these by remote management was impossible, as we soon discovered. There were no facilities, it was impossible to evacuate anyone except by occasional mercy flights by the military, and in the early 1950s I saw such cases as a six-week old baby with much of his spine destroyed by T.B., children including a young baby dying of T.B. meningitis, T.B. families living in small sod "igloos" with something like 150 square feet for a family, the walls dripping with frost in wintertime,

---

[3] In 1981 Dr. Paddon was appointed lieutenant-governor of Newfoundland.

heated only by a seal oil lamp. In winter there was often no water except what was melted and used for cooking. 'Kalak' as the Inuit called impetigo, was endemic — a filthy disease of pus and scabs, also chronic otitis and running ears almost the norm for children. Many had hearing impairments from otitis media, and not till a major Ear Surgery Programme in the 1970s were we able to improve the hearing of some of them. The infant mortality would not have been acceptable anywhere — probably even in a concentration camp.

Even after we were provided with an aircraft by the Newfoundland Government, transport was difficult. One could get to Nain fairly readily, but the high Kiglapaits Mountains, and bad weather were formidable barriers between Nain and Hebron. To be stuck 4 or 5 days was common, flying around the North, and once it was 22 days, during which time I left a busy hospital with only a junior interne in charge, a very, very busy interne, I might add. I told the Hebron people in a meeting in 1959 with Mr. Rockwood, Director of Northern Labrador Affairs and Mr. Peacock, Moravian Superintendent, and the Village Elders present, that I doubted any real improvement in their medical service or indeed the loss of life was possible while the people remained in Hebron. Previously we had persuaded several families to come south from Nutak because of multiple serious illnesses, to spend a winter near the North West River Hospital until the medical and surgical problems were controlled. Some stayed on and settled, some returned, but certainly of their own free will.

The Hebron people had other problems. With the demise of the market for arctic foxes there was little fur trapping. Their fine arctic char brought income and food, but they did not need to be in Hebron all winter for that, because it was a summer fishery, and indeed they continued to come North for the summers after they left Hebron. . . . The summer cod fishery was uncertain, and the season considerably shorter than at Nain only a hundred and forty miles south. All in all there were many reasons for leaving Hebron.

For several years the question of resettling the Hebron people was debated. In the early discussions about half the village expressed a desire to move and, in fact, did leave Hebron and settled in Nain, Makkovik and Hopedale. In the meantime, as had happened in several instances in Newfoundland, the matter became such a political football, that the government decided to cancel the operation. But by then the remaining half of the population had decided to move and, in fact, did so on their own, thus putting serious strain on accommodation in the three receiving centres. This phase of the resettlement programme, for obvious reasons, met with more difficulties and criticism than was generally the case with resettlement in the rest of Newfoundland, and opinion has been divided as to whether or not it should have been encouraged in the first place. An article in the *Evening Telegram* of October 11, 1983, quotes the former director of Northern Labrador affairs as saying, "It was apparent for some time, twenty years ago, that the social and economic factors involved would eventually bring about the abandonment of the community."

The royal commission on Labrador in its 1974 report stated categorically: "the northern resettlement programme is a failure." But this verdict was (and is) disputed by the vast majority of officials, nurses, doctors, clergymen and politicians who were intimately connected with Hebron over the past three decades, and who were in a position to gauge the feeling of the Inuit themselves. As with some such cases in Newfoundland, there were some blunders, some incompetence on the part of officialdom, and periodic nostalgia, but for almost 100 percent of those who did move, there was no desire or willingness to return. In this regard, Dr. Paddon — whose career, along with that of his father, spans seventy years of dedicated medical service to Northern Labrador — provides the following summary:

> Readjustment was of course difficult, as they had doubtless expected, there must have been times when many regretted leaving Hebron, the housing that was hastily provided was far from perfect, but their move was not a forced dismissal from Hebron by outsiders. Of course a grievance can be an asset in negotiation, it elicits sympathy, but it seems to me that our history is being rearranged to fit current social doctrines. Hebron people were still free to go back if they really wanted to, and though this is often discussed few people show any desire, thus far, to do so. I should think the amalgamation of the Hebron people with the other Inuit communities has been of great value, and has been in part responsible for the spectacular increase in Inuit population. T.B. and other problems were stamped out and the classrooms of sturdy, healthy children of today are a striking contrast to those I saw in the sod houses of Hebron only a couple decades ago.

The island of Newfoundland has often been accused of neglecting or discriminating against the population of Labrador, milking the land of its resources and leaving nothing in return. In one aspect of Newfoundland-Labrador relations — specifically, political representation in the legislature — this was certainly true. Although the British Colonial Office had recommended representation in the Newfoundland House of Assembly as early as 1863, the first popular election in which Labrador was permitted to participate was the election of the national convention in 1946. Labrador was given the right to elect one delegate. The winner was the Reverend Lester Burry, a United Church clergyman who had spent the greater part of his adult life as a missionary to Labrador. With the establishment of Responsible Government in 1949, Labrador was made a single provincial district. And although the population was not particularly large, the enormous distance to be travelled made it advisable to divide the territory in two in 1956 and, in 1962, with the emergence of Labrador City and Wabush, it was decided to carve out a third district — Labrador West. Federally, Labrador became part of the riding of Grand Falls-White Bay-Labrador, although many have argued that because of its size, Labrador should be made a federal riding in its own right, despite its small population.

Although heavily involved during World War II, Labrador's relationship with defence matters did not end with the termination of the conflict. During the Cold War and the Korean conflict, additional bases were built and all were strengthened. In addition to the large installation at Goose, other bases were placed at Cartwright, Hopedale, Saglek Bay, and Fox Harbour. These affected resident population both economically and culturally, although not always for the better. Fishermen doing unskilled — and, in time, skilled — work were paid at what to them were astronomical rates, allowing them to enjoy amenities and luxuries that many of them had never known previously. Dog teams soon gave way to snowmobiles, the rough diet of salt fish, smoked salmon and caribou or seal meat was replaced, in part at least, by the more sophisticated (although perhaps less nutritious) offerings of the miniature supermarket. The bases tended to become part of the community family, with their dances, movies and other entertainment. Whatever other effects the bases may have had on the Lake Melville and the coastal people, one thing was certain: never again would the people be willing to accept the type of life they had known prior to World War II, the Cold War, and confederation with Canada.

One unhappy by-product of this affluence, as well as American and Canadian sophistication, was the rapid increase in alcohol consumption. Historically, the Moravian Mission, the Roman Catholic Church, the Grenfell Association, the Methodist (United) Church, and the Hudson's Bay Company had all opposed or discouraged the consumption of alcohol by Native groups. Inevitably, however, such restrictions that did exist gave way before Native demands for equal treatment. Could the white clerks and officials in Hopedale be permitted to have beer or spirits in their homes and the Native next door not be permitted the same? Could the white workers at Goose be permitted to visit the bar for a beer after work, and the Inuit working with him be deprived of the same right? Notwithstanding the issue of constitutional rights, however, the simple fact remained that the rise of alcohol consumption in Labrador, as in other parts of the province, had been accompanied by a rise in violent crime and, in particular, a serious increase in neglect and abuse of women and children. Labrador is not, of course, unique in this respect. But when added to all its other difficulties — periodic unemployment, distance, climatic extremes, isolation and illiteracy — the net result was to negate much of the prodigious effort of religious and medical organizations to build and maintain an acceptable standard of life for all concerned.

At this point, I hope my readers will forgive me if I pause to take issue with what I feel is either a particularly objectionable or unjustly vague statement made by the 1974 royal commission on Labrador. In doing so, my own conclusions can be summarized. In the beginning summary of its report, the commission states that the "single broad conclusion of this Report . . . [is] . . . that Labrador has suffered from generations of neglect." "Generations" is, of course, a pretty broad term, as is "neglect." But to summarize with such an allegation without differentiating between the pre-confederation and the confederation periods, is, in my opinion, to be guilty of inaccuracy and unfairness.

In making the charge of neglect we must assume that the

industrial centres of Labrador West, of Churchill Falls and Goose Airport are not included, since these towns probably enjoy more facilities and higher standards than any town of comparable size in Canada. The fact that much of this derives from the largesse of the mining companies is not germane to the argument. For several years Happy Valley suffered from both neglect and injustice but that was quickly remedied once the situation was made fully known to the government. Certainly one must regard as significant the following major improvements made in Happy Valley and North West River during the past two decades: title to land, assistance in housing, a water and sewage system, a hospital, a vocational school, electricity, government offices, connection with the government-built road from Goose to North West River, the major bridges over Goose and North West Rivers, modern schools, an air-mail service, an air ambulance service, housing for the Montagnais Indians (who formerly camped on the south bank of North West River), a new hospital at North West River, and a new dormitory for boarding students. Considering that in 1952 Happy Valley was largely a collection of illegal shacks, the above achievements, excluding those relating to North West River, could hardly represent a "generation" of neglect. If so, then every town on the island of Newfoundland could be described as "neglected," since not one of them received as much help and attention during the twenty-two-year period from 1952 to 1974 as did Happy Valley. Given these facts, we may reasonably conclude that the term "neglected" could not have been meant to apply to the mining, hydro, and airport towns, including North West River. That leaves the coast.

None of the coastal settlements are large, even by Newfoundland standards. Forteau, L'Anse aux Loups, Mary's Harbour, Cartwright and Nain are the largest, with populations ranging from 400 to about 1000.[4] The others range from 2 or 3 families to about 100. The average coastal community, therefore, has about 25 families. But with radios, telephones or wireless at strategic points on the coast, and with air ambulance helicopters available most of the time, few are cut off from prompt medical and hospital attention for any length of time. And with

---

[4] The actual figures given in the 1981 census for five of the largest coastal communities are: Nain, 938; Cartwright, 658; L'Anse au Loup, 589; Forteau, 520; and Mary's Harbour, 408.

the Grenfell main hospitals at St. Anthony and at Happy Valley-Goose Bay, as well as fourteen cottage hospitals or nursing stations scattered along the coast, and a modern hospital ship, it is difficult to find a case for neglect in medical services. In one of his last statements before retiring, Dr. Gordon Thomas, the superintendent of the International Grenfell Association, said that the medical service to the coastal residents of Labrador was "among the best in any rural outport area in the world." Medical authorities in Newfoundland were generally agreed that the medical services for coastal Labrador were usually superior to those available to comparable stretches of coastline in Newfoundland.

When Newfoundland became a province of Canada in 1949, Labrador automatically qualified for the various federal social benefits — old age pensions, family allowances, unemployment insurance, veterans benefits, blind pensions, and others. Welfare officers were stationed at larger centres and travelled almost continuously up and down the coast. The only difference between the service in Labrador and that on the island was that, because of the distance involved, the officers were given smaller case loads than were their counterparts in Newfoundland.

Road-building in Labrador started on a modest scale in 1953, eventually resulting in a road from the Quebec border (near L'Anse Eclair) to Red Bay, a distance of fifty miles. A road was also built to link up Happy Valley-Goose Bay with North West River. These roads necessitated the building of three major bridges over the Pinware, Goose and North West rivers. Another large bridge was built over St. Mary's River. The Red Bay Highway was linked to Newfoundland by means of a ferry across the Strait of Belle Isle, which operated with large government subsidies. A short but valuable three-mile road was built around Cartwright harbour to join up the Grenfell facilities, including the hospital, with the community itself. Wharves were built in nearly every sizeable harbour on the coast: Mary's Harbour, Port Hope, Simpson, Cartwright, Makkovik, Hopedale, Postville, Davis Inlet and Nain. Fish plants were built at Makkovik and Nain, and community stages were built at a number of places, including Forteau, West St. Modeste, Black Tickle, Charlottetown and Capsan Island. Most of the larger communities were given or were provided with the means to acquire electrical power generated by diesel motors. During the period, larger and better schools were built at L'Anse Eclair, Forteau, West St. Modeste, Mary's Harbour, Cartwright, Davis Inlet and North West River. The last two were of special interest in that they were built for the exclusive use of the two Indian groups in Labrador.

Largely as a result of the town councils established with Newfoundland government encouragement and funding, most of the larger communities were given the means to acquire an adequate water supply, either by means of artesian wells or by feeding from a brook or pond. The provision of new housing, especially for native families, was both an important and costly programme undertaken in "receiving" centres like Nain, and the two Indian communities of Davis Inlet and North West River. This was done partly as a means of giving the Indians a better chance to segregate T.B.-infected patients who, so long as they remained in their canvas tents, were a focus of infection for others. Other government or Grenfell building included the provision of cottage hospitals or nursing stations at Nain, Makkovik and Hopedale to supplement the work being done by other stations up and down the coast. Another little-known programme involved making repairs to, or building, paths and emergency shelters for winter travelling. Other improvements were also made in air mail, freight, and wireless services.

This list could be continued, but enough has been cited to indicate that there was nothing essentially different from the overall treatment afforded to coastal Labrador and that given to coastal Newfoundland. If anything, the only difference lies in the total expenditure by governments and organizations which, if computed for similar lengths of coastline on the island of Newfoundland, and on Labrador, or on a per capita basis, would show that Labrador has received more attention. If this is so, then it is only what is right, given the hardship and deprivation endured so long by a courageous and hard-working people. But no benefit is derived from alleging "neglect" and related charges. All it does is to help perpetuate a myth.

11 FRIENDS AND ENEMIES

The dominant role played by Smallwood from 1949 to 1971 tends to obscure the parts played by other members of the administration. They were nevertheless integral parts of the whole governmental process during that period, and this chapter examines some of the personalities involved. It is only regrettable, given the constraints of space, as well as my desire to provide a certain measure of thoroughness, that I have not been able to mention all those people who served.

The first provincial election was held in May 1949, following which Premier Smallwood announced his cabinet. The one man who was at Smallwood's right hand from the May election in 1949 until the summer of 1971 was Leslie R. Curtis, a former law partner of Sir Richard Squires, and generally acknowledged to be one of the ablest lawyers in Newfoundland. As attorney-general and minister of justice he advised the government on the legal implications wherever indicated. While conservative in nature, and inclined to be suspicious and cynical regarding motives, his ability to burrow through an impasse or to ride out a crisis served Smallwood and the cabinet well on numerous occasions.

Charles H. Ballam had been a labour organizer before going into politics. He was elected to the national convention in 1949 where he supported confederation. He became Newfoundland's first minister of labour in 1949, a portfolio he held until 1966. As such he was noted for his loyalty and common sense. Most of the progressive labour legislation of the period was the result of his recommendations.

James R. Chalker was for a period the only businessman in the cabinet, where he served for the entire period from 1949 to 1971. Modest and sensible, he was also loyal and reliable. Smallwood grew to rely on him to plan and oversee important ceremonial functions, especially royal visits.

William J. Keough, the youngest member of the original cabinet, had also been a supporter of confederation in the national convention. He remained a loyal and conscientious supporter of Smallwood until his sudden death in 1971.

Samuel J. Hefferton had been a teacher and for several years was president of the Newfoundland Teachers Association. Smallwood invited him to take the portfolio of education in 1949. During his tenure, Memorial College became a university, and a teacher's salary scale based on experience, academic qualifications and responsibility was introduced — the first in Newfoundland's history.

Edward S. Spencer had been a surveyor and practical engineer before entering the Smallwood cabinet as minister of public works, which at that time included highways. He was loyal and hard-working.

Philip J. Lewis, a well-known lawyer, had been in public life in the 1920s and returned to it as a member for Harbour Main-Bell Island early in the Smallwood era. At no time would he accept a portfolio but agreed to become chairman of the royal commission set up to prepare the case for Newfoundland for the financial review under Term 29 of the Terms of Union.

Dr. James M. McGrath had had a long and varied experience in public health before coming into the cabinet as minister of health. Under his guidance Newfoundland's health programme became one of the best in Canada.

Dr. G.A. Frecker had had a distinguished career as an educator, serving as deputy minister of education for fifteen years. As such, and as minister of education for eight years, he played a leading role in Newfoundland's educational revolution.

John T. Cheeseman had been in the legislature in the 1920s and returned to public life as fisheries minister in the Smallwood administration. In the interim he had been in the fish business and a senior fisheries officer with the Commission of Government. When a royal commission to study conditions on the south coast of Newfoundland was set up, Cheeseman was appointed chairman. His report served as a blueprint for subsequent government action in that part of the province.

Myles P. Murray was a lawyer and a veteran of World War II, eventually becoming president of the Newfoundland Command of the Canadian Legion.

Eric C. Jones had been an educator and magistrate and a member of the South Coast royal commission before accepting a cabinet appointment to the highways portfolio where he held the complete respect of his colleagues.

Beaton J. Abbott had been a school principal and then a magistrate before entering politics. As the highest ranking layman within the United Church hierarchy he enjoyed enormous respect from that body.

C. Max Lane had been a school principal and magistrate, and before entering the cabinet as minister of fisheries, had been president of the Newfoundland Federation of Fishermen and, later, head of the Newfoundland Brotherhood of Woodworkers. His wide familiarity with Newfoundland outports enabled him to deal competently and intelligently with the fisheries and related activities.

Other members of the Smallwood cabinets were Edward Russell, Herbert L. Pottle, Gregory Power, John Crosbie, Clyde Wells, T. Alex Hickman, H.R.V. Earle, all of whom defected from the cabinet and either withdrew from public life, or joined the Conservative party. The role these ministers played both in and without the cabinet will be examined later.

The legislature, of course, consists of more than cabinet ministers, and any government must have the support of its private members to stay in power. Most of these back-benchers were of high calibre, some eventually becoming cabinet ministers while others went on to achieve fame in other fields. Williams Adams, Addison Bown, William Callahan, Eric Dawe, Philip Forsey, Charles R. Granger, Gerald Hill, Arthur Johnson, Dr. Hubert Kitchen, Roy Legge, John Mahoney, Aiden Maloney, Dr. Noel Murphy, Stephen A. Neary, John A. Nolan, W.A. Oldford, Herman W. Quinton, Edward Roberts, William N. Rowe, Michael Sinnott, James J. Spratt, Harold Starkes, Captain Uriah Strickland, Oliver L. Vardy, George Warren, Captain Earl Winsor, Gordon A. Winter and Melvin Woodward— all entered the cabinet, although some for only a short period before the defeat of the Liberals in 1971.

Of the above list, Roberts, William Rowe and Neary each successively became party leader, while Mahoney became a judge of the Supreme Court, and Adams a judge of the St. John's District Court. Of the other backbenchers, Arthur Mifflin became chief justice (Appeals) of Newfoundland, Nathaniel Noel became a Supreme Court judge, while Rupert Bartlett became a county judge and Geoffrey Carnell became judge of the Citizenship Court. Others were successful and respected business and professional men. Smallwood's skill in attracting candidates was nowhere more evident than in his choice of Speakers of the House of Assembly. The first Speaker was Reginald Sparkes, who had had a rich background in education as a school principal and supervising inspector. Sparkes set a high standard which his successors, John Courage and George Clarke (both lawyers), followed successfully. The result was a standard of general decorum which contrasted markedly with that of earlier Assemblies in Newfoundland.

From what I have said so far it is obvious that I held a high opinion of the quality and dedication of the Liberal caucus. But that opinion is not so partisan that I can deny the fact that the Conservatives were equally successful in attracting men of high ability, loyalty and perseverence. The PCs' problem was not one of quality but of quantity: from the May election in 1949 until their victory in the fall of 1971, the most they had in the House at one time was seven members. In the 1966 election, for example, only three Conservatives were elected out of a total of forty-two. Between 1949 and 1970, the party had nine leaders.

Here again, space does not permit even a thumbnail sketch of all who sat opposite the government during the Smallwood era. But the following should be noted: Peter J. Cashin was the son of a former prime minister of Newfoundland. He obtained the rank of major in World War I and entered public life in 1923, becoming finance minister in the Squires' administration of 1928. His defection in 1932 helped to bring about the collapse of the government. Cashin was a powerful speaker but his fierce independence, and political unreliability and unfettered invective probably kept him from becoming an effective leader.

William J. Browne, a Rhodes Scholar and a lawyer, was first elected in 1924 and served in the last Responsible Government before Commission of Government. In the interim he became a judge, but returned to public life in 1949 to serve in the House of Commons. After being defeated, he re-entered provincial politics in 1954, but returned to federal politics in 1956 and later served as solicitor general in the Diefenbaker administration.

James D. Higgins was, without doubt, Newfoundland's best-known criminal lawyer when he entered public life in 1951. Earlier he had been deputy mayor of St. John's. With a keen wit and a sparkling personality, Higgins was one of the most popular politicians in the Conservative camp. He came to grief politically after he repudiated his party's stand on the Term 29 Dispute, and was later appointed to the Supreme Court of Newfoundland.

John G. Higgins was also a Rhodes Scholar, a lawyer and a recognized classical scholar. He served briefly as leader of the Conservative party from 1949 until 1951, and subsequently was summoned to the Senate of Canada.

Malcolm Hollett was a Rhodes Scholar who became a senior magistrate after his discharge from the Newfoundland Regiment in 1917. A good speaker and a convincing debater, he opposed confederation in the national convention and became leader of the Conservatives in 1953. He was summoned to the Senate in 1961.

James J. Greene was a Rhodes Scholar who became a lawyer and subsequently leader of the Conservative party in 1959 when the Conservatives elected only three members. Greene discharged this responsibility admirably, considering his lack of political experience and the one-sided nature of the debates. After sitting for seven years, Greene retired to practise law.

Gerald R. Ottenheimer studied at Memorial, and Fordham, as well as the Universities of Rome, Paris and Ottawa. Subsequently he joined the faculty at Memorial before becoming director of adult education for Newfoundland and Labrador. He became leader of the Conservative party of Newfoundland in 1967, but retired after several years to complete his law studies at the Sorbonne before returning to public life as minister of education in the Moores administration.

Dr. Noel F. Murphy was a well-known medical practitioner when he entered public life as the member for Humber East. He became leader of the Opposition in 1966, and of the Progressive Conservative party that same year. He proved to be a skilled analyst and, with the help of several of his colleagues, he frequently kept the government on the defensive. He carried a double political burden since he had become mayor of Newfoundland's second largest city, Corner Brook, in 1966. In 1971 he joined Smallwood's cabinet.

Although it has been only a dozen years or so since the demise of the Smallwood era, it is already encrusted with mythology. Of all the myths none has been more persistent, nor swallowed more easily, even by many Liberals, than the perception that Smallwood was not only a dictator but that he took care to surround himself, if not with incompetents or worse, then at least with a bunch of flunkeys and bootlickers ready to rubber-stamp whatever he ordered.

The fact is that fifty outstanding lawyers, magistrates, educators, municipal leaders, businessmen, sea captains, medical doctors, company executives and trade unionists served at one time or another in the Smallwood Cabinet. Those who knew J.T. Cheeseman, Dr. James McGrath, Philip J. Lewis and Gregory Power can only be amused at the charge that they allowed themselves to be yes-men, pushed around by a power-mad egotist who rode roughshod over them. If the charge were true, no one has yet answered a question I posed several years ago when asked about it: "If true, why did we spend endless hours, day after day, week after week, year after year at cabinet meetings?" The truth is that on countless occasions the premier brought suggestions and plans before the cabinet only to withdraw them when, after lengthy debates, it became clear to him that there was either no consensus or that there was strong opposition. Conversely, over the twenty-two-year period, there were occasions when cabinet ministers submitted proposals about which Smallwood expressed some reservations or objections, but which he allowed to be adopted because the cabinet as a whole felt otherwise. It goes without saying, of course, that no major programme was likely to be adopted if the premier firmly disagreed with it. Smallwood was a strong leader and, like all such men, laid himself open to the charge of being dictatorial.

It is ironic that the Progressive Conservative Opposition from 1949 to 1971 fell victim to another piece of mythology — this one almost the inverse of that ascribed to the Liberals. Repeatedly, from the earliest days of the administration, one heard the charge that the Opposition was too weak to face up to Smallwood. The only real weakness in the Opposition was in their numbers, although, as Smallwood demonstrated in the national convention, numerical superiority is not always the only prerequisite for emerging the winner. Having only between three and seven members at any one time on the Conservative side, however, clearly made it almost impossible to mount an effective force. Yet these few members were no ordinary handful: Cashin and Browne had served in the legislature during the turbulent 1920s and early 1930s; Cashin was one of the best orators in Newfoundland, his only peers being Smallwood and Gordon Bradley; and, as a speaker and debater, Hollett was almost their equal. Browne was a tireless worker with bulldog perseverance. Of the twenty or so who served in opposition at one time or another, four had been Rhodes Scholars, eight were lawyers, and one a prominent medical doctor. Notwithstanding the quality of these men, however, it was still Smallwood and the Liberal party who were identified with the benefits of confederation; no opposition could hope to defeat the government during the first two decades following the union with Canada. But the small group kept hammering incessantly at what they termed the government's blunders and excesses, and kept alive the spirit of defiance and hope of ultimate victory. But that victory had to wait until the members of the new generation, who had not really experienced anything against which to compare the blessings of confederation, were able to throw their political weight around. Much of their inspiration and ammunition had been supplied, however, by the small group who kept fighting when nearly everyone else knew it was hopeless.

Earlier in this chapter I listed a number of ministers who, for various reasons, defected from the Smallwood administration. Defections were not confined to the cabinet, however, and among the earliest to leave were two backbenchers, Harold Horwood and Samuel Drover.

Horwood had been one of Smallwood's chief helpers in the confederation campaign. He ran and was elected in the 1949 provincial election in Labrador, then only one district. But in the 1951 general election, to the surprise of many, he did not seek re-election. There was some doubt as to why he had left politics, since he had not until then expressed any great dissatisfaction with the government. Some felt that he intended to seek a senior post in the civil service; others that he had gotten out because of his disappointment in not having been appointed to the cabinet; and still others thought he wanted to carve out a literary career. Whatever the original reason, it soon became clear that Horwood no longer wished to support either Smallwood or the Liberal party. As a columnist for Newfoundland's largest daily newspaper, the *Evening Telegram*, he brought his considerable literary talents to bear in launching attack after attack on the character and record of the Smallwood administration and individual members in it.

A number of Liberals simply ignored his invective, feeling that his tendency towards extremism in his columns would eventually defeat their purpose. The fact is, however, that during the years he was a columnist and editor of the paper, large numbers of voters, especially in St. John's and other urban centres, were undoubtedly influenced against Smallwood and his regime. This probably helped to explain the failure of the Liberal party to gain consistent support in centres such as St. John's and Grand Falls.

Drover had been a member of the Newfoundland Ranger[1] Force and, in that capacity, had served for some years in White Bay. He had no difficulty in getting the Liberal nomination and was elected with a substantial majority in the 1949 provincial election and again in 1951. Even before the 1951 election, however, he had expressed some dissatisfaction and frustration with the government's failure to do more for his extensive district. (It included the area from Cape St. John into White Bay proper and down the entire east coast of the Great Northern Peninsula to the Strait of Belle Isle.) Like other members for rural districts, Drover wanted for his constituents more

---

[1] A police force created in 1934, modelled loosely on the Royal Canadian Mounted Police.

hospital services, more nursing services, roads, electricity, water and sewer services — little of which had been forthcoming up to the time of his defection. Plagued by personal problems, especially a period of bad health, Drover finally crossed the House to oppose the Liberals. Eventually he announced his decision to join the CCF Party (now NDP), for which he was a candidate in White Bay South (the district of White Bay had, in the meantime, been divided in two), but failed to get more than 15 percent of the vote in the 1956 election. Unlike Horwood's turning away from the Liberals, it cannot be said that Drover's defection seriously harmed either the administration or the party. Most party supporters in rural areas appreciated the reasons for Drover's discontent and sympathized with him, but felt that the government was entitled to more time in order to solve the great problems caused by isolation, scattered population, and a precarious economy. It is worth noting that by 1966 the area had additional hospital, medical and nursing services, road connections, electricity and, in the large communities, water and sewer services.

The first cabinet minister to leave the cabinet and party was Edward Russell, a former teacher, magistrate and director of cooperatives with the Newfoundland government. Russell had been a brilliant student at Memorial College, had prospered under Commission of Government (which he supported against confederation) and, if one may judge from his memoirs, had been a somewhat reluctant entrant in the political field. Some of his colleagues felt that his occasional profession of humility hid a very strong pride and, albeit less successfully, a contempt for those whose intellects fell short of his own. Others, including Smallwood, felt that he was totally unfitted by temperament to be part of a political machine. In March, 1951, at the time of his second resignation (he had sent Smallwood his resignation in 1950 and then reconsidered) he gave as one of his reasons his belief that Newfoundland was headed for financial collapse. Some years later, in his *Political Memoirs* and in other writing, he elaborated on the other reasons for his defection, which included his general dissatisfaction with the government's economic development policy and, in particular, what he regarded as Smallwood's cavalier disregard for traditional approaches to economic problems.

In the light of history, it can be seen that some of Russell's fears of provincial bankruptcy were not well grounded. Smallwood did proceed with his industrial programme; and while a number of the new industries eventually went under, Newfoundland's credit in the world's money markets remained as good as that of the wealthiest provinces of Canada. In fact, it is a matter of record that at no time during the whole Smallwood era did Newfoundland have any difficulty raising loans on standard terms and conditions on the strength of its own credit, despite the dire predictions of imminent financial disaster that were made periodically by enemies (and some friends) of the administration.

Russell later ran as a Progressive Conservative in a federal election in Bonavista-Twillingate but, to probably no one's surprise (including his own), he was swamped by his Liberal opponent, J.W. Pickersgill.

Peter Neary was probably correct in his assessment that Russell's resignation had little practical effect. Added to the others, however, it helped to swell the total opposition.

After a period as an insurance underwriter, Russell returned to his university studies, and in time was appointed to the English department at Memorial. His plays and other writings based on Newfoundland outport life received national acclaim, and at the time of his death in 1977, he was generally regarded as one of Newfoundland's outstanding literary figures.

Herbert L. Pottle was a member of Smallwood's first cabinet in 1949. His academic credentials included a Ph.D. from the University of Toronto, and his early professional experience had been largely in the field of education. For some years, as an executive officer with the government department of education, he had administered United Church education in Newfoundland. From that position he had moved to become the director of child welfare and the first judge of the St. John's juvenile court. Pottle had always been active in the United Church, and was probably one of the two most highly respected laymen of that church. (The other was B.J. Abbott.) Consequently, it was no surprise to anyone when, following the death of Sir John Puddester, the United Church member of the Commission of Government, Pottle was appointed to the vacancy.

Pottle, as it may be remembered, was a key figure in the

confederation debate. The first referendum in June, 1948 gave Responsible Government the edge over confederation by several thousand votes, but Commission of Government was so far behind the other two that it had to be dropped in the second referendum. The over 20,000 votes cast for Commission of Government were far more than were necessary to give the victory to either Responsible Government or confederation. It was, therefore, a matter of vital interest to both sides as to what the Newfoundland members of the Commission would do. The vice-chairman of the Commission, Sir Albert Walsh, one of the three Newfoundland members, took no public stand. But in the interim between the two referenda, both Herman W. Quinton, a highly popular Anglican, and Dr. Pottle, publicly announced their support for confederation with Canada — an act which may well have turned the tide in favour of the cause.

It goes without saying that Smallwood was extremely grateful to the two commissioners, and as soon as the opportunity presented itself he invited both into the cabinet. Pottle became minister of the newly created department of public welfare[2] which, in effect, involved starting from scratch and organizing a new office which could meet the heavy challenge being presented by new federal and provincial welfare measures.

Smallwood's respect for Pottle was shown in a number of ways, some small but nonetheless significant. For example, whether because of his church background or his Commission of Government position, Pottle was the only man in cabinet whom Smallwood never addressed by his first name. It was always "Doctor Pottle." In other ways too, Smallwood deferred to Pottle, as indeed did other members of the cabinet. He was regarded as a leader in the field of welfare and, accordingly, the other ministers were inclined to accept his recommendations without question. In my own experience, I recall only one instance where an important recommendation from him was rejected by cabinet, a record unmatched by any other minister.

Smallwood's confidence in Pottle was so great that, when a major department lost its minister because of illness or political defeat or retirement, Smallwood would ask Pottle to take

---

[2] Quinton joined the Smallwood cabinet as finance minister in 1949, and was summoned to the Senate in January, 1951.

over the department concerned for a lengthy period. Acting ministers, appointed during a regular minister's absence, were very common, but in Pottle's case this did not apply. On several occasions for months at a time, in addition to carrying the substantial work load of his own department, he would also carry other heavy departments. He assumed the additional duties willingly enough, but my own impression was that he worked too hard. (I had been deputy minister for public welfare for three years while Pottle was minister, a post which, of course, put me in daily contact with him.)

Pottle's resignation came as a bolt from the blue to all his colleagues, including the premier. The latter was planning to go to a federal-provincial conference within a few days, and Pottle had earlier indicated his pleasure at being invited to be one of the premier's party. In fact the tickets had already been issued when Pottle took the dramatic step, just as a night session of the Assembly was about to adjourn, of rising on privilege and after bending over to whisper a few words in the premier's ear, announced that he was resigning from the administration on the grounds that he no longer had confidence in its policies, especially those relating to economic development.

To say that Smallwood was shocked by Pottle's defection would be an understatement. Nor was his dismay entirely political. It is both interesting and revealing to note that in the final chapter of his memoirs, Smallwood lists only five "wounds" in his political life. One of the five was Pottle's resignation.

In the final paragraph of his resignation statement Pottle wrote "I have no other employment ready at hand" — something which a few of his critics, including an earlier defector, Edward Russell, refused to accept. Within a few months Pottle had accepted a position in Toronto with the United Church of Canada, which had been unfilled for a year. He continued to take close interest in Newfoundland politics, however, as his book *Dawn Without Light*, reveals. It is obvious in this erudite but, in the opinion of some, biased work, that the bitterness he felt in 1955, for whatever reasons, far from dissipating, had intensified with the years.

The political effects of Pottle's defection were not particularly striking. Government critics applauded the move as confirming their conviction that Newfoundland was headed for disaster. A subsequent effort by one or two persons to organize a movement to support Pottle politically was stillborn and, as was shown by the next provincial election, few, if any, of Smallwood's supporters were affected. Many, while still respecting Pottle's integrity and ability, felt that he was not cut out for the hurly-burly of party politics and that, while not supportive of his unexpected attack on Smallwood and, by implication, his cabinet colleagues, he had done the sensible thing by resigning.

Gregory Power was Smallwood's chief lieutenant in the confederation struggle. Possessed of a mordant wit, and well-armed with a vast arsenal of verbal weapons, he realized very early that trying to answer confederation's opponents with reason and logic was a waste of time. Instead, he selected ridicule as his weapon of choice. In the confederate newspaper, to which he was the principal contributor, he left his readers rocking with mirth as he assailed Chesley Crosbie, Donald Jamieson and others who were advancing weighty and serious arguments for Responsible Government, only to have them torn to tatters by the unanswerable satire contained in Power's letters, poems and articles.

Power ran and was defeated in the first federal election after confederation, and for the next two-and-a-half years marked time politically while holding the post of chairman of the Board of Liquor Control. But this did not prevent him from serving as Smallwood's chief advisor and almost constant travelling companion. Subsequently, in the provincial election of 1951, he ran and was elected in his native district of Placentia-St. Mary's, and was appointed minister of finance. When the next cabinet shuffle took place, Power became highways minister. Probably his chief contribution to that department was in introducing a policy of mechanized maintenance to replace the time-honoured but obsolete "pick and shovel, wheelbarrow, horse and cart" practices which were now inadequate to meet the ever-increasing demands for improved roads and bridges.

Power continued to be Smallwood's best friend and closest confidante until 1958, when it became apparent that some strains were developing in the relationship. Some have attributed this to Power's disagreement with Smallwood's approach to the International Woodworkers of America (IWA) problem.

My own feeling is that, while Power may have had reservations regarding the government's policy in dealing with the IWA crisis, it was not the main reason. Rather, it was something more personal and prosaic.

In private life Power had been a chicken farmer—for a while, at least, the largest egg and chicken producer in Newfoundland. With his family, Smallwood too had included chicken raising among his extensive agricultural activities on their farm at the Roaches Line, eventually equalling and perhaps surpassing Power's enterprise. The basic disagreement between Smallwood and Power seemed to hinge around the degree of government control necessary or desirable for that industry. Power was fiercely independent in his approach and was intensely proud of his achievement in this field. Smallwood favoured legislation and regulations to provide an umbrella which would cover all egg and chicken production in the province, whether individual farmers like Power wanted it or not.

Little if anything was known publicly about this controversy, although several of his cabinet colleagues were aware of Power's strong feelings. He had been heard to threaten that if the proposed policy were adopted he would "get out." Whatever his reasons, however, by the winter of 1958–59 Power was no longer attending cabinet meetings, and by April of 1959 Smallwood accepted his resignation. The estrangement lasted for some ten years before a reconciliation finally took place and their life-long friendship was renewed. Power's break with Smallwood had been more personal than political. At no time had he "crossed the House," nor did he proclaim allegiance to another party. Thus his actions did not have strong political results, nor were they intended to. From the time of his resignation he simply abstained from public affairs.

In the 1966 provincial election a number of new faces appeared on the political scene, about half of them lawyers and several still in their twenties. Among the group were T. Alex Hickman, a native of Grand Bank, who had built up a large law practice in St. John's[3]; Clyde K. Wells, a young, promising and personable lawyer, practising in Corner Brook; and John C. Crosbie, deputy mayor of St. John's.

---

[3] Hickman was appointed chief justice of Newfoundland (Trials Division) during the Clark regime.

174

Crosbie had had a brilliant academic career in law and economics and, after being elected, entered the cabinet as minister of municipal affairs. The following year he became minister of health which he held until May 1968, when he resigned from the Smallwood cabinet and sat as a Liberal Reform member until 1971, at which point he joined the Conservative party. He maintained his seat in St. John's West in the fall election that year and became minister of finance in the Moores administration early in 1972. (Of his subsequent career as a provincial minister, then a member of Parliament, then finance minister in the Clark administration, and finally as a serious leadership contender in the 1983 Progressive Conservative federal leadership convention, nothing further will be discussed here, since these developments are outside our chronological frame of reference.) His activities between 1966 and 1971, however, require more than passing attention, since, in the opinion of many, it was Crosbie's increasing attacks on Smallwood that did more than anything else to bring about the 1971 stalemate which led to the Liberal defeat early in 1972.

John Crosbie was the grandson of two well known politicians — Sir John Crosbie and Andrew Carnell. Sir John was involved in politics from the time of Morris until the defeat of the Conservative party in 1928. He never became prime minister although many believed he aspired to that post. His son, Chesley (John's father) headed the movement for Responsible Government and economic union with the United States, and came near to beating confederation, which would have probably given him the premiership. John Crosbie's maternal grandfather, Andrew Carnell, had attempted unsuccessfully to get elected to the House of Assembly, although he fared extremely well in municipal politics being elected mayor of St. John's for four terms. Politically, then, John Crosbie's family background had been a mixture of exciting successes and frustrating failures.

Crosbie's predominant characteristics were industry, a caustic wit, an analytic mind, and boundless ambition. When all this was added to his own and his family's popularity, especially in the St. John's area, it was clear that Crosbie could make a valuable contribution to his party, and could be a dangerous antagonist to anyone opposing him. One strange aspect of the Crosbie saga was the failure of Smallwood at the beginning to appreciate Crosbie's talents and potential. In fact, when it was first suggested that Crosbie be recruited into the Liberal party (Crosbie was waiting impatiently for such a development) Smallwood turned thumbs down on it. It was not until Crosbie had run in the St. John's municipal election and had beaten a number of seasoned politicians to become deputy mayor on his first attempt that Smallwood began to change his mind.

It was almost inevitable that two such strong-minded men would clash. And when economic programmes involving John Doyle and John Shaheen, whom Crosbie regarded as adventurers, were under consideration, that is what happened. Usually supported by Clyde Wells, Crosbie was frequently critical of some of Smallwood's actions. Matters came to a head, however, when Smallwood proposed some interim financing amounting to $5 million for Shaheen's Come-by-Chance oil refinery venture.

It was clear to all of us in the cabinet that the breaking point was rapidly approaching. No longer was it a matter of whether or not the break would come; it was simply when. For my part, the biggest danger was not Crosbie's and Wells' inevitable defection from the cabinet, but the certain deleterious effect it would have on the federal election to be held in June, 1968, a date only a few weeks away. Since both Crosbie and Wells were still Liberals (their quarrel was not with the party as such, but with Smallwood), I took it on myself to plead with each of them separately not to take any serious step until after the election. They assured me they would not. Next I approached the premier with the same request and received the same assurance.

What happened subsequently to nullify their promises is a mystery. The immediate cause was Smallwood's insistence on a decision respecting the interim financing. When this passed cabinet, Crosbie and Wells resigned. Charges and counter-charges were now being hurled back and forth publicly, and by the time the election was held it was evident that the defection of these two able, popular and respected lawyers had done enormous damage to the Liberal cause. In the 1965 federal election the Liberals had taken all seven seats, most of them with overwhelming majorities; in the 1968 election these figures were nearly reversed, with the Conservatives taking six

176

seats. While it had been recognized that the Conservatives had been making gains in Newfoundland, no one expected that in an election where Liberals on the mainland, under Trudeau, made overwhelming gains, the Newfoundland Liberals would be almost obliterated. There was and is no doubt in my mind that the actions of Crosbie and Wells in leaving the cabinet and denouncing Smallwood cost the party at least four, and possibly five federal seats.

The 1968 defeat of the Liberals was the first that Smallwood had experienced since he took office in 1949. It caused a state of shock that no amount of rationalizing could alleviate. Most people, including many of his friends, felt that the election results, even though they were federal, indicated an increasing desire to see him retire from public life after so many years of service. Perhaps it was these considerations which led him, some weeks after the election, to announce a leadership convention to be held in 1969 which would select his successor. The first and, for some months, the only serious candidate to appear was Crosbie. Systematically and with little regard for the expenses involved, he set up an organization which he felt would lead him to a victory. During the succeeding weeks Smallwood began to look with some apprehension at the gains that reports and rumours were giving Crosbie. He approached me, and later Donald Jamieson (now the only Newfoundland Liberal in the House of Commons), urging one or the other of us to run. For reasons which he never made public Jamieson turned down the idea. It is possible that he felt, as I did, that Smallwood was beginning to regret his decision, and that eventually he would reconsider it. He continued to urge me to run, and as the months went by I saw that Crosbie was contacting more and more potential delegates from all over the province. There was, however, no doubt whatever in my mind that Jamieson, Richard Cashin, I, and possibly one or two others, given Smallwood's support, could defeat Crosbie. Accordingly, in early January, I announced my candidacy. In my statement I stressed that I was running because Smallwood had stated unequivocally that he was not running. I emphasized that if Smallwood did run then I would not be a candidate. Following my announcemnt, the premier made a public statement in which he expressed his pleassure over my decision. Six months later, however, Smallwood announced that he had changed his mind and intended to run. Shortly, thereafter, I announced that I was withdrawing and that my efforts — and, I hoped, those of my pledged supporters — would be behind Smallwood. For the record, when the convention was held in late October, those delegates who had agreed to support me, practically without exception, supported Smallwood. A good example was my own district of Grand Falls. That district was entitled to fifteen delegates. They had all agreed to support me, and when the convention was held, all fifteen supported Smallwood.

There were two other casualties in this whole affair — T. Alex Hickman and his friend H.R.V. Earle. The former waited until about a month before the convention to announce his candidacy. While Hickman was generally likeable and was regarded as a hard-working, competent lawyer, no one gave him a chance to win. Perhaps he foresaw the possibility of garnering enough votes to become a king-maker. If so, then disappointment lay ahead. Of the 1710 votes cast, he received 187. Smallwood's advantage over Crosbie was by more than 600 votes.

Earle was a respected and conscientious businessman who had made valuable contributions to the educational, civic and church life of St. John's. Both Hickman and Earle felt that a cabinet minister should be able to run for the leadership of his party, or support any candidate of his choice without jeopardizing his cabinet seat. They were, of course, correct in stating that examples of this principle were to be found in other political jurisdictions. But Smallwood was not a person to look kindly at such an idea. Within the House of Assembly were at least eighteen Liberal backbenchers who had supported Smallwood loyally through thick and thin, some of them dating as far back as 1949. A number of these private members, especially the older ones, had waited patiently year after year in hope of getting a cabinet post. For the premier to have kept in his cabinet persons who had done their best to overthrow him at the convention would have tried the loyalties of the faithful to the limit — perhaps beyond it. In any event, neither Hickman nor Earle was invited to return to the cabinet. Both of them eventually found their way into the ranks of the Conservative party and, in time, into the Moores administration.

Smallwood had retained the leadership of the party, but at

tremendous cost, both financially and in other ways. Valuable members had been lost from the cabinet, and while there were plenty of young and able members to take their places, the dispossessed were bound to do harm to the party. More serious still was the fact that far from being an ordinary leadership convention where, when the shouting is over, the party closes ranks and girds itself to meet the common foe, the 1969 convention became, in fact, a civil war. When it was over there was no real closing of the ranks. Many of the dissident Liberals, especially university students and young professionals, ended up campaigning against the Liberal party and strongly supporting the Conservatives. A small minority, disillusioned with the orthodox Liberals, joined the New Democratic party.

The 1969 leadership convention was totally unnecessary. There was no strong ground-swell threatening Smallwood's position as premier and party leader. Resources, both in men and money that could have been used to fight the next general election went down the drain. The Party was split, unnecessarily and, as it turned out, irrevocably. This self-inflicted wound was probably the one thing that, more than anything else, precipitated the demise of the Liberal party of Newfoundland in 1971.

12 SMALLWOOD AND OTTAWA

PICKERSGILL

B oth enemies and friends of Smallwood have been unanimous in their belief that the invitation extended by Smallwood to J.W. Pickersgill to enter Newfoundland politics was one of the most important moves made during the Smallwood era. Pickersgill and Smallwood had met in 1947 when the former was a special assistant to Prime Minister King, and Smallwood was visiting Ottawa to get information that he might use in his fight for confederation. King was absent at the time, but by good luck the acting prime minister, Louis St. Laurent (the person destined shortly to succeed King) was available, and thanks to Pickersgill's good offices, Smallwood was able to meet with him.

Pickersgill's interest in Newfoundland had pre-dated his meeting with Smallwood but was intensified by Smallwood's enthusiasm. As assistant to St. Laurent he acted as an advocate for Newfoundland, especially when the Canadian government's interest in the possibility of confederation seemed to flag. When union took place, Newfoundland's representative in the federal cabinet was Gordon Bradley, who had played such an important role in bringing about confederation. As secretary of state, however, there was little of a direct nature that Bradley could do in Newfoundland's interest. His physical condition, too, seemed to have deteriorated through the years, and he lacked both the energy and the federal expertise to meet Smallwood's expectations. Clearly the time would soon arrive when Bradley would want to retire from active politics. This would leave two vacancies, one in the federal riding of Bonavista-Twillingate, which Bradley represented in the House of Commons, and the other, Bradley's seat in the federal cabinet. The hope was, of course, that one person would fill both posts, and on this matter Smallwood sought the advice of the federal official he knew best — Pickersgill, who by now was clerk of the Privy Council, the most influential and prestigious post in the entire federal civil service. The net result of their discussions was that Pickersgill agreed to resign from his post, run in Bonavista-Twillingate and, if elected, represent Newfoundland in the federal cabinet. In the meantime, Bradley agreed to accept a summons to the Senate.

The election was held in 1953 and everything went as planned. Pickersgill's qualifications for his new duties were most imposing. He had spent many years at the seat of power in Ottawa. He knew almost everyone of any consequence both in the political as well as the civil-service fields. He was familiar with the massive quantities of legislation passed over the years, and his agile mind was ever working to find ways in which that legislation could be applied to help solve Newfoundland's problems. Among his accomplishments were the establishment of Terra Nova National Park, the borders of which he elongated in such a way as to make Canada responsible for a maximum amount of the Trans Canada Highway within the park; establishment of the experimental fish plant at Valleyfield; the building of innumerable wharves, marine works, post offices, public buildings and breakwaters; the establishment of the Atlantic Development Board, which poured millions of dollars into Newfoundland for projects such as the Bay d'Espoir hydro development; the institution of ferry services to islands of the northeast coast; and the building of a paved road from the Trans Canada Highway to Argentia that would tie in with a new ferry service to mainland Canada.

Other projects for which Pickersgill was primarily responsible — or which, without his support, would never have been brought to fruition — were the 90:10 formula for completing the Trans Canada Highway in the Atlantic provinces (of which Newfoundland was the chief beneficiary); the establishment of Term 29 as a constitutional right; a subsidy for the Strait of Belle Isle ferry service; the sharing of federal-provincial properties at the American bases of Pepperrell and Stephenville; and the elimination of the federal tax on privately financed power developments, thus materially assisting in making the Churchill Falls project feasible. But Pickersgill's greatest achievement, in the minds of most Newfoundlanders, and certainly the one that benefitted the people more than did any other, was his fight to get unemployment insurance for the men (and women) who caught the fish — a fight he won single-handedly.

One remarkable aspect of the relationship between Pickersgill and Smallwood was the fact that two such strong-willed, independent-minded men could work together so harmoniously without any major schisms developing. It was a tribute to the intelligence and dedication of the two that at no time was there a really serious possibility of confrontation either federally or provincially. And this in spite of the fact that Pickersgill did not hesitate, on behalf of his constituents, to interfere or at least lobby about provincial matters. Pickersgill was, in fact, Newfoundland's ambassador in Ottawa, and the ombudsman for the large riding of Bonavista-Twillingate.

Diefenbaker

From 1947 until 1957 Newfoundland's relations with the federal government were on the whole polite and quite pleasant. Prime Minister St. Laurent was universally respected; federal benefits kept pouring into the province in the form of family allowances, old-age pensions, unemployment insurance, veterans' allowances, public works such as wharves, lighthouses, post offices, federal buildings, and shared-cost programmes in agriculture, health, welfare and so on. But right from the time of union — in fact, even before it — a basic question had troubled the negotiators[1] and, after union, the government. Under the Terms of Union, Newfoundland lost most of its money-raising powers (as had other provinces) which traditionally were the customs and excise taxes and duties. But it still retained its responsibility for most of the basic services such as education, social welfare, health, and transportation.

---

[1] One of them, Chesley A. Crosbie, refused to sign the terms on the grounds that the financial terms were inadequate for Newfoundland's needs.

The question was whether or not Newfoundland, over the long haul, would be in a financial position to meet its responsibilities. The possibility existed that the people of Newfoundland, with their federal benefits and with the economic improvements resulting from federal stimulation, might be relatively prosperous; meanwhile the Newfoundland government could be perennially bankrupt, or, at best, existing in a state of poverty.

Because no one could anticipate what conditions would be like within a few years, Term 28 (of the Terms of Union) included a federal transitional decreasing grant spread over a twelve-year period. But even more important in the long run was Term 29, which stated:

> In view of the difficulty of predicting with sufficient accuracy the financial consequences to Newfoundland of becoming a province of Canada, the Government of Canada will appoint a Royal Commission within eight years from the date of Union to review the financial position of the Province of Newfoundland and to recommend the form and scale of additional financial assistance, if any, that may be required by the Government of the Province of Newfoundland to enable it to continue public services at the levels and standards reached subsequent to the date of Union, without resorting to taxation more burdensome, having regard to capacity to pay, than that obtaining generally in the region comprising the Maritime Provinces of Nova Scotia, New Brunswick, and Prince Edward Island.

The Newfoundland co-authors of the Terms of Union regarded this Term as Newfoundland's lifeline. Such was the importance attached to it by Newfoundland that the whole province supported the government's decision to set up a royal commission of its own to prepare Newfoundland's case for submission to the commission outlined under Term 29. One of the province's ablest lawyers, Phillip J. Lewis, who was a minister without portfolio in the Smallwood administration, was appointed chairman. In due time, the commission made its report which set the amount required for Newfoundland to meet the standards prescribed in the Term at $15 million annually. The federal royal commission was under the chairmanship of Chief Justice McNair of New Brunswick, formerly premier of that province. When the federal royal commission reported, it recommended that Ottawa should pay Newfoundland $8 million annually. No expiry date was recommended.

Newfoundland was deeply disappointed over the amount recommended, and urged the Canadian government to be more generous than the commission had been. But when the Canadian government announced its decision, to the dismay and indignation of practically everyone in the province and many outside, Prime Minister Diefenbaker stated that Ottawa would pay Newfoundland $8 million annually for five years "in final and irrevocable settlement" of the federal obligation under Term 29. Newfoundlanders as a body expressed their resentment in a variety of ways. One political result was that the Conservative party in Newfoundland split down the middle and was almost obliterated in the succeeding provincial election. The federal decision was widely perceived in the province as a unilateral destruction of a clause designed to protect Newfoundland's interest. What Ottawa was saying was that after five years, no matter what financial or economic condition Newfoundland might be in, no matter how burdensome taxation was in the attempt to maintain public services, all obligation on Ottawa's part would cease. This action, the Newfoundland people declared, was arbitrary, unfair, dictatorial and illegal. Premier Smallwood undertook a campaign across Canada designed to educate the people to the significance of Term 29, and to engender support for Newfoundland's cause. That support was forthcoming in abundant measure.

At the federal-provincial first ministers' conference, several of the non-Liberal premiers expressed support for Newfoundland. "I don't know why he [Diefenbaker] did it," said one Social Credit premier. "The amount involved, while important to Newfoundland, was only peanuts in the federal budget." Another well-known and respected Conservative premier did not mince his words. Speaking directly to the prime minister, he said, "For God's sake, Prime Minister, give Newfoundland what she is entitled to and let us get on to other business." Diefenbaker at first refused to budge on the issue, although urged to do so from all quarters. It was rumoured in the Conservative party that he recognized the magnitude of the blunder he had made and would like to have stepped back, but he felt that such an action would have been a grave reflection on the office of the prime minister.

Eventually he agreed to extend the $8 million grant for another five years after 1962. But this did not deal with the basic principle of Newfoundland's constitutional rights in the matter. In any case, Diefenbaker's concession probably came too late to undo the damage that had been done.

It is often asked why Diefenbaker risked being charged with unilaterally breaking the intent and spirit of the Terms of Union. Some attributed it to his chagrin that Newfoundland was not a party to the Diefenbaker landslide in the 1958 federal election. Another reason sometimes put forward was that he simply read a statement prepared by one of his ministers or aides, without realizing the seriousness of its implications. Whatever the reason, there was no doubt that he did himself and his party serious harm by his stand. All Canada had welcomed Newfoundland into confederation. They knew the new province had special problems requiring special measures for solution. The last thing that the average Canadian wanted was to see this new province treated in a parsimonious or vindictive manner. What no one could understand was how Diefenbaker could arbitrarily set a five-year time limit to Canada's obligation under the Term. Conceivably, Newfoundland could have been worse off in 1963 than in 1958, even with a taxation load far heavier than that in the three Maritime provinces. Needless to say, Diefenbaker's political opponents were quick to seize the advantage. Lester Pearson, leader of the Liberal party, announced that when his party once more formed the administration, one of their first acts would be to undo the injustice done to Newfoundland. It is now a matter of history that Pearson kept his word.

Term 29 was not the only point of contention between Diefenbaker and Smallwood. Following on the heels of that quarrel, a loggers' strike took place in Newfoundland. Given the importance of lumber and paper mills to the province's economy, the strike had serious potential consequences for the people of Newfoundland. Indeed, many Newfoundlanders were shaken in a way that, apart from the fight for confederation, they had not experienced since the religious and political riots of a hundred years earlier. In this case, however, there were also serious national and even international reverberations. But before dealing with this contentious issue, some background information is desirable.

186

The Newfoundland loggers had started to unionize in 1936 with the formation of the Newfoundland Lumberman's Association. Within the next two or three years, three more unions were formed. In 1939, a woods labour board was formed, consisting of representatives from the four unions and from the Grand Falls and Corner Brook mills under a government-appointed chairman. The board met regularly and, among other things, discussed loggers' grievances. For seventeen years the loggers had not gone on strike; considerable progress had been made in improving conditions of work but there was still a degree of discontent, as was revealed when the IWA (International Woodworkers of America) strike started in 1958.

At that time it was difficult to generalize about conditions in the lumber camps, since conditions tended to vary from camp to camp. Some were relatively hygienic, with good food and reasonably comfortable surroundings, probably as good as many loggers enjoyed at home; other camps were operated under almost primitive conditions, where dirt and discomfort were part of everyday life.

In 1956 H. Landon Ladd, a senior officer in the International Woodworkers of America (the IWA), offered the Newfoundland Lumberman's Association an opportunity to affiliate with the IWA. The offer was refused. In spite of this, however, the IWA set up an office in December 1956 and began to solicit support. By May of 1958 it was certified as a bargaining agent for the AND (Anglo-Newfoundland Development Co.) loggers collectively, and for the twenty-four contractors cutting pulpwood for Bowaters. During the summer of 1958, negotiations between IWA and the Anglo-Newfoundland Development Company failed to reach agreement on two basic issues — higher wages and shorter working weeks. As customary under the law, the minister of labour was requested to set up a conciliation board. In December the board recommended a 16 percent increase over two years and a reduction of the work week from sixty to fifty-four hours. The union accepted the report, but the company rejected it. Accordingly, the union called for a strike to start on December 31, 1958. For the next three months chaos reigned in central Newfoundland, and for the rest of Newfoundland the whole thing became a nightmare. The company tried to operate some of its camps, and some loggers resorted to violence to stop them. The violence was not just against those contractors and loggers who did not want to strike. From physically blocking company roads strikers were soon stopping vehicles on the public highway; if the strikers felt the vehicle was in any way identified with the non-strikers it was turned back or, in some cases, simply overturned. Assaults were made on company camps and in some cases the occupants were forced into the snow, inadequately clothed in sub-zero weather.

For six weeks, apart from urging strikers to keep the peace, the Newfoundland government took no action, although requests to do so came from every segment of the population — including strikers themselves. Then, on February 12, Smallwood gave a province-wide speech in which he stated that the IWA strike had failed, that the loggers should form another union and that he was willing to go to Grand Falls, accompanied by Max Lane, head of the Federation of Fishermen, to help in forming that union. The response was overwhelming, and several thousand men converged on Grand Falls. The union, called the Newfoundland Brotherhood of Woodworkers, was set up, and this was followed by a special session of the Newfoundland Legislature in which Smallwood's motion to decertify the IWA as the sole bargaining agent for the loggers was unanimously adopted. There was probably more support for this measure from every part of the province and from every segment of the population than for any other measure in Newfoundland's history.

When it was seen that the IWA was unable to stand against the Newfoundland government, an appeal was then made to the International Labour Organization in Geneva, which referred the matter to the federal minister of labour, Michael Starr, who in turn requested a statement from Premier Smallwood. The reply, in part, to Starr's letter is given below:

> I thank you for your generosity in forwarding to me the letter and enclosures that you have received from the I.L.O.
> The I.W.A. entered Newfoundland quite lawfully and operated quite lawfully for two years or more. They then called a strike of loggers employed by the Anglo-Newfoundland Development Company, and this was quite lawful.

Smallwood went on to allege that the I.W.A. in a public statement called upon their striking members to break the law of the land and that for more than five weeks a "veritable reign of terror" existed. According to Smallwood, it was because of this "bloody violence" that he introduced into the House of Assembly legislation to decertify the I.W.A., which measure was passed unanimously. Smallwood continued:

> The decertification of the I.W.A. meant merely the ending, by the Legislature, of the monopoly they had enjoyed of the right to negotiate with the employers; to conclude agreements with the employers, and generally to conduct themselves as a trade union in Newfoundland has not been affected at all. They no longer enjoy a monopoly of the right to operate as a union and to represent the loggers of the A.N.D. Company, and in actual fact another union, the Newfoundland Brotherhood of Woods Workers, has meanwhile been organized and has negotiated contracts with the employers. The new Brotherhood has several thousands more members than had the I.W.A. at their peak.
>
> My action, taken as Premier of this Province, in introducing the decertification legislation into the Newfoundland Legislature, and the action of the Leader of the Opposition in supporting it, and of all the Members in voting for it received the all-but-unanimous approval of the people of Newfoundland. All Newfoundland newspapers, without exception, all radio stations, all religious bodies and virtually all the citizens supported our stand.
>
> If the I.L.O. is anxious to know the full truth about the I.W.A., the I.W.A. strike, and the action taken unanimously by the Legislature of the Province, and all the reasons for this action, it might be advisable for them to send highly qualified persons to Newfoundland to conduct an investigation into this matter. I would be happy to assist them in the making of a thorough-going, impartial enquiry into all these matters.

The responsibility for maintaining law and order in central Newfoundland rested with the RCMP, in accordance with an agreement signed between the Government of Canada and the Government of Newfoundland in 1957. Clause 13 of that agreement provided for contingencies and emergencies of the kind that were developing in the Grand Falls area. It reads as follows:

> Where in the opinion of the Attorney General of the Province an emergency exists within the Province requiring additional members of the force to assist in dealing with such emergency,

> Canada shall, at the request of the Attorney General of the
> Province, increase the strength of the Division as requested, if
> in the opinion of the Attorney General of Canada, having
> regard to other duties and responsibilities of the force such
> increase is possible.

To Newfoundlanders, and indeed to all other provinces having similar agreements with Ottawa, the intent of the clause was as simple as it could possibly be. If the attorney general of the province declared an emergency, and if there were no special conditions in other parts of the nation that would preclude sending reinforcements, then the attorney general of Canada had no choice but to make the additional police available.

In the case of the loggers' strike it was the RCMP itself that first declared the emergency and asked for assistance. According to Superintendent Parsons, head of the RCMP in Newfoundland, he lacked sufficient strength to maintain law and order. When advised of this, the Newfoundland attorney general, L.R. Curtis, immediately contacted the federal justice minister, Davie Fulton, to make the formal request. In the meantime Parsons contacted the head of the RCMP in Canada, Commissioner Leonard Nicholson, to alert him to the seriousness of the situation and to request his support in getting reinforcements. Fulton then gave the order to collect the extra police and fly them to Gander. This action was being undertaken when the order was countermanded by Prime Minister Diefenbaker. When apprised of this, Commissioner Nicholson, who was nearing retirement after a long and honourable career in the Force, resigned. All of Canada was shocked. Diefenbaker had not only broken an agreement between Canada and its newest province, but he had humiliated his until-then-popular minister of justice and had so compromised the chief commissioner of the RCMP that he felt obligated to sacrifice his career in protest against the probably illegal and certainly arbitrary action of the prime minister. Many observers felt that Fulton, too, should have resigned — a step which would have been applauded by the great majority of the Canadian people and might well have changed the course of the minister's political future.

On March 11 a confrontation took place between the RCMP

aided by the Newfoundland Constabulary sent from St. John's, and several hundred loggers, as a result of which Constable William Moss, a young and promising member of the constabulary, was brutally killed by a blow to the head. This brought the whole crisis to fever pitch and for a while a small-scale civil war appeared possible. In the meantime it was clear — from letters to members, radio and newspaper commentaries, church leaders, the leaders of some other unions — that the Newfoundland government had, apart from those loggers who were members of or sympathized with the IWA, virtually complete support not only from the Newfoundland people but, increasingly as time went on, from many people right across Canada. Even some portions of the labour movement gave their support, either directly or tacitly.

One example of how strongly the Newfoundland people, or at least one group of Newfoundlanders, felt about the issue was manifested when the Reverend J.R. Muchmore, secretary of the United Church's Board of Evangelism and Social Service, criticised the government's action regarding the IWA. He advised Fulton that the RCMP should not be brought further into the issue and that the matter should be handled by law-enforcement agencies in Newfoundland. On learning of Muchmore's statements, the United Church in Newfoundland erupted. The indignation was heightened by the fact that at the time the premier, the lieutenant-governor, the opposition leader, the mayor of St. John's, the president of Memorial University, the attorney-general, the minister of public welfare and the minister of education were all adherents or members of the United Church. In fact, one of the group, B.J. Abbott, was chief lay representative from Newfoundland to the General Council of the United Church. Any of these men could have contacted Muchmore and thereby prevented pre-judgements based on ignorance, as well as the unacceptable comments and advice which embarrassed and provoked the whole United Church in Newfoundland. The people demanded and received assurance that Muchmore was not speaking for the United Church. As to why Muchmore decided to pontificate on the matter without at least consulting one or two United Church leaders in Newfoundland, no one could offer an answer. Presumably he did discuss the issue with someone outside Newfoundland, although regrettably one who knew no more about the actual circumstances in Newfoundland than did Muchmore himself.

One question that has intrigued many observers is why the critics who saw so much that was wrong, indeed reprehensible, in the actions of the government and the House of Assembly, apparently saw nothing wrong in Diefenbaker's decision, unilaterally, to break the agreement between the two governments regarding the RCMP — particularly given the fact that the decision did alarm every provincial premier and attorney general in Canada which had a similar agreement with the federal government. As one premier (not Liberal) phrased it: ''If he [Diefenbaker] can get away with this, we could wake up some morning and find we had no police force.''

Whether it was the passing of the legislation or the knowledge that, apart from several thousand loggers, the vast majority of the Newfoundlanders wanted the IWA out, or whether it was the overwhelming victory that Smallwood received in the 1959 provincial election, the union gradually withdrew from Newfoundland, a *de facto* concession of defeat. The antagonism did not all disappear overnight, however, and controversy still rages from time to time over the legitimacy of the government's action in decertifying the IWA and in making other legislative amendments. One fact seems to stand out: given the same circumstances, those members of the legislature and of the cabinet who were responsible for taking action against the IWA would do the same thing again, whether it was that union or any other body. During the strike, the two paper companies threatened that if the IWA prevailed they would close down. Some thought this to be an attempt at blackmailing the government into action. But what the government knew, and what has since been apparent on several occasions, was that the two mills were sometimes only marginal operations in the best of circumstances. If a mill encountering problems closed down in Maine or Quebec (as some of them have), it would be a regrettable misfortune. In Newfoundland, it would be a catastrophe.

The resolution of the two major confrontations between Diefenbaker and Smallwood did not signal the end of the bitterness between the two. A third soon emerged. As part of the ''lend-lease'' deal in World War II between Britain and the United States, the latter was given the right to build several large military bases in Newfoundland — one of which was the Air Force base on the banks of historic Quidi Vidi Pond, named Fort Pepperrell. One clause in the agreement obligated the United States to return the property to the Newfoundland government when the lease period had expired, or when the United States decided to vacate the bases. That time came in 1960 and the Newfoundland government took the view that since the deal had been made before Newfoundland joined Canada, the property should revert to the province. The federal government had a different view, however, and insisted that it, and not Newfoundland, was now the responsible agent in the matter. The quarrel went on for nearly two years, but was eventually settled amicably with an agreement which gave Newfoundland most of the valuable installations, including a hospital and some excellent residential buildings, that she was anxious to acquire. In return for Ottawa's concessions to Newfoundland, the prime minister requested Smallwood to withdraw the suit that Newfoundland's attorney general had lodged in the Supreme Court of Canada against the federal government for breaking the police agreement. A number of us in the Newfoundland government felt that it was almost certain that Newfoundland would win the case and that, as a matter of principle, Ottawa should not be let off the hook. But against that was the fact that litigation could go on for months or even longer and the Pepperell issue, in the absence of any conciliatory spirit in Ottawa, might result in Newfoundland being left with empty hands.

And so, of the three major disputes between Diefenbaker and Smallwood, the Pepperrell issue was solved by negotiation; the police matter became less urgent with the withdrawal of the IWA, although it left some still unanswered questions; and the argument over Term 29 was resolved by a change of government in Ottawa.

For twenty-five years many political observers have wondered why Diefenbaker adopted such a hostile and unyielding posture in his dealings with Newfoundland. Some, including Smallwood, have speculated that it was the province's poor Conservative returns in the 1958 election that soured him against Newfoundland in general and Smallwood in particular. During the election Diefenbaker had visited several large centres in Newfoundland and had been met with overwhelming enthusiasm by thousands of voters. Diefenbaker could hardly be blamed, then, for assuming that Newfoundland's voting support would be as strong as in the other nine provinces. But Smallwood had assembled his forces and set out to negate the potential Diefenbaker landslide in Newfoundland. For example, Smallwood, with one and at times two or three of his cabinet ministers, engaged a private railway car which travelled from St. John's to Port aux Basques, stopping at every place of any size and, at the larger centres holding rallies. There is no doubt that Smallwood, by invoking Liberal loyalties, and, in particular, common gratitude, was able to stem the Diefenbaker tide in Newfoundland. The result was that, far from winning five or six of the seven seats, he won only two. Newfoundland's five Liberal seats did not matter much in 1958. But in the 1962 and, particularly, in the 1963 election, the six and then seven Newfoundland seats helped to unseat the Conservative party.

Finally, it should be noted that the beginning of Diefenbaker's decline began with his treatment of Newfoundland over the Term 29 and the police issues. There were tens of thousands of Newfoundlanders and people of Newfoundland descent live in every province of Canada. They and the many other thousands of politically non-aligned voters who wanted to see Newfoundland become a happy and prosperous component of confederation showed their displeasure and disgust in the only way open to them. In less than six months the polls showed that Diefenbaker's popularity had begun to plummet. How much the decline was the result of his treatment of Newfoundland is difficult to ascertain. But in the absence of other serious economic or political problems during the period, the Newfoundland connection must be given a significant share of responsibility.

Smallwood, Winters and Trudeau

Apart from Prime Ministers St. Laurent and Pearson, as well as J.W. Pickersgill, the public figure in Ottawa with whom Newfoundland had the longest and most intimate relationship was Robert H. Winters, a native of Lunenburg, Nova Scotia. (That relationship actually preceded the beginning of Winter's political career, since his father, the captain of a Lunenburg banking schooner, had frequently visited Newfoundland in quest of bait, or to take shelter from a storm.) Winters first entered federal politics in 1945 under the leadership of Mackenzie King and entered the cabinet in 1948, becoming minister of resources and development in 1949. In this capacity, he signed the memorandum of agreement respecting the Trans Canada Highway, in June, 1950, with E.S. Spencer signing for the Newfoundland government.

Winters had a most impressive set of credentials for public life. He was personally handsome and genial, had graduated from Mount Allison University and then had gone on to take two degrees in science and engineering at the Massachusets Institute of Technology. He served as an engineer in World War II, attaining the rank of lieutenant-colonel. Added to these qualifications were his ability to speak clearly and logically, and his dedication to hard work. Those who knew him early in his career were convinced that, if he cared to, he would some day become a political leader of the first rank.

Winter's promising political career was temporarily suspended by his electoral defeat in 1957. But he moved easily to the business world and in a short time became president of Pro Algom — a subsidiary of Rio Tinto, one of the world's largest mining conglomerates — and a director of a number of other important companies. In 1963 he became chairman and chief executive officer of Brinco, a position which brought him into frequent contact with Smallwood. In 1965 Winters returned to politics and was elected in the November general election, and was appointed to the new Pearson cabinet.

Within a couple of years, it became evident that the prime minister was thinking of retirement and that a leadership conference would soon be forthcoming. It was not long before prospective leaders were announcing their intentions, but Winters was not among them. Smallwood was most concerned that the new leader should be one not only familiar with Newfoundland's special problems, but sympathetic to her needs — all of which pointed to Winters. Smallwood made no secret of his preference for Winters, a stand which was supported by the big majority of Newfoundland Liberals and many non-Liberals as well. There was no doubt that Winters was held in enormous respect by most Newfoundlanders, and that he was liked by all who had come in contact with him. Consequently, there was considerable satisfaction among those who were close to the premier when, following Pearson's resignation, Winters informed Smallwood privately that he would be a candidate.

I first met Winters when he and I were guest speakers at a great banquet at the Royal York Hotel given by the Newfoundland residents of Toronto. It was March, 1949, the night that Newfoundland became a province. Shortly thereafter two general elections were called: the provincial in May and the federal in June. At the request of Premier Smallwood, Prime Minister St. Laurent deputized two of his ablest ministers, Paul Martin and Robert Winters, to come to Newfoundland to assist in the campaign. Since Smallwood had committed himself to a blitz campaign in eastern and northern Newfoundland, he asked me to be the host for our two visitors, who were to confine their activities to St. John's and the Avalon Peninsula. As a result of our work together, I got to know both Winters and Martin[2] very well. Over subsequent years, I met Winters casually during my visits to Ottawa following union, but during the time he served as Brinco's chairman I had many more opportunities to meet him, both in Labrador and, especially, during his many visits to St. John's. On those occasions he would invariably lunch with Smallwood in the premier's private dining room in the Confederation Building. Since, along with Attorney-General Curtis and one or two other cabinet ministers, I was a permanent guest of the premier (at no expense to the treasury), I was privy to just about all the discussion that went on between Smallwood and Winters, including both Churchill Falls and Winters' leadership plans.[3]

(I should mention here that as each candidate for the federal leadership publicly announced his intentions, he asked for, or was given the chance to select from among the local Liberals someone to be his "contact" as well as his advisor in planning meetings, press conferences, and other events. I was deeply honoured when Winters asked Smallwood for his

---

[2] Some twenty-two years later it was Martin, as government leader in the Senate, who introduced me to Canada's Upper House.

[3] Since all these conversations took place in a private dining room, I could not, in common courtesy, reveal details about them without first obtaining the premier's consent. This was the only part of this book that I felt should first be referred to him.

approval, which was freely given, to have me act as his "Man Friday" in Newfoundland.)

Although Winters had not made a public declaration of his intention to run, Smallwood (and many other Newfoundlanders) were sure he would and relaxed, secure in the belief that, first, of all the potential candidates (Trudeau had not entered the picture) Winters was the most likely to win, and second, Newfoundland owed it to Winters to support him because of the contribution he had made to the province, especially on the Churchill project. Several weeks went by and then, as a bolt from the blue, came the telephone call from Winters informing Smallwood that he had decided not to run. For a full half-hour Smallwood pleaded and argued. But his formidable talents of persuasion were in vain. Winters was adamant, and a stricken Smallwood finally conceded defeat. There were, of course, a half-dozen or so other candidates, but none who, in Smallwood's estimation, possessed qualifications that were as favourable to Newfoundland as Winters did. And so, for some weeks, the matter was left up in the air.

In the meantime, plans were going ahead for a constitutional conference, and to this end, Minister of Justice P.E. Trudeau, at the prime minister's request, made a cross-country trip to confer with all the premiers individually. On the day of Trudeau's arrival Smallwood was unable to wait in St. John's until Trudeau had met other commitments and accordingly, asked me to take the justice minister out after dinner to the premier's home on the Roache's Line, some forty-odd miles from St. John's. With Trudeau was Don Jamieson, soon to become prominent in federal politics. We spent the evening discussing constitutional and other general matters. Little was said about the leadership question. But all three of us were deeply impressed by the obvious brilliance of this newcomer to politics.

Our next meeting with Trudeau was at the constitutional conference itself, in February, 1968, where he distinguished himself, not only by his bilingual skill in debate but, in particular, by his handling of the arguments put forward by the Quebec delegation. It was probably this experience, more than anything else, that led Smallwood to the conclusion that in Trudeau, Liberals all across Canada had a political winner — a man who both by logic and emotion was converted to the ideal of regional equalization embodied in the phrase "co-operative federalism." Never slow to jump at a chance — but not, in this case, before consulting a number of his key political advisers — Smallwood contacted Trudeau to say that if he would run for the Liberal leadership, he (Smallwood) believed that the Newfoundland people and the delegation to the leadership convention would support him. To the best of my recollection, Smallwood was the first political leader to see in Trudeau the answer to Liberal prayers right across Canada. Then, without warning, another bolt fell. Winters called to say that he had changed his mind, that he would be running after all, and that he was counting on Newfoundland's support.

This time Smallwood was more than flabbergasted. He was deeply embarrassed, but had no choice except to tell Winters that, on the basis of Winters' earlier decision, the Newfoundland Liberal caucus, and by inference, the delegates, were committed to support Trudeau. It was now Winters' turn to plead and argue. But he was unable to obtain a firm commitment from Smallwood. One concession (an obvious one) that Smallwood was able to give, however, was that the Newfoundland delegation would have the right to vote as they wished. In the final analysis, since it was by secret ballot, no one would know how each delegate had voted. But this was of only partial comfort to Winters, knowing well that with the hold Smallwood had on Newfoundland Liberals, the majority would not undertake what might be considered disloyalty to their leader. Winters continued to solicit a public declaration of support from Smallwood and apparently continued to believe right up to the start of the convention that when the chips were down Smallwood would go for Winters rather than Trudeau.

As the convention was getting under way, Smallwood came out publicly to announce his support for Trudeau. This was a blow of the first magnitude to Winters, a fact which he realized and expressed to me before any voting started. Winters' bitterness was intensified after the actual voting started, when, at one stage, it was very likely that the swing to Trudeau could be stemmed if the Newfoundland delegation were to support Winters. This did not happen, however, and the course of Canadian history was changed. Trudeau won the leadership and, shortly after, an overwhelming election victory. A year later Bob Winters died suddenly at the age of fifty-nine. Whether the strain of losing the election precipitated his tragic demise is one of the imponderables of history. What is more certain, however, is that it was Winters, not Smallwood, who helped to bring about the former's defeat in the race for the Liberal leadership.

13 THE SMALLWOOD RECORD

REFLECTIONS OF HIS PEERS

From the day that he resigned (or was dismissed) from the Smallwood Administration until Smallwood's collapse from power, John Crosbie was the premier's inveterate political antagonist. Indeed, many observers believe that Crosbie's unrelenting, implacable hostility was the most significant factor in precipitating Smallwood's political downfall.

In the events leading up to the actual split, with each man seeming to be more worried as to who would shoot first, Crosbie persisted in claiming to be a Liberal. (Indeed, both he and Wells supported the Liberals in the federal election that took place in June, just a few weeks after the break with Smallwood.) According to Crosbie, his quarrel with Smallwood resulted from the latter's habit of undertaking expensive and risky industrial projects without proper feasibility studies, and without due regard for business principles.

In a recent discussion with me, when invited to express his views regarding Smallwood's overall career in public life — his biggest mistakes, his sins of omission, as well as his greatest achievements — Crosbie reiterated his view that Smallwood's errors were largely in the field of economic development. These included not only the earlier small projects of the Valdmanis period but also the biggest ones, especially the Come-By-Chance, Brinco and Churchill Falls, and the Linerboard projects. Here he felt that Smallwood had taken unnecessary risks, and allowed himself to be manipulated not only by Doyle and Shaheen, but by Donald Gordon, Robert Winters, the Rothschildes, and others connected with the BRINCO-Churchill Falls project. He felt that Smallwood would have done well to join forces with Quebec, as Levesque had suggested, for a joint development of Churchill — an idea that Smallwood has consistently rejected as immoral, given that the companies making up BRINCO had accepted Newfoundland's invitation with full confidence in the province's integrity. Crosbie suggested, too, that Smallwood was guilty of serious omission in his somewhat lackadaisical approach to the whole off-shore matter and that a *modus operandi* should have been adopted in the 1960s when it first became a live issue. Finally, Crosbie faults Smallwood's personality-centred approach to politics as the reason for his failure to leave a viable party behind him. These criticisms aside, however, Crosbie stated that Smallwood made great contributions to the good of Newfoundland, especially in the fields of social welfare and education. In addition, his effective representation of interests in national debates attracted attention and respect from the rest of Canada. To use Crosbie's words: ''Smallwood brought Newfoundland into the twentieth century.''

Clarence Powell was a former outport magistrate who subsequently became director of local government, then deputy minister of municipal affairs and, finally, chairman of the board of public utilities. In these latter positions he presided over the growth of municipal government on a scale probably unprecedented in any part of the world: for example, in 1949 only three towns had full water and sewer services; in 1971 there were 199. Similarly impressive statistics extended to growth in municipal fire brigades, recreational facilities, electrification and joint housing programmes. But in spite of these phenomenal developments, for which he could claim a good deal of credit, when asked what he considered to be the most far-reaching programme undertaken by the government during the Smallwood era, Powell listed education and roads.

Powell did not approve all government programmes, however. The most ill-advised and detrimental, in his view, was the policy of job-creation through ''new industries,'' implemented for the most part during the early part of the administration. Allowing the Churchill Falls (Labrador) Corporation

(CFCO) to enter into a contract with Hydro-Quebec without providing for rate revisions, and neglecting the possible effects of inflation on revenue, was Smallwood's most serious error of omission, Powell believes, followed by the government's funding of water and sewers, municipal paving and other municipal projects without requiring property taxes and town plans. But Powell's overall view is generally that too much emphasis has been placed in retrospect on the government's lack of foresight, and he points out that other provincial governments, as well as the federal government itself, have all made unwise decisions resulting in huge losses of public money.

On other issues, Powell believes that the real cause of the confrontation between the IWA strikers on the one hand and the government and people on the other was a recognition that the IWA would establish a logging elite which would destroy the traditional fisherman-logger relationship and lead to economic turmoil and distress. Although the IWA was crushed, the swing to a logging elite gained sufficient momentum over time to defeat the opposition. On the resettlement programme, Powell accepts the inevitability of centralization — a process which, he says, started voluntarily and which, quite properly, the government felt that it had to assist.

Aiden Maloney was born and raised in a fishing community in Bonavista Bay. His early background was in commercial fishing, and eventually he became manager of one of the largest fish plants on the south coast. He spent most of his four-year tenure in the Smallwood administration as minister of fisheries. Maloney feels that one of Smallwood's most significant achievements was his attempt, if only partially successful, to persuade the government of Canada to institute a national fisheries policy similar to that which had been set up for agriculture. One result of this effort was the enactment of the Salt Fish Act and the establishment of the Canadian Salt Fish Corporation, of which Maloney was the first head. In Maloney's words, "That initiative played and continues to play an important part in the lives of thousands of our people around the coasts of Newfoundland and Labrador."

In general, Maloney gives high marks to the tremendous energy and drive with which Smallwood dedicated himself to the task of improving conditions in Newfoundland. Maloney credits Smallwood and, by inference, the great majority of Newfoundlanders, with having done the right thing in opposing the IWA. But those character traits which were so effectively used by the premier in that struggle were also the cause of occasionally extreme measures he took to provide jobs for Newfoundlanders. In this, Smallwood found himself faced by the same predicament from which no Newfoundland premier has ever been able to extricate himself, except for the artificial and temporary prosperity afforded by two world wars.

C.A. Knight, referred to earlier in Chapter 5, was a highways engineer who had spent most of his professional life in the departments of public works and later of highways. He was respected for his ability and integrity. As a deputy minister in a key department of government he had frequent contacts with the premier as well as with all cabinet ministers and members of the legislature. Knight ranks the Smallwood government's education programme as its number one achievement, followed by the roads programme. He approved the government's policy of assistance in resettlement, as well as the massive provincial parks programme. As an engineer he was particularly pleased with the government's Urban and Rural Planning Act which, he feels, protected the highways and prevented runaway ribbon development, even then a problem in many parts of Newfoundland.

Knight believes that the government's commitment to the Come-By-Chance refinery was ill-advised and that a better use could have been found for Bay D'Espoir power than giving it at subsidized rates to the Erco chemical plant at Long Harbour. He feels, too, that the new industries programme was less than prudent, although he does not attribute any long-term detrimental effects to it. In retrospect he thinks Smallwood took the right stand during the IWA strike and that Smallwood's fight for and victory in bringing about confederation will, in the long run, outweigh any shortcomings he may have displayed as premier. One interesting observation made by Knight is that while in his early years as premier Smallwood was very much a one-man government, he did not continue as such. As time went on, his regime became less individualistic, with cabinet ministers assuming greater responsibility in their respective departments.

H.R.V. Earle's role in the Smallwood-Crosbie leadership

struggle was related in the previous chapter and needs no reference here. But his views on the Smallwood era, during part of which he had been first a private member and then an active cabinet minister, are of interest. Among Smallwood's major achievements, he lists the establishment of Memorial University as well as the technical and vocational institutions. Other programmes receiving high marks from Earle are those for roads, hospitals and welfare homes for adults and children, assistance to fisheries and agriculture, assistance to the needy, and the raising of the standard of living generally.

On a less complimentary note, Earle points to Smallwood's ventures in the field of industrial development as his largest failures. Many of the projects which proved to be unsound had been undertaken without proper independent research. This applied also to Smallwood's dealings with what Earle calls "unscrupulous entrepreneurs." There was unnecessary overexpenditure on capital account, and the government undertook current account expenditures — notably, free tuition and grants to university students — which it could not afford. One reason for these mistakes, Earle feels, was insufficient consultation by the premier with cabinet ministers and senior civil servants. On other issues, Earle disapproved of some aspects of the resettlement programme, alleging that in some cases people were encouraged to move to settlements where they were worse off than they had been before. He thinks that Smallwood acted as any strong man should have acted with regard to the IWA and Diefenbaker episodes and that the outcome was not to Smallwood's discredit. But Earle feels most strongly that the premier should have retired as soon as he had the Churchill Falls project under way. Had he done this, Smallwood would have escaped much of the unfair criticism subsequently heaped upon him.

Earle's appraisal of Smallwood is generally positive. While regarding Smallwood as quick-tempered and "somewhat naive and gullible," he expressed admiration for his "unbounded enthusiasm," his great oratorical ability, his capacity for grasping ideas, his ability to become absorbed in work, and his loyalty to his friends. Although Smallwood was "uninformed and careless in finance," he was nevertheless a committed and true Newfoundlander who "was very necessary for his time."

Stuart R. Godfrey came to Newfoundland from England as

a young boy and, after attending Memorial University College, entered the department of the auditor-general following re-organization of the Newfoundland civil service by the Commission of Government. Later he moved into the department of education and, in 1949, to the new ministry of public welfare as assistant deputy minister. In 1964 he resigned from the Newfoundland civil service to become commissioner of public welfare for the city of Ottawa and subsequently commissioner of social services for the regional municipality of Ottawa-Carleton, a post he held until his retirement. Because of his wide-ranging and unusual background his views on the Smallwood record are of special interest.

Godfrey feels that both practically and symbolically the decision of the new government in 1949 to divide the traditional pairing of health and welfare by creating a new ministry of public welfare was necessary to ensure that the social rights of poor and other disadvantaged Newfoundlanders were properly represented. Also, it was necessary for the recruitment and training of personnel in the field of social welfare. A vital corollary was the implementation of the massive road-building programme.

On the negative side Godfrey appears to have had little confidence in the government's early economic (industrialization) policy, the "develop or perish" message of which implied scaling down the labour-intensive inshore fishery in favour of new industries. Godfrey also feels that while abandonment of traditional settlement locations was probably inevitable, and that the reasons for the resettlement program were justified, they were not interpreted and implemented effectively. Further, the government's handling of the IWA issue was a classic example of abuse of political power, and Godfrey describes himself as being "shaken" by the total support that the government received in this matter from the entire legislature and, by implication, from the church institutions, without full regard to the basic rights and social conditions of an important part of the labour force.

E.P. Henley was born in St. John's, served as a bomber command pilot during World War II, worked subsequently in the aviation industry at Gander, and later became director of tourism in Newfoundland. His avocation was the dramatic arts. Henley's reflections on the Smallwood era are that the govern-

206

ment was to be commended for its excellent road-building programme, its interest in arts and culture centres, and its achievements in education. Of the many contacted in researching this book, Henley is one of the few who had praise for the Smallwood administration's economic development programme.

Henley views the government's handling of the IWA situation as a realistic response, given that if allowed to go on unopposed, the IWA might well have had catastrophic effects on the two paper mills and, therefore, on the economy generally. The resettlement programme, on the other hand, was the most controversial undertaken by the government: Henley's words, "the conception was sound but the implementation was poor" and the government made the serious mistake of overlooking the issue's "emotional impact." The government's approach to the fisheries was, he feels, too political, but the most serious omission, which he describes as a "major oversight," was the failure of the 1948 negotiators to ensure adequate and reasonably priced transportation for Newfoundland. Regarding Smallwood himself, Henley says: "In general I think he did a commendable job. Things were happening during the period of his administration. If nothing else they were exciting times."

J.A.G. MacDonald was born in Nova Scotia and came to Newfoundland as a young man to serve as construction engineer with the department of public works (later, highways). Subsequently he became chief highways engineer, then deputy minister of highways, and finally chairman of the board of commissioners of public utilities. MacDonald feels that the most valuable programme undertaken by the government was the building of roads to connect, where possible, all the communities in Newfoundland, and the additional programme of paving those roads. On the questions of Smallwood's contribution to Newfoundland, MacDonald is succinct: "Time has proved . . . [Smallwood] . . . wrong on several issues . . . [but] there are many monuments from the Smallwood era that will live longer than any of us."

Gregory Power was discussed in the previous chapter. Here it is only necessary to say that for nine years following confederation he was Smallwood's closest friend, after which there was a long period of estrangement until the 1970s when the relationship was re-established. Power's summary of Small-wood and the period is brief and to the point: of all the government's programmes, the greatest was the construction of roads, which brought the historic isolation of the Newfoundland people to an end; economic development was the least profitable of all the Government's activities; and, as for Smallwood himself, Power feels that overall the pluses outweigh the minuses.

C.M. Lane was born the son of an outport fisherman and as a young man was a fisherman himself. He became a teacher, then a magistrate, then general secretary of the Federation of Fishermen. Later he entered active politics, becoming in time minister of fisheries. Lane believes that Smallwood made the basic mistake of trusting some of his friends too much, especially those who were regarded as "experts." Further, he regards much of the criticism of the new industries and, later, of Churchill Falls and other developments as having been grossly unfair and largely the product of hindsight. Smallwood was right in attempting to develop new industries, he states, and the fact that some of them were expensive failures is no proof that they should not have been undertaken.

James R. Chalker was a member of the first cabinet following the 1949 election, where he remained until the 1971 election and Smallwood's resignation. Although he enjoyed a long and very successful business career, it is interesting to find that of all Smallwood's achievements, Chalker singles out those in the fields of education and transportation as the most important. On the other hand, of all its mistakes, the government's worst was to rush into the industrialization programme without proper investigation. As a result, the German entrepreneurs were able to use the programme for their own ends. In spite of the failures, Chalker feels that the stimulating effect of the industries in providing labour and in utilization of local materials was not given adequate credit.

Chalker readily admits that it is difficult to evaluate the government's record without resorting to the wisdom of hindsight. Nevertheless, on looking back, he feels that the fisheries was one area where government action in the very early days might have made a difference. In particular, since Newfoundland production was so inferior compared with the competition, Chalker feels that Newfoundland should have brought over fishermen from western Europe and Iceland who would have trained Newfoundland fishermen in those new techniques which had given the Europeans superiority in world markets. (Indeed, it is quite possible the idea could have worked, particularly given the precedent set by Scottish entrepreneur Lewis Miller, who established the biggest lumbering industry in Newfoundland's history. Miller realized that the Newfoundland workers had to be trained in the skills of logging if the business was to compete with similar enterprises in Canada and Europe. To this end he brought over from Sweden some 60 experienced loggers and their families, for whom he built houses in Lewisporte, Glenwood and Millertown. Not only did Miller's projects benefit, but when they closed down in the early 1900s a number of the group found further opportunities when the Anglo-Newfoundland Development Company started their great enterprise at Grand Falls.)

Chalker feels that Smallwood's ultimate defeat was inevitable — if only because any political party tends to lose its popularity after a lengthy period in power. People simply get "fed up" with the status quo, often forgetting the accomplishments of the present government. This was certainly the case in 1971, when thousands of young voters had either not been born in 1949 or were too young to remember the revolution in living standards brought about by confederation. "We were there too long," Chalker admits, but, in the nautical style of the yachtsman, he maintains that Smallwood was nevertheless "a good skipper."

THE MAN AND THE ERA

Having considered the opinions of his peers, it is interesting to note the views of Smallwood himself with respect to his own achievements and failings. His greatest triumph cannot be disputed: without Smallwood, Newfoundland would not have become a province when it did, and in all probability would not have become a province at all. Yet confederation actually preceded the Smallwood era. What of the era itself?

Judging from his numerous speeches over the years, Smallwood's opinion of his own achievements has varied from time to time. Recently however, he appears to have taken the greatest and most consistent satisfaction in having helped to revolutionize education in Newfoundland. Next to education, he seems to consider the vast road and bridge programme as having the most effect on the Newfoundland people — although it can be argued that this was a necessary condition for the improvement of education, as well as other major programmes. Third on the list of Smallwood's endeavours, and for which he has frequently been dealt with unfairly, is the rejuvenation of the fisheries — probably the most complex and frustrating task ever undertaken by a Newfoundland government.

Of his weaknesses, Smallwood is most likely to mention his tendency to trust people automatically — something for which on several occasions he had to pay dearly. Included in his disappointments was the lack of Canadian capital that came into Newfoundland to develop its resources, thereby forcing him to go first to Germany and, later, to Britain in search of investors. In addition, he has chided himself for his failure to pursue more vigorously a search for salt and oil on the Island of Newfoundland. Had commercially exploitable bodies of salt been discovered, the foundation would have been laid for other industries to locate in Newfoundland. Land-based oil discoveries would have contributed greatly to Newfoundland's economy, but these were hampered by lack of basic research and exploratory drilling.

Unemployment was one of Smallwood's greatest concerns, although there were many businessmen and some politicians who felt that in his eagerness to solve the problem, he did not pay enough attention to ordinary business practices. Another serious, if less evident lack of attention was in regard of both education and secondary road building. These two needs were fundamental: so long as they were not met, progress in other areas could not take place. Changing Memorial College to a university was not very meaningful if the physical plant was too small. Consolidation of schools, both elementary and secondary, was impossible without roads. Yet a casual look at the 1949-1957 capital budgets for these two all-important items reveals a pitifully small expenditure for the two. Indeed, it was not until 1958, following two conferences on education, that a massive attempt was made (successfully) to cope with every phase of education, including the university, as well as the vocational and technical institutions. In the same way, while some attention was given to the Trans-Canada Highway, comparatively little attention was given in the early years to building and later paving secondary roads. The argument was used that Newfoundland could not afford to spend any more than it did. But here, too, it was a matter of assigning priorities, in which case there were valuable lessons which could have been learned from the history of Scandinavia, Iceland, and other small countries of Europe. Admittedly, some progress was made on the basic capital services, but far less than should have been made, particularly given the Commission of Government legacy of wide spread educational and social neglect.

In 1935 I was a census enumerator in one of the more prosperous areas of Newfoundland. There were 18 communities in my district, and I was quite familiar with all of them. My records showed that over 20 percent of the adults listed were illiterate. The actual number was nearer 30 percent, since the enumerator had no choice but to accept the answer given to the question "Can you read and write?" My subsequent experience all over Newfoundland and Labrador led me to the conclusion that, if literacy is defined by ability to read and understand an ordinary newspaper paragraph, then in 1949 at least 40 percent of all adults in the province were illiterate — by far the highest rate of any comparable region in Canada or the United States. It is not too surprising, therefore, that surveys made by sociologists and anthropologists in the 1940s showed that by every socio-economic measurement, Iceland, with a narrower economic base and an even harsher climate, surpassed Newfoundland. Certainly one reason for this astounding disparity must have been the fact that every adult in Iceland was literate.

The 1966 election was an unqualified victory for the Liberals who won thirty-nine seats against three for the Progressive Conservatives. This margin was not unexpected. During the four years that had elapsed since the provincial election of 1962, the new university had been vastly enlarged, the College of Trades and Technology and the College of Fisheries had been built, new large schools were everywhere in evidence, the Trans-Canada Highway had been completed, a network of secondary roads — many of them paved or in process of being paved — had linked communities in all parts of the province, including the Baie Verte and Great Northern Peninsulas. In 1966, "Come Home Year" had brought thousands of former Newfoundlanders, as well as Canadians and Americans of Newfoundland descent, to the island. In their ready enthusiasm for the unparalleled improvements they saw wherever they turned, thousands of tourists became, perhaps without meaning to, ardent supporters of the Smallwood and the Liberal cause. That summer a triumphal motor tour from St. John's to Port Aux Basques carried Smallwood and his entourage, at times stretching several miles in length, over the newly finished Trans-Canada Highway. Everywhere there was a sense of accomplishment and euphoria which stood in vivid contrast to the frustration and pessimism so common throughout Newfoundland's history. It came as no surprise, therefore, when in August of that year Smallwood announced a provincial general election for September 8. Given the mood of the electorate, the Progressive Conservatives could do little more than try to hold onto their seven out of the forty-two seats. Even in this they failed: their outport seats went back to the Liberals, as did several of their St. John's seats. Three of the seats won by the Liberals were by acclamation and in a number of others the Progressive Conservatives made only a token effort. The Liberals won thirty-nine seats, the P.C.s three.

The October 1971 election told a different story. As massive as the Liberal majority had been in 1966, so now were their losses. The best the Liberals could claim was a tie in the number of seats, but they could not deny the large majority obtained by the Progressive Conservatives in the popular vote. For some weeks frantic negotiations were carried on *sub rosa*, many of them involving the member for Labrador West, Thomas Burgess, who had been elected by the Newfoundland Labrador Party. Matters were complicated by the discovery, after a recount for St. Barbe South had been ordered, that the poll clerk had burned the original ballots. The whole issue was brought to a head when the Liberal member for Bay de Verde resigned his seat, thus giving the Lieutenant-Governor an opportunity to dissolve the legislature and order another general election to take place on March 24, 1972. This time the Liberal defeat was decisive. The Progressive Conservatives won 33 seats, the Liberals 9. The popular vote was equally decisive: 126,507 for the Conservatives and 77,849 for the Liberals. Smallwood did not run in the 1972 election. For all practical purposes his regime came to an end in October 1971, after twenty-two and a half years in control of the Newfoundland government. What happened, then, between September 1966 and October 1971 to bring about such a dramatic reversal of Liberal fortunes?

The easy answer to the question is that the people felt it was time for a change, and to a certain extent this argument has some validity. Historically, voters in pre-confederation Newfoundland had not been in the habit of giving their prime ministers lengthy terms of office. Even the most successful leaders could not manage more than two consecutive mandates. Whiteway was premier for separate periods, the longest being about seven years. Sir James Winter was elected in 1897 and badly defeated in 1900. As premier, Bond lasted eight years and was succeeded by Morris who resigned after eight years. Squires was prime minister three times but never more than four years at a stretch. There is a tendency, therefore, for Liberal apologists to say, "What could we expect after twenty-two years in office?" But this argument is not a very strong one, and can be disproved with a bit of simple arithmetic. The 1966 election, in which the Liberals lost three seats, showed the Liberals to be considerably stronger than they had been in 1962 when they lost eight seats. Put another way, it meant that after more than thirteen years in office the Liberals started to pick up strength. Outside of Newfoundland there is ample evidence to indicate that length of tenure is not enough in itself to bring about defeat. Alberta, for example, kept Premier Manning in power for twenty-five-and-a-half years and still continued to elect a Social Credit government until 1971 — a total of twenty-eight years. An even more decisive argument is to be found in Ontario which has elected a Progressive Conservative government for 42 years without interruption. Clearly other reasons besides the 22 years of Liberal tenure should be invoked to explain the Newfoundland situation. Some of these were not hard to find.

The period from 1965 to 1971 was one of increasing unrest among workers generally and with certain groups in particular. Nurses, for example, claimed with justification that they were underpaid. Their negotiations with their employers, the several hospital corporations, did little to satisfy their grievances, although there was little the hospitals could do, since they

213

depended largely on fixed government grants. For its part, the government resisted increasing the grants for fear that in doing so other groups would take a harder stand in wage negotiations. Eventually some of the nurses decided to go on strike for more money. At that point the government felt it had no choice but to pass legislation making hospital strikes illegal. This action pleased some people, but resulted in the almost total loss of political support from nurses — now a large, influential and articulate group — and of other medical groups as well.

Another group, deservedly popular with the general public, was the Newfoundland constabulary. The members of the force, all living in St. John's and faced with ever increasing costs in rent, school fees, clothing and other basic expenses, were notoriously underpaid. Although prolonged negotiations had been undertaken, no progress was made. Finally, the constabulary was forced to take the unprecedented step threatening strike action. Public opinion was clearly with the police, but the government remained intransigent — at least, until the leading churches issued a joint statement publicly criticising the government's stand and calling on it to show more consideration for the police. Only then did the government agree to the needed salary increases. But politically the damage was done. The police knew that the government had given in, not because of concern for the welfare of the police, but because public opinion, led by the churches, had left them with no choice. The police felt they owed no gratitude to the government for their higher salaries.

Still more trouble was to follow. In 1970 negotiations for a new salary scale started between the Treasury Board, representing the government, and a committee representing the Newfoundland Teachers' Association. The association's demand was for a flat 26 percent increase in all teachers' salaries, a figure which Treasury Board and the government felt it could not afford. The counter-offer by the government was for an immediate increase averaging 14 percent for the first year and another 10 percent for the second year. The Association rejected this offer and since the government would not move from its position, recommended to its membership that they initiate a policy of selective withdrawal of services, the practical effect of which was that a number of the larger schools was closed for periods of nearly a month. Finally the Association relented and advised its members to resume normal work, at which point the government proceeded to implement its offer.

Judging from media reports and other forms of public expression, the teachers' demand for an immediate 26 percent increase had been received with little sympathy by the people of Newfoundland, so the government lost little immediate support from the general electorate for its stand. But once again it had made an enemy in a highly organized and extremely vocal group, and the provincial election was less than a year away. Consequently, when the election was called in October 1971, the great majority of Newfoundland's 7000 teachers, as well as their families, reversed their traditional support for Smallwood and began actively campaigning against the Liberal Party.

There were, of course, other causes for discontent. And while none in itself could have profoundly affected the outcome of a general election, the cumulative effects could be disastrous. Newfoundland's economy during the years 1970 to 1971 were the most unsettled of the entire Smallwood era: a general strike at the mining town of Buchans carried on month after month, and the New Democrats began to gain ground there at the expense of the Liberals; the mill at Grand Falls had three major shutdowns each lasting for three weeks; there had been ominous talk of a complete or near-complete shutdown at Corner Brook; finally, there were reactions of outrage at hints that the government might nationalize the Bowater industry in Newfoundland. And again the NDP profited. Perhaps more serious than any of these developments, however, was the fact that the student body at Memorial University, approaching 10,000 by 1971, were bitterly disillusioned over the government's decision to reduce or even abolish some categories of the student aid which had been introduced with so much fanfare only two or three years earlier. They, too, were more politically potent than their numbers would indicate: coming from every part of Newfoundland, most of them now able to vote, their opinions of the government were bound to have an effect on both their families and friends. So it was that by the spring of 1971 the Liberal government had effectively alienated the great majority of the university students, teachers, nurses and policemen. The significance of this becomes more apparent when we look at some of the 1971 election tallies. A changeover of 35 votes would have given the Liberals the District of Carbonear; 54, the District of Ferryland; 38, the District of St. Mary's; 125, the District of Lewisporte; 45, the District of Burgeo and La Poile. In total, a changeover of fewer than 300 votes could have given the Liberals a total of 25 seats with 15 for the PCs, or a Liberal majority of 10 seats in the House, a respectable majority by any Newfoundland standard.

The simmering discontent of the electorate was attributable not only to economic factors. There was considerable dissatisfaction with education, which went far beyond the teachers and university students. The Roman Catholic Church, the largest in Newfoundland, had reason to feel injured: without prior consultation with the churches, the government decided in 1964 to set up a Royal Commission on Education.[1] Of the thirteen people appointed to the commission (twelve commissioners and an executive secretary) only three belonged to the Catholic Church. The chairman and secretary were well-known educators who belonged to the Anglican Church. Although no public statements were made at the time, there were many who felt that on such an all-important matter as education, the Catholic Church, representing 37 percent of the population of Newfoundland, should have had stronger representation, especially since the United Church, representing only 20 percent of the population, had six members on the commission. Whether this resentment was reflected in the election results of 1971 or not can only be guessed. But an examination of the election returns shows that of the ten or eleven districts traditionally regarded as Catholic seats, only two were won by the Liberals.

The blunders made by the Liberals in events leading to the 1971 election must be seen as only part of the reason for their defeat. There were logistical errors as well. Why, for example, was the election put off to such a late day? Historically, the intervals between elections had been from a minimum of two-and-a-half years to four years, yet the 1971 election was not held until five years and one month after that held in 1966. By the summer of 1970 it was apparent that the Liberal Party

---

[1] Other aspects of the Royal Commission on Education are given in Chapter 6.

was slipping, but it was equally clear that the Party still had enough public support to win substantially had the election been held at that time. But 1970 was allowed to slip by and so too was the greater part of 1971. As that summer passed several of us in the Party expressed our concern. In particular I was fearful of what would happen once the academic year started. There was no doubt the teachers were out "to get" the Liberals and the students would be only too happy to get back to University, where they could organize and be organized. I could foresee the spectre of marches and demonstrations around Confederation Building, all taken in and broadcast by television crews. Strategically, it was clear that the election should be called for not later than the day after Labour Day, when teachers would have just arrived back at their classrooms and when students would be in the final days of their summer work or busy getting ready to return to St. John's. This advice, made by others as well as myself, was rejected. The result was that when the election was held in late October, several thousand teachers — especially in the St. John's, Gander, Grand Falls and Corner Brook areas — had had time to plan their campaign to bring about the downfall of the Liberal government. Thus, the 1971 election, which would have been won had it been held any time between the first of June and first week of September, was allowed to go down the drain.

It is difficult to know who was advising Smallwood during the period from 1966 to 1971. Certainly it was not the senior members of the cabinet on whose judgement he had relied so often in earlier years, as can be seen in the following illustration. When the 1966 provincial election was called, C.R. Granger, the federal member for Grand Falls-White Bay-Labrador, had vacated his seat and run for the District of Gander — which he won handily. In 1967 J.W. Pickersgill also resigned his federal seat, thus making it necessary to find someone to represent Newfoundland in the federal cabinet. There were two obvious choices available: Richard Cashin, who had won several elections in St. John's West, and Donald Jamieson, who, while relatively new to federal politics, was well seasoned in public matters. To the surprise of many, Smallwood decided to recommend C.R. Granger, even though it would mean opening up the Gander District. When I heard of the impending change I pointed out that we were placing a sensitive seat at risk (the previous incumbent had won it only by 250 votes) and we might well lose it in a by-election. I was assured this would be impossible, that the Liberal candidate had been a popular mayor of the town of Gander and would "sweep" the election. Nevertheless, I argued, the large towns of Bishop's Falls and Botwood, which were in Gander District and which together then had a larger population than did the town of Gander, were not likely to be impressed by the candidate's municipal credentials. Furthermore, I did not think the people of Gander would be happy about losing their popular provincial member, Granger, whom they had elected by a large majority only a few months earlier. In the event, Granger resigned, ran federally and was elected with a greatly reduced majority. In the Gander by-election held to replace the Liberal Granger, the Progressive Conservative candidate was elected by a good majority.

In the opinion of many observers the Gander by-election was crucial to the fortunes of the Liberal Party. Only once before (in St. Barbe South) had the solid wall of Liberal outport strength been breached by the PCs, and that had been regarded as a fluke. But now it had been done again in a Liberal stronghold. And so the PCs celebrated their victory, secure in their own minds that Gander had signalled the beginning of the end for the Liberals.

There were perhaps a half-dozen instances where the premier was obviously wrongly advised, and one of them concerned my own home of Lewisporte. Harold Starkes had been elected there several times by strong majorities. In the September 1966 general election, Starkes received 2287 votes to his opponent's 810. In late June or early July, while talking with a small group of Liberal leaders, I was told that Starkes would not be running for Lewisporte and that a replacement had been found for him. When I inquired as to the reason for this unexpected change, I was told first, that Starkes would not win in Lewisporte, and second, that since 30 percent of the Lewisporte people were Pentecostal, a young man who belonged to that church had been given the "green light." After considering this information for a moment, I asked if they were aware of the religious affiliation of the other 70 percent of the population. To my astonishment no one seemed to know that Lewisporte was one of the largest United Church centres in Newfoundland. Still more surprising to me personally was the fact that although my grandfather was one of the three families who founded that Methodist (now United Church) community, and I had been born and raised there, no one had bothered to ask my advice. My own district of Grand Falls was next door to Lewisporte and, having made numerous visits to that community, I knew the area well. Had I been consulted, I would have had to advise the Liberal planners not to rely on Pentecostal affiliation to elect a candidate in Lewisporte. As it was, in the 1971 election the Pentecostal Liberal candidate for Lewisporte was defeated by James Russell, grandson of William Russell, one of the Methodist founders of Lewisporte. The district that had prided itself on being called "Sir Robert Bond's"[2] district, was now in the hands of the Progressive Conservative party and the Liberals were left wondering why such disastrous steps had been taken with such little research into the possible results.

These are but two instances where Smallwood was given and accepted wrong advice. Why this change in advisers and who gave him the advice I do not know. Space does not permit dealing with several other cases where similar mishandling of districts led to their being lost from the Liberal fold. It seems certain, however, that given a planning committee set up in 1969 or early 1970, with experience and without personal axes to grind, a general election held any time before the first of September 1971, and preferably in the fall of 1970, would have resulted in a substantial Liberal victory. This is not hindsight but simply a repetition of what several of us tried to drive home at the time.

Smallwood had his faults and virtues, of course, and as is inevitable for any public figure, his enemies tried to emphasize and exaggerate the faults while his friends tended to do the opposite. There were examples where he allowed flattery to interfere with his good judgement, and other examples where his perspective was clouded by a fear of other potential leaders. But he was not alone in these traits — Churchill, de Gaulle, F.D. Roosevelt, Sir Richard Squires and Mackenzie King all possessed similar characteristics to some degree.

---

[2] For most of his political life Sir Robert Bond represented the three-man District of Twillingate which included the present District of Lewisporte.

Moreover, when considering Smallwood's faults against his accomplishments, there is no doubt as to which had the greatest significance.

This boy from an outpost of Empire did achieve fame, not just in Newfoundland, but at the international level. Those who were attracted by his eloquence, his ability to think abstractly, to get at the essence of an idea, his utter fearlessness, his unfailing memory, his unflagging energy and industry included more than the semi-literate Newfoundland voter. Among them were the Queen and Prince Philip, Winston Churchill, Lester B. Pearson, Louis St. Laurent, Edmond de Rothschild, Lord Beaverbrook, Sir Eric Bowater, Richard Nixon, John Kenneth Galbraith, and dozens of others. To mix so freely and impressively with so many of the world's great and influential, Smallwood clearly had to be a man of exceptional ability and style.

The Smallwood era ended in the fall of 1971 when the premier was no longer in a position to impress his views and aspirations on the Newfoundland people. To many Newfoundlanders it was a case where finally the mills of the gods had performed their duty; to others it was a tragedy of Grecian dimensions. On the one hand were charges of patronage, irresponsibility and ineptitude resulting in misuse of public resources; on the other, blessings from those old enough to remember what things had been like before Smallwood — the poverty, privation, deprivation, and the all-prevailing fear of tomorrow. Perhaps we are still too near to the period and the man to draw up a valid balance sheet. Whatever his faults and shortcomings, they were not more heinous nor were they publicized more than were those of Whiteway, Bond, Morris and Squires — four political giants in Newfoundland history. No political leader worked harder or suffered more disappointments. But none secured more successes. Smallwood is still very much with us, but some day he will require an epitaph. The difference between his and Sir Christopher Wren's may be merely the difference between the singular and the plural.

BIBLIOGRAPHY

AKYEAMPONG, Ernest Bugya. "Labour Laws and the
 Development of the Labour Movement in Newfoundland,
 1900–1960." Unpublished Master's Thesis, 1967, Memorial
 University of Newfoundland, St. John's.
ALEXANDER, David. "Economic Growth in the Atlantic Region,
 1880–1940." Fredericton: *Acadiensis*, Autumn 1978.
ALEXANDER, David. "Newfoundland's Traditional Economy and
 Development to 1934." *Acadiensis*, Spring 1976.
AMMON, Lord. *Newfoundland, the Forgotten Island*. London:
 Victor Gollancz, 1944.
AMULREE, Lord. (Chairman). *Report of Newfoundland Royal
 Commission, 1933*. London: His Majesty's Stationery Office,
 1934.
ANSPACH, Lewis. *A History of the Island of Newfoundland*.
 London: Sherwood, Gilbert and Piper, 1827.

BARKHAM, Selma. "The Basques: Filling a Gap in our History."
 Canadian Geographical Journal, February/March 1978.
BARKHAM, Selma. "The Spanish Province of Terranova." *The
 Canadian Archivist*, vol. 2, #5, 1974.
BELLOWS, G.R. "The Foundation of Memorial University College,
 1919–1925." *Newfoundland Quarterly*, Summer 1925.
Benevolent Irish Society, St. John's, Nfld. Centenary Volume,
 1806–1906. Cork: Guy, 1906.
BERTON, Pierre. *My Country: The Remarkable Past*. Toronto:
 McClelland and Stewart, 1976.

BILOUS, Marlene Sonia. "Federal Attempts at Relieving Regional Economic Disparity: Newfoundland's Experience with DREE." Unpublished Master's Thesis, Memorial University of Newfoundland, St. John's, 1973.

BIRKENHEAD, Lord. *The Story of Newfoundland*. London: H. Marshall and Son, 1920.

BLACKBURN, Robert H., ed. *Encyclopedia of Canada (Newfoundland Supplement)*. Toronto: University Associates of Canada, 1949.

BLAKENY, C.H. *Canada's Tenth Province*. Moncton: Moncton Publishing Company, 1950.

BLAND, John. *Letters to Newfoundland Governors*. 1797–1800. Newfoundland Archives, St. John's.

BOLT, Canon G.H. *Codner Centenary*. St. John's, 1923.

BONNYCASTLE, Sir Richard H. *Newfoundland in 1842*. London: Henry Colburn, 1842.

BOWN, Addison. *Newfoundland Journeys*. New York: Carlton Press, 1971.

BOWN, Addison. "Old Time Politics in Newfoundland." St. John's: Newfoundland Historical Society, 1970.

Bowring Magazine. Bedford, England: Sidney Press. Summer 1961.

BRIFFETT, Frances B. "The History of the French in Newfoundland previous to 1714." Master's Thesis, Queen's University, 1927.

BRIFFETT, Frances B. *Little Stories About Newfoundland*. Toronto: J.M. Dent and Sons, 1939.

BRIFFETT, Frances B. *The Story of Newfoundland and Labrador*. Toronto, J.M. Dent and Sons, 1954.

BROSNAN, The Very Reverend Michael. *Pioneer History of St. George's Diocese, Newfoundland*. Corner Brook: Western Publishing, 1948.

BROWNE, W.J. "A History of Agriculture in Newfoundland." *Newfoundland Quarterly*. Summer 1942 to Autumn 1947.

BROWNE, W.J. Lecture. "Finance and Politics, 1900–1934." St. John's: Newfoundland Historical Society, October, 1979.

BRUCE, Harry. *Lifeline*. Toronto: Macmillan of Canada, 1977.

BRUCE, Sister M. Teresina. "A Historical Study of Family, Church and State Relations in Newfoundland Education." Doctoral thesis. University of Ottawa, 1963.

BRUCE, Sister M. Teresina. "The First Forty Years of Educational Legislation in Newfoundland." Master's thesis. University of Ottawa, 1956.

222

BUFFETT, Rev. F.M. *Story of the Church in Newfoundland*. Toronto: General Board of Religious Education, 1939.

BURKE, V.P. "Newfoundland's Various Forms of Government." *Newfoundland Quarterly*, June 1942.

BURSEY, W.J. *The Undaunted Pioneer*. St. John's: Privately printed, 1977.

BUTLER, Victor. *The Little Nord Easter: Reminiscences of a Placentia Bayman*. St. John's: Memorial University of Newfoundland, 1975.

CABOT, William B. *In Northern Labrador*. London: John Murray, 1912.

CARTWRIGHT, Frederick F. *Disease and History*. New York: Thomas Y. Crowell Company, 1972.

CARTWRIGHT, George. *Labrador Journal*. (Ed. C.W. Townsend). Boston: Vance Estes and Company, 1911.

CASHIN, Peter. *My Life and Times, 1890–1919*. Breakwater Books, 1976.

CELL, Gilian T. *English Enterprise in Newfoundland, 1577–1660*. Toronto: University of Toronto Press, 1969.

CHADWICK, St. John. *Newfoundland — Island into Province*. Cambridge University Press, 1967.

CHANG, M. "Newfoundland in Transition." Master's Thesis. Memorial University of Newfoundland, 1974.

CHAPIN, Miriam. *Atlantic Canada*. Toronto: Ryerson Press, 1956.

CLARK, Richard L. "Newfoundland, 1934–49." Doctoral dissertation. University of California, 1951.

COCHRANE, J.A. and Midgley, C. *An Economic Geography of Newfoundland*. Exeter, England: A. Wheaton, 1936.

COCHRANE, J.A., and A.W. Parsons. *The Story of Newfoundland*. Toronto: Ginn and Company, 1949.

COGSWELL, Fred. "Newfoundland 1715–1880." *Literary History of Canada*. University of Toronto Press, 1965.

COLLETT, Thomas E. *The Church of England in Newfoundland (Correspondence)*. St. John's: Joseph Wood, 1853.

COPES, Parzival. *St. John's and Newfoundland — An Economic Survey*. St. John's: Newfoundland Board of Trade, 1961.

CREWE, N.C. "A Slade Monograph." Newfoundland Quarterly, Fall 1963, Spring 1964, Summer 1964, Fall 1964.

CROSBIE, J.C. Article. "Local Government in Newfoundland." Toronto: *Canadian Journal of Economics and Political Science*. August 1956.

CUFF, Harry A. "Commission of Government in Newfoundland — A Preliminary Survey." M.A. thesis, Acadia University, 1959.

CUFF, Harry. "Political Developments in Newfoundland during World War II." *Arts and Letters Competition*. St. John's: Government of Newfoundland, 1964.

CUNNINGHAM, Wm. B. "Newfoundland Finance with Particular Reference to the Union with Canada, 1949." Master's thesis, Brown University, 1950.

DAVEY, J. *Fall of Torngak (Moravian Mission in Labrador)*. London: Partridge, 1905.

DAWSON, Samuel E. "The Voyages of the Cabots in 1497 and 1498." Royal Society of Canada, 1894.

DAY, J. Wentworth. *Newfoundland, the Fortress Isle*. Fredericton: Brunswick Press, 1960.

DEVINE, P.K. and O'MARA. *Notable Events in the History of Newfoundland*. St. John's: Trade Review Office, 1900.

DOWNING, John. *A Brief Narrative concerning Newfoundland*. London: Colonial Papers, 1676.

DOYLE, Gerald S. *Old-Time Songs of Newfoundland*. St. John's, Gerald S. Doyle, 1955.

DUNCAN, Norman. *Dr. Grenfell's Policy*. London: Hodder and Stoughton, 1911.

DUNPHY, Sister M. Alexandra. "A History of Teacher Training in Newfoundland, 1726–1955." Bachelor of Education thesis, Mount St. Vincent College, 1956.

DYKE, A. Prince. "Community Inventory of Labrador." St. John's: Department of Labrador Affairs, March 1969.

DYKE, P. "Knowing More about Labrador." *Newfoundland Stories and Ballads*. St. John's: Summer/Autumn 1969.

EGGLESTON, Wilfred. "Newfoundland: The Road to Confederation." St. John's: Ottawa: Department of External Affairs, 1974.

ENGLAND, George Allan. *The Greatest Hunt in the World*. Montreal: Tundra Books Ltd., 1969.

ENGLISH, L.E.F. "First Constitutional Suspension." *Arts and Letters Competition*. St. John's: Government of Newfoundland, 1955.

ENGLISH, L.E.F. "Historic Newfoundland". St. John's: Government of Newfoundland and Labrador, 1968.

ENGLISH, L.E.F. *Outlines of Newfoundland History*. London: T. Nelson, 1929.

FARIS, James C. *Cat Harbour: A Newfoundland Fishing Settlement*. Toronto: University of Toronto Press, 1972.

FAY, C.R. *Life and Labour in Newfoundland*. Toronto: University of Toronto Press, 1956.

FAY, C.R. "The Channel Island and Newfoundland." *Newfoundland Quarterly*, March 1955.

FEARN, Gordon F.N. "The Commercial Elite and Development in Newfoundland." Newfoundland Historical Society, March 1976.

FEILD, Bishop Edward. *Journals: 1845, 1846, 1848*. London: Society for the Propagation of the Gospel, 1845, 1846, 1849.

FELTHAM, John. "Sir William Coaker and the Political Activities of the F.P.U." Newfoundland Historical Society, February 1968.

FELTHAM, J. "The Development of the Fishermen's Union in Newfoundland." Master's thesis, Memorial University, 1959.

FIELD, Agnes M. "The Development of Government in Newfoundland, 1638–1813." Master's thesis, University of London, 1924.

FLYNN, T.J. "Letters on Newfoundland History." *Newfoundland Quarterly*, 1921–1923.

FOX, Arthur. "The Newfoundland Seal Fishery." *Newfoundland Quarterly*. Summer 1966.

FRECKER, G.A. *Education in the Atlantic Provinces*. Toronto: Gage, 1956.

GABRIELSON, Dr. Ira. *The Wildlife of Newfoundland*. St. John's: Queen's Printer, 1955.

GARDNER, John. "The First Atlantic Crossing." *Atlantic Advocate*, October, 1966.

GODFREY, Stuart R. "Introduction of Social Legislation in Newfoundland." *Newfoundland Historical Society*, April 1979.

GODFREY, Stuart R. *Social Welfare in Newfoundland*. Unpublished manuscript. Ottawa, 1979.

GOSLING, William, G. *Labrador*. London: Alston Rivers, 1910.

GOSSE, Edmund. *Life of Philip Henry Gosse*. London: Kegan Paul, Trench, 1890.

GOUDIE, Elizabeth. *Woman of Labrador*. Toronto: Peter Martin Associates, 1973.

GREENE, J.P. "The Influence of Religion in Politics of Newfoundland 1850–1861." Thesis, Memorial University, 1970.

GRENFELL, Wilfred T. and others. *Labrador, the Country and the People*. New York: Macmillan, 1909.

GRENFELL, Wilfred T. *Down North on the Labrador*. New York: Fleming H. Revell, 1911.

GRENFELL, Wilfred T. *A Labrador Doctor*. London: Hodder and Stoughton, 1920.

GRENFELL, Wilfred T. and others. *Labrador*. New York: The Macmillan Company, 1922.

GRENFELL, Sir Wilfred T. *Forty Years for Labrador*. London: Hodder and Stoughton, 1934.

GRENFELL, Sir Wilfred T. *Romance of Labrador*. London: Hodder and Stoughton, 1934.

GRENFELL, Sir Wilfred T. *Labrador Log Book*. Boston: Little, Brown, 1938.

GUNN, Gertrude. *The Political History of Newfoundland, 1832–1864*. Toronto: University of Toronto Press, 1966.

GURNEY, H. *Economic Conditions in Newfoundland, 1935*. London: H.M. Stationery Office, 1935.

GUTSELL, B.V. *An Introduction to the Geography of Newfoundland*. Ottawa: King's Printer, 1949.

GWYN, Richard. *Smallwood, The Unlikely Revolutionary*. Toronto: McClelland and Stewart, 1968.

HAMDANI, Daood Ul Hasan. "The Role of Public Finance in the Economic Development of Newfoundland, 1949–1964." Unpublished Master's thesis, 1966, Memorial University of Newfoundland, St. John's.

HANDCOCK, Dr. W.G. Article. "The Poole mercantile community." Memorial University of Newfoundland, 1984.

HANDCOCK, Gordon W. "Patterns of English Migration and Settlement in Newfoundland." *Newfoundland Historical Society*, December 1978.

HARPER, John M. *History of Newfoundland and the other Maritime Provinces*. St. John's: J. and A. McMillan, 1876.

HARRINGTON, Michael. "The Prime Ministers of Newfoundland." St. John's: *The Evening Telegram*, 1962.

HARRINGTON, Michael F. *Sea Stories from Newfoundland*. Toronto: Ryerson Press, 1958.

HARRIS, C. Alexander. "Newfoundland 1783 to 1867" and "Newfoundland 1867–1921." *Cambridge History of the British Empire*. Cambridge University Press, 1930.

HARRIS, Leslie. *Newfoundland and Labrador—A Brief History*. Toronto: J.M. Dent and Sons, 1968.

HARRIS, Leslie. "The First Nine Years of Representative Government, 1832–1841." Master's thesis, Memorial University, 1959.

HARVEY, Moses. *Newfoundland in 1897*. London: Sampson Low, Marston, 1897.

HARVEY, Moses. *Newfoundland in 1900*. New York: The South Publishing Company, 1900.

226

HARVEY, Moses. *Text Book of Newfoundland History*. London: Collins, 1890.

HATTON and HARVEY. *Newfoundland, the Oldest British Colony*. London: Chapman and Hall, 1883.

HEAD, C. Grant. *Eighteenth Century Newfoundland*. Toronto: McClelland and Stewart, 1976.

HEFFERTON, S.J. (ed.). *Newfoundland Who's Who*. St. John's, 1952.

HENSON, Ben. *Newfoundland Portfolio*. St. John's: Breakwater Books, 1977.

Heritage of the Sea — our case on offshore mineral rights. St. John's: Government of Newfoundland, 1978.

HERRICK, Clinton S.; Dinham, Paul S. and O'Neil, Mollie. *Continuity and Change in Newfoundland Politics*. Paper. Memorial University. 1972.

HEWSON, John. "Beothuk and Algonkian: Evidence Old and New." *International Journal of American Linguistics*, 1968.

HIBBS, R. *Who's Who in and from Newfoundland*. (3 editions). St. John's: Dicks and Co., 1927, 1930, 1937.

HIBBS, Richard. "First Roads Built in Newfoundland." *Newfoundland Quarterly*, Summer, Autumn and Christmas, 1940.

HICKMAN, G.A. "History of Education in Newfoundland." Master's thesis, Acadia University, 1941.

HICKS, George. *Newfoundland — From Shadow to Sunlight*. Typescript copy, Grand Falls, 1968.

HIGGINS, John G. Debates of the Senate. Senate Hansard. Ottawa, 1959.

HIGGINS, John G. "How the Rule of Law came to Newfoundland." *Newfoundland Quarterly*, March and June 1959.

Highway to Progress. St. John's: E.C. Boone Advertising Ltd. 1966.

HILLER, J.K. "A History of Newfoundland, 1874–1901." Doctoral dissertation, University of Cambridge, 1971.

HILLER, J.K. "Confederation Defeated: The Newfoundland Election of 1869." *Newfoundland Historical Society*, September 1976.

HILLER, James K. (ed.). "The Confederation Issue in Newfoundland, 1864–1869, Selected Documents." Memorial University, October 1974.

HILLER, J.K. "The Constitutional Crises of 1908–09. A Sub-plot." *Newfoundland Historical Society*, February 1974.

HILLER, J.K. "The Moravian Mission to Labrador." *Newfoundland Quarterly*, November 1966.

HILLER, J.K. "The Railway and Local Politics in Newfoundland, 1870–1901." Memorial University, 1973.

HILLER, James K. "Whiteway and Progress". *Newfoundland Quarterly*, March, 1972.

HILLER, J.K. and Neary, Peter. (Eds.) *Newfoundland in the nineteenth and twentieth centuries; Essays in Interpretations*. University of Toronto Press, 1980.

HOCKING, Anthony. *Newfoundland*. Toronto: McGraw-Hill Ryerson, 1978.

HOLLOWAY, Robert E. *Through Newfoundland with the Camera*. London: Sach and Co., 1910.

HORWOOD, Andrew. *Captain Harry Thomasen*. St. John's: Andrew Horwood, 1973.

HORWOOD, Andrew. *Newfoundland Ships and Men*. St. John's: Marine Researchers, 1971.

HORWOOD, Harold. *Newfoundland*. Toronto: Macmillan of Canada, 1969.

HOUSE, Edgar. *Light at Last*. St. John's: Jesperson Press, 1981.

HOWLEY, James P. *The Beothucks or Red Indians*. Cambridge University Press, 1915. Reissued by Coles Publishing Company, Toronto, 1974.

HOWLEY, Rev. M. *Ecclesiastical History of Newfoundland*. Boston: Doyle and Whittle, 1888.

HOWLEY, Rev. M. *Newfoundland at the Beginning of the Twentieth Century*. New York: South Publishing Co., 1902.

HUNTER, A.C. "Newfoundland's Debt to Captain Cook." *Newfoundland Quarterly*, Winter 1971.

HUTTON, J.E. *The History of Moravian Missions*. London: Moravian Publication Office, 1923.

HUTTON, S.K. *Among the Eskimos of Labrador*. London: Seeley Service and Company, 1912.

INGSTAD, H. *Westward to Vinland*. London: Jonathan Cape, 1969.

INNIS, H.A. *The Cod Fisheries*. Toronto: University of Toronto Press, 1954.

IVERSON, N. and Matthews, R. *Communities in Decline*. St. John's: Memorial University, 1968.

JAMES, Sister M. *Foundation of the Presentation Congregation in Newfoundland*. St. John's, 1975.

JAMES, Thomas H. *Newfoundland, Its Resources and Discovery*. St. John's: *Evening Telegram*, 1910.

JELF, R.H. *Life of Joseph James Curling*. Oxford: Fox, Jones and Company, 1909.

228

JOB, R.B. "Dr. William Carson." *Newfoundland Quarterly*, Spring 1943.

JONES, Frederick. "Edward Feild, Bishop of Newfoundland, 1844–1876." *Newfoundland Historical Society*, 1976.

JUNEK, Oscar W. *Isolated Communities — A Study of a Labrador Fishing Village*. New York: American Book, 1937.

KELLY, E.T. "The Coming of the Newfoundland Irish." Parts I and II. *Newfoundland Quarterly*, June and September 1967.

KELLY, Tom. "A Fact Sheet on Sealing." Washington, D.C. *Canada Today*, vol. 8, #10, 1977.

KELLY, Tom. "Canada Today." Washington, D.C.: November 1976.

KIRBY, H.F.G. "The Inland Postal History of Newfoundland." *Newfoundland Quarterly*, Autumn and Christmas 1944.

KLEIVAN, Helge. *The Eskimos of Northeast Labrador*. Oslo: Norsk Polarinstitut, 1966.

KENNEDY, John C. Brief to the Royal Commission on Labrador. Memorial University of Newfoundland, 1973.

"The Labrador Boundary." *Newfoundland Quarterly*, Spring 1925.

La FONTAINE, Gerald. (ed.). "Churchill Falls News." Churchill Falls, 1967–1973.

LaFOSSE, Thomas J. "Newfoundland Royal Commission on Education." Master's thesis, University of Alberta, 1971.

LAHEY, R.J. "The Role of Religion in Lord Baltimore's Colonial Enterprise." Baltimore: *Historical Magazine*, Winter 1977.

LAHEY, R.J. "Church Affairs During the French Settlement at Placentia." *Placentia Historical Society*, December 1972.

LAHEY, R.J. "Religion and Politics in Newfoundland." *Newfoundland Historical Society*, March 1979.

LAWTON, J.T., and Devine, P.K. *Old King's Cove*, St. John's, 1944.

LEE, Cuthbert. *With Dr. Grenfell in Labrador*. New York: Neal Publishing, 1914.

LEIGH, J. *Moravians in Labrador*. Edinburgh: Whyte, 1833.

LeMESSURIER, H.W. "Ancient St. John's." *Newfoundland Quarterly,* 1903–1904.

LeMESSURIER, H.W., MacDonald, R.G., Rendell, P.B., and Knight, E.E. *History of St. Thomas's Church*, St. John's, 1962.

LENCH, Rev. Charles. *An Account of the Rise and Progress of Methodism on the Grand Bank and Fortune Circuits from 1816 to 1916*. 1916.

LENCH, Rev. Charles. *The Story of Methodism in Bonavista*. St. John's: Robinson, 1919.

LESTER, Benjamin. Manuscript diary, 1791–93. Dorset County Archives, Dorchester, Dorset, England.

LIBERAL PARTY OF NEWFOUNDLAND. Building New Highroads to a Better Life. St. John's: 1964.

LIVERPOOL manuscript (Abstract of the Pulling Report). Newfoundland Archives, St. John's.

LODGE, Thomas. *Dictatorship in Newfoundland*. London: Cassell, 1939.

LOUNSBURY, Ralph G. *The British Fishery at Newfoundland*. New Haven: Yale University, 1934.

LUMSDEN, James. *The Skipper Parson*. Toronto: William Briggs, 1906.

LYSAGHT, A.M. *Joseph Banks in Newfoundland and Labrador, 1766*. Berkeley and Los Angeles: University of California Press, 1971.

MAYO, H.B. "Newfoundland and Confederation in the Eighteen-sixties." *Canadian Historical Review*, vol. 29, no. 2, 1947.

McALLISTER, R.I. (ed.). *The First Fifteen Years of Confederation*. St. John's: Dicks and Co., 1965.

McALLISTER, R.I. (ed.). *The Structure of the Newfoundland Population*. St. John's: Government of Newfoundland, 1965.

McCANN, Philip. Address. "Confederation Revisited." *Newfoundland Historical Society*, St. John's, 1983.

McCARTHY, M.J. *A History of Placentia*. St. John's: Provincial Reference Library.

McCARTHY, Michael. "History of St. Mary's Bay, 1597–1949." St. John's: *Arts and Letters Competition*, 1971.

McCARTHY, Michael J. "The Irish in Newfoundland, 1749–1800." St. John's: *Arts and Letters Competition*, 1974.

McCARTHY, Michael J. "Women of Newfoundland, 1003–1800." St. John's: *Arts and Letters Competition*, 1976.

McCORMAC, Sister M. Basil. "The Educational Work of the Sisters of Mercy in Newfoundland." Master's thesis, Catholic University of America, Washington, D.C., 1956.

McCORQUODALE, Susan. *Newfoundland, the only Living Father's Realm*. Canadian Provincial Politics: (Martin Robin, Editor). Prentice-Hall of Canada Ltd., Scarborough, 1972.

McCORQUODALE, Susan. "Public Administration in Newfoundland during the Period of Commission of Government." Doctoral Dissertation. Queen's University, 1973.

McDONALD, Ian. "The Reformer Coaker." *Book of Newfoundland*, vol. 6, St. John's: Newfoundland Book Publishers, 1975.

McDONALD Ian. (ed.). *Newfoundland since 1815*. St. John's: Memorial University, 1976.

McDONALD, Sir Gordon. *Newfoundland at the Crossroads*. Toronto: Ryerson, 1949.

McGEE, John T. *Cultural stability and change among the Montagnais Indians of the Lake Melville Region of Labrador*. Washington, D.C.: The Catholic University of America, 1961.

McGHEE, Robert, and James Tuck. *An Archaic Sequence from the Strait of Belle Isle, Labrador*. Ottawa: National Museums of Canada, 1975.

McGRATH, J.W. "James MacBraire, Merchant and Pioneer, 1795, 1840." *Arts and Letters Competition*. St. John's: Government of Newfoundland, 1970.

McGRATH, J.W. "R.G. Reid and the Newfoundland Railway." *Newfoundland Historical Society*, December 1971.

McGRATH, J.W. "The 1898 Railway Contract." *Newfoundland Historical Society*, March 1973.

McGRATH, P.T. *Newfoundland in 1911*. Whitehead, Morris, 1911.

McGRIGOR, G.D. *Newfoundland Facts and Fallacies*. London: Royal Geographical Society, 1922.

MACKAY, R.A. (ed.). *Newfoundland*. Toronto: Oxford University Press, 1946.

McLINTOCK, A.H. *The Establishment of Constitutional Government in Newfoundland*. London: Longmans, 1941.

McNAMARA, Raymond E. "The Economy of Newfoundland." Master's thesis, Columbia University, New York, 1951.

McNEILL, William H. *Plagues and Peoples*. New York: Anchor Press/Doubleday, 1976.

MacWHIRTER, W.D. "A Political History of Newfoundland, 1865–1874." Master's thesis, Memorial University, 1960.

MANLEY, Jabez W. "Popular History of Newfoundland and Labrador." St. John's: *The Pilot*, 1852.

MANNION, John. "The Irish Migrations to Newfoundland." *Newfoundland Historical Society*, October 1973.

MANNION, John (ed.). *The Peopling of Newfoundland*. St. John's: Memorial University, 1977.

MANUEL, Edith. *Newfoundland, Our Province*. Exeter: A. Wheaton and Co., 1955.

MANUEL, Edith. *St. Peter's Anglican Church, Twillingate*. St. John's: Morgan Printing Co., 1970.

MANUEL, Ella. *Woody Point, 1800*. Privately printed.

MARSHALL, Ingeborg. *The Red Ochre People*. Vancouver: J.J. Douglas, 1977.

MARSHALL, Rev. W. "Journal, 1839–42." (Methodist Missionary to Newfoundland). St. John's: United Church Archives.

MARTIN, A. "The Economic Geography of Newfoundland." Doctoral dissertation, Oxford University, 1938.

MARTIN, Robert M. *History of the British Colonies*. London: Henry and Bohn, 1844.

MASSIE, Joseph. "A Historical Account of the Naval Power of France (including a narrative of the proceedings of the French at Newfoundland)." London, 1712.

MATHER, John J. "On the Loss of Responsible Self Government and Dominion Status by Newfoundland, 1933–1934." Master's thesis, State University of Iowa, 1950.

MATHIAS, Philip. "Forced Growth; Five Studies of Government involvement in the Development of Canada." Toronto: J. Lewis and Samuel, 1971.

MATTHEWS, D. Ralph. *There's No Better Place than Here*. Toronto: Peter Martin Associates, 1976.

MATTHEWS, Keith. "A History of the West of England Newfoundland Fishery." Doctoral dissertation, Oxford University, 1968.

MATTHEWS, Keith. "Collection and Commentary on the Constitutional Laws of Seventeenth Century Newfoundland." St. John's: Memorial University, 1975.

MATTHEWS, Keith. "Historical Fence Building." St. John's: Memorial University, 1971.

MATTHEWS, Keith. "Index to who was who in the Trade and Settlement of Newfoundland." St. John's: Memorial University, 1971.

MATTHEWS, Keith. *Lectures on the History of Newfoundland, 1500–1830*. St. John's: Memorial University, 1973.

MATTHEWS, Keith. "The Reformers of 1832." *Newfoundland Historical Society*, January 1974.

MATTHEWS, Keith. "The West Country Merchants in Newfoundland." *Newfoundland Historical Society*, December 1968.

MERCER, G.A. "The Province of Newfoundland and Labrador." Ottawa: Royal Canadian Geographical Society. Revised 1968.

MERCER, Rev. W.E. "A Century of Methodism in Twillingate and Notre Dame Bay, 1831–1931." *Twillingate Sun*, 1932.

MIFFLEN, Jessie B. "Development of Public Library Services in Newfoundland, 1934–1972."

MOCKRIDGE, Rev. Chas. H. *The Bishops of the Church of England in Canada and Newfoundland*. Toronto: F.N.W. Brown, 1896.

MORETON, Rev. Julian. *Life and Work in Newfoundland.*
London: Rivingtons, 1863.

MORGAN, M.O. "Financial Affairs of the First Newfoundland
Assembly." *Newfoundland Quarterly*, June 1954.

MORGAN, M.O. and Rothney, G.O. *Historical Review of
Newfoundland.* St. John's: Appendix to the Report of
Newfoundland Royal Commission on Terms of Union,
St. John's, 1957.

MORINE, Sir A.B. *Sir Hugh Hoyles — Prime Minister 1861–65.*
St. John's: Robinson.

MORISON, Samuel Eliot. *The European Discovery of America.*
New York: Oxford University Press, 1971.

MORTON, W.L. "Newfoundland in Colonial Policy." Bachelor's
thesis, Oxford, 1935.

MOSDELL, H.M. *5000 Facts About Newfoundland.* St. John's:1922.

MOSDELL, H.M. *When Was That?* St. John's: Trade Printers and
Publishers, 1923.

MOTT, H.Y. *Newfoundland Men.* Concord: T.W. and J.R. Cragg,
1894.

MOULTON, E.C. "Constitutional Crisis and Civil Strike in
Newfoundland, February to November, 1861." Toronto:
Canadian Historical Review, September 1967.

MOULTON, E.C. "The Political History of Newfoundland,
1861–1869." Master's thesis, Memorial University, 1960.

MOYLES, R.G. *Complaints is Many and Various.* Toronto: Peter
Martin Associates, 1975.

MUNN, W.A. "History of Harbour Grace." *Newfoundland
Quarterly*, 1934–1936.

MURPHY, James. *A Century of Events in Newfoundland.*
St. John's, 1924.

MURPHY, James. *Historic Items of Newfoundland.* St. John's,
1924.

MURPHY, James. *The Colony of Newfoundland.* St. John's: Daily
Globe Publishing Co., 1925.

MURPHY, Noel F. "An Outline of History of Western
Newfoundland." *Newfoundland Historical Society*, October
1970.

MURRAY, H.E.L. "The Traditional Role of Women in a
Newfoundland Fishing Community." Thesis, Memorial
University, 1972.

MURRAY, James. *Commercial Crisis in Newfoundland.* St. John's:
Queen's Printer, 1895.

MURRAY, Myles P. "Forgotten Ferryland." *Newfoundland
Quarterly*, September 1954.

NEARY, Peter. "Canada and the Newfoundland Labour Market, 1939–49." *Canadian Historical Review*, Toronto, 1981.

NEARY, Peter. "The Writing of Newfoundland History — an introductory survey." St. John's: Centre for Newfoundland Studies, Memorial University, 1976.

NEARY, Peter, and O'Flaherty, Patrick. (eds.) *By Great Waters*. Toronto: University of Toronto Press, 1974.

NEMEC, Thomas F. "St. Shotts in Historical Perspective." *Newfoundland Quarterly*, January 1975.

NEMEC, Thomas F. "Trepassey, 1505–1840 A.D." *Newfoundland Quarterly*, March 1973.

NEMEC, Thomas F. "Trepassey 1840–1900." *Newfoundland Quarterly*, June 1973.

NEMEC, Thomas F. "The Irish Emigration to Newfoundland." *Newfoundland Historical Society*, March 1978.

Newfoundland — Canada's New Province. Ottawa: Department of External Affairs, 1950.

NEWHOOK, Fred J. "First Rejection of Confederation." *Arts and Letters Competition*. St. John's: Government of Newfoundland, 1960.

NEWHOOK, Fred J. "The Confederation movement in Newfoundland (1885–1895)." *Arts and Letters Competition*. St. John's: Government of Newfoundland, 1961.

NEWTON, Robert. *A Survey of the Memorial University of Newfoundland*. St. John's, 1951.

NICHOLSON, G.W.L. "The Fighting Newfoundlanders." St. John's: Government of Newfoundland and Labrador, 1964.

NICHOLSON, G.W.L. "More Fighting Newfoundlanders." St. John's: Government of Newfoundland and Labrador, 1969.

NOEL, S.J.R. *Politics in Newfoundland*. Toronto: University of Toronto Press, 1971.

O'DEA, Fabian A. Article. "Cabot's Landfall — Yet Again." *Newfoundland Quarterly*, Fall 1971.

O'NEIL, Paul. *The Oldest City*. Erin, Ontario: Press Porcépic, 1975.

O'NEIL, Paul. *A Seaport Legacy*. Erin, Ontario: Press Porcépic, 1976.

O'NEIL, Paul. "Lord Baltimore and the Avalon Plantation." *Newfoundland Historical Society*, October 1977.

O'NEIL, Paul, and others. *Remarkable Women of Newfoundland and Labrador*. St. John's: Creative Printers, 1976.

O'REILLY, J.A. "Priests and Prelates of the Past." *Newfoundland Quarterly*, March 1903.

PARKER, John. *Newfoundland, 10th Province of Canada*. London: Lincolns Prager, 1950.

PARSONS, Alex A. "The Great Sealing Industry." *Newfoundland Quarterly*, April 1915.

PARSONS, Alex A. "*The Newfoundland* Tragedy." *Newfoundland Quarterly*, July 1914.

PARSONS, J.G. *Newfoundland*. Toronto: Copp Clark, 1951.

PARSONS, J.J. "The Origins of Wesleyan Methodism in Newfoundland." Master's thesis, Memorial University, 1963.

PARSONS, John. *Labrador: Land of the North*. Vantage Press, 1970.

PASTORE, Ralph T. "Newfoundland Micmacs: A History of their traditional Life." *Newfoundland Historical Society*, 1978.

PATERSON, Janet. "The History of Newfoundland, 1713–1763." Master's thesis, University of London, 1931.

PEACOCK, F.W. "Some Psychological Aspects of the impact of the white man upon the Labrador Eskimo." Master's thesis, University of Montreal, 1948.

PEARSON, L.B. *Mike*. The Memoirs of the Right Honourable Lester B. Pearson. 3 vols. Toronto: University of Toronto Press, 1971–75.

PEDLEY, Charles. *The History of Newfoundland*. London: Longmans, 1863.

PERLIN, A.B. "Fifty Years of Journalism in Newfoundland." *Newfoundland Quarterly*, Winter, Spring, Summer, 1971.

PERLIN, A.B. "Life and Politics in Modern Newfoundland." *The Newfoundland Record*, August 1962.

PERLIN, A.B. "The St. Barbe Coast Issue." *Newfoundland Quarterly*, June 1970.

PERLIN, A.B. "Tragic Heritage." *Newfoundland Quarterly*, February and Christmas 1968.

PERLIN, A.B. *The Story of Newfoundland*. London: Longmans, 1959.

PICKERSGILL, J.W. *My Years with Louis St. Laurent*. Toronto: University of Toronto Press, 1975.

PILOT, Rev. W. *Geography of Newfoundland*. London: Collins, 1883.

PILOT, Rev. W. *Outline of the History of Newfoundland*. London: Collins, 1908.

PILOT, Rev. W. "The System of Education in Newfoundland." Department of Education, St. John's, 1898.

POTTLE, Herbert L. *Newfoundland Dawn Without Light*. St. John's: Breakwater, 1979.

235

POWELL, Benjamin W., Sr. *Labrador by Choice*. (Joan Cartledge, ed.) Toronto: Testimony Press, 1979.

POWER, Hon. Gregory. Address. "Joseph R. Smallwood." St. John's, 1981.

POWER, M.F. "The Micmacs." *Newfoundland Quarterly*, March 1910.

PRATT, E.J. *Newfoundland Verse*. Toronto: Ryerson Press, 1923.

PRESCOTT, Henry. *A Sketch of the State of Affairs in Newfoundland*. London: Saunders and Otley, 1841.

PROWSE, D.W. *A History of Newfoundland*. London: Macmillan, 1895.

PROWSE, D.W. "History of Roadmaking in Newfoundland." *Newfoundland Quarterly*, March 1903.

PROWSE, D.W. Article. "Newfoundland and New England." *Newfoundland Quarterly*, March 1902.

PULLING, Capt. G.C. Report, 1792. Liverpool papers, British Museum.

QUINN, David B. "The Argument for the English Discovery of America between 1480 and 1494." *Geographical Journal*, September 1961.

QUINN, David B. (ed.). *The voyages and colonizing Enterprises of Sir Humphrey Gilbert*. London: The Hakluyt Society, 1940.

REEVES, John. *History of the Government of the Island of Newfoundland*. London: J. Sewell, 1793.

Report and Documents Relating to Union of Newfoundland with Canada. Ottawa: Department of External Affairs, 1949.

RICHARDSON, Boyce. Article. "Joey". St. John's: Alternate Press, 1972.

RICHARDSON, Boyce. "I" *The Story of Joey Smallwood. The Last Post*. Canadian Journalism Foundation, Montreal 1972.

RICHARDSON, C.A. *Certain Aspects of the Educational System of Newfoundland*. St. John's, 1933.

ROBB, Andrew, and Roberta Edgecombe. *A Cost Benefit Analysis of the Newfoundland Resettlement Programme*. Memorial University of Newfoundland, 1969.

ROGERS, J.D. *Newfoundland: Historical and Geographical*. Oxford: Clarendon, 1911.

ROTHNEY, Gordon O. "British Policy in the North American Cod Fisheries." Doctoral dissertation, University of London, 1939.

ROTHNEY, Gordon O. "The History of Newfoundland and Labrador from 1754 to 1783." Master's thesis, University of London, 1934.

ROTHSCHILD, Edmund de. "Brinco: The Early Days."
Fredericton: *Atlantic Advocate*, July 1967.

ROWE, Francis. "Early Banking in Newfoundland."
Newfoundland Quarterly, Fall 1971.

ROWE, Frederick W. *Blueprint for Newfoundland Education*.
St. John's: Department of Education, 1958.

ROWE, Frederick W. "Newfoundland and Labrador." *World Book
Encyclopedia*. Chicago: Field Enterprises, 1964.

ROWE, Frederick W. *The Development of Education in
Newfoundland*. Toronto: Ryerson Press, 1964.

ROWE, Frederick W. *Education and Culture in Newfoundland*.
Toronto: McGraw-Hill Ryerson, 1976.

ROWE, Frederick W. *Extinction — The Beothuks of
Newfoundland*. Toronto: McGraw-Hill Ryerson, 1977.

ROWE, Frederick W. *History of Newfoundland and Labrador*.
Toronto: McGraw-Hill Ryerson, 1980.

ROWE, Frederick W. "Myths of Newfoundland." *Newfoundland
Quarterly*, Winter 1979.

ROWE, Melvin. *I have Touched the Greatest Ship*. St. John's: Town
Crier Publishing Co., 1976.

ROWELY, O.R. *The Anglican Episcopate of Canada and
Newfoundland*. London: A.R. Mowbray, 1928.

RUSSELL, F.W. "Financing Education in Newfoundland, 1960–61
to 1970–71." Master's thesis, Memorial University, 1973.

SAUNDERS, S.A. "The Economics of Newfoundland." In
Newfoundland. R.A. MacKay (ed.). Toronto: Oxford
University Press, 1946.

SENIOR, E. "The Origin and Political Activities of the Orange
Order in the 19th Century." Master's thesis, Memorial
University, 1959.

SEVERIN, Timothy. "The Voyage of Brendan." *National
Geographic*, December 1977.

SEVERIN, Tim. *The Brendan Voyage*. New York: McGraw-Hill
Book Company, 1978.

SHAW, Lloyd W. "Education in Newfoundland." Master's thesis,
Mount Allison University, 1943.

SHERK, Susan (ed.). "Fogo Island." *Decks Awash*. Memorial
University, August 1978.

SHERK, Susan (ed.). "Municipalities." *Decks Awash*. Memorial
University, September 1977.

SHORTIS, H.F. *Pioneers of Conception Bay*. St. John's: *Daily
News*, 1910.

SISSONS, C.B. *Church and State in Canadian Education*.
Toronto: Ryerson Press, 1959.

SMALLWOOD, Joseph R. *Coaker of Newfoundland*. London: The Labour Publishing Co. Ltd., 1927.

SMALLWOOD, Joseph R. *The New Newfoundland*. New York: Macmillan, 1931.

SMALLWOOD, Joseph R. *Surrogate Robert Carter*. St. John's, 1936.

SMALLWOOD, Joseph R. (ed.). *The Book of Newfoundland*. Vols. I–VI. St. John's: Newfoundland Book Publishers, 1937, 1967, 1975.

SMALLWOOD, Joseph R. *Newfoundland Handbook and Gazetteer, 1940 and 1941*. St. John's: Long Bros., 1940, 1941.

SMALLWOOD, Joseph R. *I Chose Canada*. Toronto: Macmillan of Canada, 1973.

SMALLWOOD, Joseph R. "Resettlement." Letter. *Decks Awash*. Memorial University, February 1977.

SMALLWOOD, Joseph R. *Newfoundland Miscellany*. St. John's: Newfoundland Book Publishers (1967) Ltd., 1978.

SMALLWOOD, Joseph R. *Dr. William Carson*. St. John's: Newfoundland Book Publishers (1967) Ltd., 1978.

SMALLWOOD, Joseph R. *No Apology From Me*. St. John's: Newfoundland Book Publishers (1967) Ltd., 1979.

SMALLWOOD, Joseph R. and ENGLISH, L.E.F. *Stories of Newfoundland*. St. John's; The Newfoundland Gazette, 1945.

SMITH, J. Harry. *Newfoundland Holiday*. Toronto: Ryerson Press, 1952.

SMITH, N. *Fifty-two years at the Labrador Fishery*. London: Stockwell, 1936.

SMITH, Philip. *Brinco: The Story of Churchill Falls*. Toronto: McClelland and Stewart Ltd., 1975.

SMITH, Warwick. "Reverend Laurence Coughlan." *Newfoundland Historical Society*, March 1942.

SQUIRE, Harold. *A Newfoundland Outport in the Making*. Eastport: Harold Squire, 1974.

STEWART, Robert, *Labrador*. Amsterdam: Time-Life International, 1977.

ST. JOHN, W.C. *Catechism of the History of Newfoundland*. Boston: Press of George C. Rand, 1855.

STORY, George M. "Christmas Mummering in Newfoundland." Toronto: University of Toronto Press, 1969.

STORY, George M. "Judge Prowse (1834–1914)." *Newfoundland Quarterly*, Spring 1971.

SUMMERS, Wm. F. "Geographical Analysis of Population Trends in Newfoundland." Doctoral Dissertation, McGill University, 1956.

SUMMERS, Wm. F., and SUMMERS, Mary E. *Geography of Newfoundland*. Toronto: Copp Clark, 1965.

SWAIN, Hector. "Charles Lench, Missionary." St. John's: Newfoundland and Labrador Archives, 1974.

SWEETLAND, William (pseudonym W. Avalonis). "Aborigines of Newfoundland." *Royal Gazette*, St. John's, January 1862.

TAIT, R.H. *Newfoundland*. New York: Harrington, 1939.

TANNER, V. *Newfoundland-Labrador*. Cambridge: Cambridge University Press, 1947.

TAYLOR, Griffith. "Newfoundland." Toronto: Canadian Institute of International Affairs, 1946.

TAYLOR, J.G. "Iron Men in Wooden Ships." *Newfoundland Quarterly*. Spring 1965.

TAYLOR, T.G. "Newfoundland, A Study of Settlements." Toronto: Canadian Institute of International Affairs, 1946.

THOMAS, Gordon. *Surgery in the Sub-Arctic*. St. Louis: *Journal of Thoracic and Cardiovascular Surgery*, Vol. 70, 1975.

THOMAS, Gordon. W. "Pulmonary Tuberculosis in Northern Newfoundland and Labrador." *New England Journal of Medicine*, September 1954.

THOMAS, Gordon W. and John S. Whittaker. "Extirpative Surgery for Pulmonary Tuberculosis." *Canadian Medical Association Journal*, 74, 1956.

THOMPSON, F.F. *The French Shore Problem in Newfoundland*. Toronto: University of Toronto Press, 1961.

THOMS, James R. (ed.). *Newfoundland and Labrador Who's Who*. St. John's: E.C. Boone Advertising Ltd., 1968.

THOMS, James R. *Who's Who*. St. John's: Creative Printers, 1975.

TITCOMB, Frederick G. "The Economic Rivalry for Newfoundland and Bank Fisheries to 1783." Master's thesis, Columbia University, 1935.

TOCQUE, Philip. *Newfoundland As It Was and As It Is in 1877*. London: Sampson Low, 1878.

TUCK, James A. *Aboriginal Inhabitants of Newfoundland's Great Northern Peninsula*. St. John's: Publication #3, Department of Economic Development.

TUCK, James A. "An Archaic Indian Cemetery in Newfoundland." *Scientific American*, June 1970.

TUCK, James A. "A current summary of Newfoundland Prehistory." *Newfoundland Quarterly*, Summer 1971.

TUCK, James A. "The Norse in Newfoundland." Toronto: *Canadian Collector*, March/April 1975.

TUCK, James A. *Newfoundland and Labrador Prehistory*. Ottawa: National Museum of Man, 1976.

TUCKER, E. *Life and Episcopate of Edward Feild*. London: W. Well Gardner, 1877.

TUCKER, Ephraim W. *Five Months in Labrador and Newfoundland during the Summer of 1838*. Concord, New Hampshire: Boyd and White, 1839.

TUCKER, Rev. H.W. (ed.). *Classified Digest of the Records of the Society for the Propagation of the Gospel in Foreign Parts*. London, 1701–1892.

UPTON, L.F.S. "The Extermination of the Beothucks of Newfoundland." *Canadian Historical Review*, June 1977.

VALLIS, F. "Sectarianism as a Factor in the 1908 Election." *Newfoundland Quarterly*, January 1974.

WALLACE, Dillon. *Lure of the Labrador Wild*. New York: Fleming H. Revell Co., 1905.

WALLACE, Dillon. *The Long Labrador Trail*. Toronto: Fleming H. Revell Co., 1907.

WALSH, A.J. (Chairman). *Report of the Newfoundland Fisheries Development Committee*. St. John's: Government of Newfoundland, 1953.

WARREN, P.J. (Chairman). *Reports of the Royal Commission on Education and Youth*. 2 Vols. St. John's: Government of Newfoundland and Labrador. 1967–

WARREN, P.J. "Financing Education in Newfoundland." Doctoral Dissertation. University of Alberta, 1962.

WHITBOURNE, Richard. *Discourse and Discovery of the New-Foundland*. London: 1622.

WHITE, William. "A History of Trinity." *Newfoundland Quarterly*, 1956–1957.

WHITELEY, William H. "Newfoundland, Quebec, and the Administration of the Coast of Labrador, 1774–1783." *Acadiensis*, Fall 1976.

WHITELEY, William H. *James Cook in Newfoundland, 1762–1767*. Newfoundland Historical Society, 1975.

WHITEWAY, Louise. "Towards an Art of Architecture in Newfoundland." *Arts and Letters Competition*. St. John's, 1952.

WICKS, René. "Newfoundland Social Life, 1750–1850." *Newfoundland Quarterly*, Summer 1974.

WILLSON, Beckles. *The Tenth Island*. London: Grant Richards, 1897.

WILSON, Harold F. *The Newfoundland Fishery Dispute*. St. John's: S.E. Garland, 1904.

240

WILSON, Rev. William. *Newfoundland and Its Missionaries*. Cambridge, Mass.: Dakin and Metcalf, 1866.

WINTER, H.A. "Memoirs." *Newfoundland Quarterly*, Winter and Summer 1976.

WINTON, Henry. *A Chapter in the History of Newfoundland for the Year 1861*. St. John's: Henry Winton, 1861.

WIX, Edward. *Six months of a Newfoundland Missionary's Journal*. London: Smith, Elder, 1836.

YONGE, James. *Journal*. London: Longmans, Green, 1963.

YOUNG, Arminius. *One Hundred Years of Mission Work in the Wilds of Labrador*. Stockwell, 1931.

YOUNG, Ewart, Editor. *Dateline Labrador*. Vol. 2, Nos. 3 and 4. Wabush, Labrador, 1967.

NEWSPAPERS, PERIODICALS, LEGISLATION, REPORTS, ETC.

Atlantic Advocate, 1949–1971. University Press of New Brunswick, Fredericton.

Atlantic Advocate. Articles on Resettlement in Newfoundland, Fredericton, October 1967.

Aurora, The, Labrador City, 1970–1980.

Barrelman, The, St. John's, 1939–1940.

Bay Roberts Guardian. Bay Roberts, 1946–1948.

Canada. Bureau of Statistics. Province of Newfoundland Statistical Background. Ottawa, 1949.

Canada. Department of External Affairs. Newfoundland (booklet). Ottawa, 1949.

Canada. Department of Public Works. Report. Trans-Canada Highway. 1949–1971. Ottawa.

Canada. Government of Canada and Newfoundland. Agreement. Trans-Canada Highway. Ottawa, 1950.

Canada. Government of Canada and Newfoundland. Agreement. Department of Regional Economic Expansion. Ottawa, 1971.

Canada. Statistics Canada. *A Statistical Portrait*. Ottawa, 1983.

Canada. Terms of Union of Newfoundland with Canada. British North America Act, 1949.

Carbonear Herald and Outport Telephone, The, Carbonear, 1879–1882.

Clarenville Packet. Clarenville, 1969–1984.

College of Fisheries. Annual Reports, 1965–1974.

Colleges of Trades and Technology. Annual Reports, 1964–1974.

Colonial and Continental Church Society. Annual Reports, 1823–1872.

Compass, The, Carbonear, 1968–1984.

Daily Colonist, The, St. John's, 1886–1893.

Daily News. St. John's, 1894–1984.

Daily Review. St. John's, 1899–1910.

Daily Star. St. John's, 1913–1921.

Decks Awash. Department of Extension, Memorial University of Newfoundland, 19(?).

Diocesan Magazine, Centenary Number, 1939.

Evening Chronicle. St. John's, 1907–1912.

Evening Herald, The, St. John's, 1890–1920.

Evening Mercury, The, St. John's, 1886–1893.

Evening Telegram, The, St. John's, 1879–1984.

Express, The, St. John's, 1864.

Fishermen's Advocate, The, St. John's, 1910–1924, and Port Union, 1924–1984.

Free Press, The, St. John's, 1901–1908.

Gazette, The, St. John's, 1807–1963.

Gander Beacon. Gander, 1959–1963.

Grand Falls Advertiser. Grand Falls, 1946–1984.

Great Britain. Dominions Office. Newfoundland Annual Reports of the Commission of Government for the years 1935, 1936, 1937, 1938. London: H.M. Stationery Office.

Great Britain. Newfoundland Royal Commission, 1933. London: H.M.S.O., 1933 (Amulree Report).

Lewisporte Pilot, Lewisporte, 1962–1984.

Memorial University College. Presidential Reports, 1925–1949.

Memorial University of Newfoundland. Presidential Reports, 1950–1983.

Mercantile Journal, The, St. John's, 1826–1827.

Methodist Missionary Society. Report. London, 1833.

Monitor, The, St. John's, 1948–1984.

Morning Chronicle, The, St. John's, 1865–1881.

Morning Courier and General Advertiser. St. John's, 1844–1878.

Newfoundland. Acts.

_____ _____ College of Trades and Technology Act, 1969.

_____ _____ Fisheries College Act, 1964.

_____ _____ Local School Tax Act, 1954, 1957, 1970.

_____ _____ Memorial University Acts, 1949, 1957.

_____ _____ Newfoundland Teachers' Association Act, 1952, 1957.

_____ _____ Public Libraries Act, 1952.

_____ _____ School Attendance Act, 1942.

_____ _____ Teacher Training Act, 1963.

_____ _____ Technical and Vocational Training Act, 1963.

_____ _____ University Fees and Allowaces Act, 1966–1967.

_____ _____ Vocational Education Act, 1952.

Newfoundland. Census Returns, 1857, 1869, 1874, 1891, 1901, 1911, 1921, 1935, 1945.

_____ Church of England Superintendents of Education. Annual Reports, 1874–1919.

_____ Commission of Enquiry into the Present Curriculum of the Colleges and Schools in Newfoundland. Report. St. John's, 1934.

_____ Commission of Enquiry on the Logging Industry. Sir Brian Dunfield (Chairman). Report. Queen's Printer, St. John's, 1960.

_____ Committee on Education. Report. Newfoundland Convention, 1946–48.

_____ Conference on Education, 1958. Report. St. John's, 1958.

_____ Conference on Teacher Shortage, 1957. Report. St. John's, 1957.

_____ Department of Education. Annual Reports, 1920–1973.

_____ Department of Education. *Monthly News Letters*. St. John's, 1968–1971.

_____ Department of Finance. Budget Speeches, 1927–1984.

_____ Department of Health. Annual Reports.

_____ Department of Public Welfare (Social Services and Rehabilitation). Annual Reports, 1951–1983.

_____ Division of Child Welfare. Annual Reports, 1946–1950.

_____ Education Acts, 1836, 1838, 1843, 1851, 1852, 1853 1858, 1866, 1870, 1874, 1876, 1887, 1892, 1898, 1903, 1916, 1920, 1927, 1935, 1952, 1960, 1968, 1969.

_____ Department of Mines and Resources. Annual Reports. St. John's, 1949, 1955.

Newfoundland. House of Assembly. Journal, 1833–1933.

_____ _____ Legislative Council Journal, 1833–1933.

_____ _____ Proceedings, 1903–1933.

_____ Labrador Conference, 1956. Report. St. John's; Queen's Printer, 1956.

_____ Labrador Conference. Report. St. John's; Queen's Printer, 1967.

_____ Methodist Superintendents of Education. Annual Reports, 1874–1919

_____ Newfoundland Fisheries Development Committee. (A.J. Walsh, Chairman). Report, 1953.

_____ Northern Newfoundland Conference, 1956. Report. St. John's: Guardian, 1956.

_____ Roman Catholic Superintendents of Education. Annual Reports, 1874–1919.

_____ Royal Commission on Agriculture. (A.M. Shaw, Chairman). Report. St. John's: Queen's Printer, 1955.

_____ Royal Commission on the Economic State and Prospects of Newfoundland and Labrador. Report. St. John's: 1967.

_____ Royal Commission on Forestry. (Major-General Howard Kennedy, Chairman). Report. St. John's: Queen's Printer, 1955.

_____ Royal Commission on Unemployment. (Lester Coombs, Chairman). Government of Newfoundland, 1958.

_____ Southern Newfoundland Conference. Report. St. John's: Guardian, 1956.

_____ Newfoundland Statistics, 1949–1964. Government of Newfoundland and Labrador, 1964.

_____ Statutes. St. John's, 1833–1984.

Newfoundland Express. St. John's, 1830–1876.

Newfoundland Gazette. St. John's, 1807–1984 (See Royal Gazette).

Newfoundland Government Bulletin. St. John's, 1943–1951.

Newfoundland Journal of Commerce. St. John's, 1936–1970.

Newfoundland Mercantile Journal. St. John's, 1816–1827.

Newfoundland Patriot, The. St. John's, 1834–1878.

Newfoundland Quarterly. St. John's, 1905–1984.

Newfoundland Stories and Ballads. St. John's, 1954–1974.

Newfoundland Vindicator. St. John's, 1841–1842.

Newfoundland Year Book. Guardian Limited. St. John's. 1955.

Newfoundlander. St. John's, 1827–1884.

Newfoundlander, The. St. John's, 1949–1954.

North Star. St. John's, 1872–1881.

Observer's Weekly. St. John's, 1934–1962.

Pilot, The, St. John's, 1852–1853.

Public Ledger and Newfoundland General Advertiser. St John's, 1820–1882.

Royal Gazette and Newfoundland General Advertiser. Later Newfoundland Gazette. St. John's, 1807–1890.

St. John's Daily News and Newfoundland Journal of Commerce, St. John's, 1860–1880.

St. John's Advertiser, The, St. John's, 1875–1879.

Sentinel and Conception Bay Advertiser, The, Carbonear, 1836–1844.

Society for the Promotion of Christian Knowledge. Reports, 1813–1842.

Society for the Propagation of the Gospel. Annual Reports, 1792–1904.

Standard and Conception Bay Advertiser, The, Harbour Grace, 1860–1894.

Star and Newfoundland Advocate, The, St. John's, 1840–1846.

Telegraph, The, St. John's, 1856–1875.

Terra Nova Advocate and Political Observer, The, St. John's, 1876–1889.

Times, The, St. John's, 1860–1865.

Times and General Commercial Gazette, The, St. John's, 1832–1894.

Trinity Enterprise. Trinity, 1909–1910.

Twillingate Sun. Twillingate, 1945–1952.

Twillingate Sun and Northern Weekly Advertiser, The, Twillingate 1880–1892.

Weekly Herald. Harbour Grace, 1854.

Weekly Herald and Conception Bay General Advertiser. Harbour Grace, 1845–1854.

Weekly Record and Trinity Bay Advertiser, The, Trinity, 1886–1897.

Western Star, The, Curling and Corner Brook, 1900–1905 and 1947–1984.

INDEX